WARRIORS AND NATION BUILDERS

WARRIORS AND NATION BUILDERS:

DEVELOPMENT AND THE MILITARY IN AFGHANISTAN

By Andy Tamas

CANADIAN DEFENCE ACADEMY PRESS

Canadian Defence Academy Press
PO Box 17000 Stn Forces
Kingston, Ontario   K7K 7B4

Produced for the Canadian Defence Academy Press
by 17 Wing Winnipeg Publishing Office.
WPO30372

Cover Photo Credits:
Base Photo, CFB Kingston (Boots and Sandals)
Silvia Pecota, March 2006

Library and Archives Canada Cataloguing in Publication

Tamas, Andy, 1943-
Warriors and nation builders : development and the military in Afghanistan / by Andy Tamas.

Issued by: Canadian Defence Academy.
Produced for the Canadian Defence Academy Press by 17 Wing Winnipeg Publishing Office.
Includes bibliographical references and index.
ISBN 978-1-100-10164-4 (bound).--ISBN 978-1-100-10165-1 (pbk.)
Cat. no.: D2-228/1-2008E (bound).--Cat. no.: D2-228/2-2008E (pbk.)

1. Canada--Armed Forces--Afghanistan. 2. Afghan War, 2001- --Participation, Canadian.
3. Canada--Foreign relations--Afghanistan. 4. Afghanistan--Foreign relations--Canada.
5. Democratization--Afghanistan. 6. Nation-building--Afghanistan. 7. Postwar reconstruction-
-Afghanistan. I. Canadian Defence Academy II. Canada. Canadian Armed Forces. Wing, 17
III. Title.

DS371.412 T36 2008   958.104'7   C2008-980347-7

Printed in Canada.

1 3 5 7 9 10 8 6 4 2

DEDICATION

This book is dedicated to my family and especially my wonderful wife Susie, who *does* have a sense of adventure, and to my mother, Angela Szepesi, an exemplary trooper in the "Army of Light" and the members of the Canadian Forces, our diplomats and development personnel – and those of other countries – who willingly put themselves in harm's way to build a better world, and most importantly, to the people of Afghanistan and other similar fragile states who want little more than a society that works.

Table of Contents

Foreword

I am delighted to introduce *Warriors and Nation Builders: Development and the Military in Afghanistan*. This book represents an important addition to CDA Press. Written by Andy Tamas, an experienced and well-respected development worker, it provides insights into the "Development" pillar of the vaunted "3D" (Diplomacy, Development and Defence) approach.

Ongoing operations in Afghanistan have done much to advance a greater understanding and practice with regard to the integrated "Whole of Government" approach to dealing with conflict in the contemporary security environment. However, this inclusive methodology unquestionably creates challenges for leaders. Only recently have we begun to accept the reality that success depends on an effective, co-operative military-civilian integrated approach to most operations in the contemporary environment. Very few of the conflicts we face are a function of an exclusive military problem. Rather, most are the result of political, economic and social dysfunction that is exacerbated by and prolonged as a result of insecurity. As a result, military presence and/or force is but one tool to remedy the problem. Moreover, it is normally ineffective without the corollary political and economic levers to fix the larger underlying problems. In short, both military and civilian decision-makers have come to realize that without security, there can be no reconstruction and development. However, similarly, it is now understood that without reconstruction and development, there can be no long-lasting security.

This volume is but one small contribution to the body of developing knowledge that promotes greater understanding in the realm of 3D, particularly as it relates to the Canadian Forces. Written from a civilian point of view by an experienced development worker who understands both the civilian and military perspectives of development within the context of Afghanistan, *Warriors and Nation Builders* provides excellent insight and knowledge, and is a must read for all professional officers. In short, it describes the complex business of nation building so warriors can better collaborate with their development partners in the effort to "win" in Afghanistan, as well as similar campaigns in other regions to help fragile states become sustainable peaceful societies.

FOREWORD

In closing, I wish to reiterate the importance of this book for those in the profession of arms, as well as in other government departments. At the Canadian Defence Academy Press, we hope that it will both enlighten and educate those who serve in, and who interact with, the profession of arms in Canada.

Colonel Bernd Horn
Chairman
CDA Press

Preface

"You development workers are nothing but a bunch of Birkenstock-wearing, granola-munching tree huggers."

– Colonel Mike Capstick,
Commander, SAT-A, Kabul, September 2005

The title of this book reflects a reality of contemporary peace and security operations in which both military and development inputs are needed to help build sustainable societies. As stated in the Foreword of the US Army's 2006 *Counterinsurgency* manual:

Soldiers and Marines are expected to be nation builders as well as warriors. They must be prepared to help re-establish institutions and local security forces and assist in rebuilding infrastructure and basic services. They must be able to facilitate establishing local governance and the rule of law. The list of such tasks is long; performing them involves extensive coordination and cooperation with many intergovernmental, host-nation, and international agencies.

Scholars have written that "the challenge of rebuilding after war is essentially a development challenge in the special circumstances of a war-torn society... (an) understanding of best practice in development ... must underpin responses to the plight of war-torn countries. War is not a single catastrophic event but a devastating way of life closely associated with chronic poverty and social injustice. Peace is not a quick fix but a development process that begins, and can be nurtured, long before ceasefires are brokered, and which needs to be sustained through years of postwar recovery."[1]

I was invited by the Canadian Forces Leadership Institute to write this monograph after participating in a conference and a seminar in Kingston in which I shared a number of insights and impressions gained in 2005/06 while living and working for a year in Kabul with Colonel (Col) Mike Capstick, 15 other soldiers and other Department of National Defence (DND) personnel as a member of the Strategic Advisory Team in Afghanistan

(SAT-A). I was hired by the Canadian International Development Agency (CIDA) as a capacity development worker and was embedded in this team of strategic planners, analysts and public affairs specialists in one of the first missions operating under Canada's policy of "3D" (Diplomacy, Development and Defence) or what later came to be known as a "Whole of Government", or an "Integrated Approach" to Canada's international activities. This book focuses on two of these three "Ds": Development and Defence.

The monograph begins with a brief description of recent changes in the military's requirements, the origins of 3D, how the SAT came to find itself in Kabul, and what we did while we were there. The main focus of the rest of the book is on my perceptions of the development side of military-development collaboration in an important part of a counter-insurgency and peace-building operation: the strengthening of communities and the institutions of state in the complex environment of a "security" campaign so the host government can address its own needs, and countries like Afghanistan can be helped to become stable, prosperous societies and full participants in the community of nations.

Conflicts such as the current counter-insurgency campaign in Afghanistan are not just military activities, and sustainable peace is not achieved with weapons alone. While security is a prerequisite for nation building, development work is an essential element in this campaign. Although there are many similarities in how development and military personnel go about their business, there are important differences that need to be better understood and incorporated into all levels of a campaign if the mission is to succeed. This book addresses these issues.

I was a participant-observer in a small part of Canada's Afghanistan campaign, and had ample opportunity during my time with them to learn how my military colleagues thought and operated. It has been an ongoing adventure: since completing my stint with SAT-A in August 2006, I have been a faculty member at the Pearson Peacekeeping Centre's United Nations Integrated Mission Staff Officers Course in Cornwallis, Nova Scotia. I also subsequently returned to Afghanistan to work with the United Nations Development Program (UNDP) as the Chief Technical Advisor in a new Coaches and Advisors Program for public sector capacity development, and later as an Institutional Development Advisor (DEVAD) to help the Afghanistan Civil Service Institute (ACSI) develop a strategic plan. When

I returned to Kabul with UNDP in late 2006, and again in 2007, I had the opportunity to see development from another perspective and to interact socially and professionally with Afghans and my military, development and diplomatic colleagues from many countries in this collaborative and multi-faceted peace-building initiative.

Since completing my SAT mission I have been mulling over, and sifting and sorting through the many impressions I accumulated in my time in Afghanistan, and have had productive exchanges with a number of colleagues in our development, diplomacy and defence establishments. I have also drawn on the experience of members of the Canadian Forces (CF) who served in similar peace and security campaigns in Haiti, the Balkans, the Middle East and other parts of the world. These exchanges have broadened and enriched my initial thoughts about the complexity of the issues the world is facing at this point, and the evolution of our collective ability to intervene and strengthen the capacity of fragile, post-conflict states so they can steadily increase their ability to manage their own affairs.

Several military acquaintances have said that they wish they had read a book such as this before they were deployed and found themselves in the midst of a campaign where they were facing a range of issues for which they had received little preparation. I hope this monograph lives up to their expectations.

I received a great deal of help in writing an earlier paper on development-military collaboration in working with communities as part of a counter-insurgency campaign, and also in preparing this monograph. I am thankful for the input from Afghan co-workers, the many military and development colleagues and others who encouraged this effort, and the Canadian Forces Leadership Institute personnel who found my comments and preliminary efforts worthy of greater elaboration. My son Peter, a professor in the development studies program at St. Francis Xavier University in Antigonish, Nova Scotia, has been a particularly helpful collaborator. Although I have benefited greatly from all this support, this book does not reflect the official views of any agency of the United Nations (UN), the Canadian or Afghan governments, or any organization or individual who provided assistance; I alone am responsible for the thoughts and opinions expressed here.

I hope readers find this work helpful in their efforts to build sustainable peace in Afghanistan and wherever else development and military actors work with host-country agencies to improve the lives of the people we serve.

I'll close this Preface with an email from a US Army officer serving with the International Security Assistance Force (ISAF) who read my previous paper on development-military collaboration in working with communities in a counter-insurgency:

> Sir,
>
> Got done reading your article, and I think that it needs to be read by every leader in the military before they come into theatre (so they understand the complexities of dealing with the local population).
>
> That being said, have you considered an additional paragraph in the beginning – "How much development work needs to be done?" The main point is that you can't do all of the work, since that makes the local government look inefficient and powerless. You can only do as much work as the local government can manage/control.
>
> Classic example – USAID [United States Agency for International Development] builds a school, but the local government can't hire teachers or buy equipment. So the empty school is now a symbol of the local government's lack of power whenever someone walks by it. Or a hideout for bad guys.
>
> Hope this helps.[2]

So do I. Happy reading.

Andy Tamas
Almonte, Ontario
Canada
March 2008

Introduction

Over the past few decades it has become increasingly evident there is a need for greater collaboration between the military and the field of international development. With the changing nature of warfare – no longer primarily a conflict between two opposing standing armies – and the need to incorporate civilian agencies such as UNDP and CIDA in peace and stability missions, the military needs to learn more about what is beyond the third block of the Three Block War or the humanitarian dimension of full-spectrum operations. Likewise, the development field needs to learn more about how the military operates so the collaboration can be a two-way street. This monograph focuses mainly on responding to the military's needs, and will also be useful for members of the international development community and others such as diplomats and host-country government personnel.

Development-related goals are now essential factors in achieving military success, particularly in counter-insurgency campaigns where the community and its sometimes tenuous relationship with the host government are key factors in how the society operates. One of the most effective tools in what is being called Fourth Generation Warfare is helping to build a society where people have more to gain by laying down their arms and becoming engaged in the local economy than by continuing to fight – in other words, by having a decent job in a stable secure society, with an adequate income to support their families.

Most planners and leaders of military operations traditionally have not focused on issues such as community development, governance, literacy, public administration, policing, agriculture or strengthening the private sector. These and other essential dimensions of stability and an effective counter-insurgency campaign are outside the military's areas of expertise – they are seen as somebody else's responsibility. However, because of the dangers of operating in many of the areas where the military is engaged in peace and security missions, civilian development personnel often cannot do their work to strengthen local systems. They may sometimes require military escorts and other supports to help them go about their business. This impacts the effectiveness of civilian personnel, and increases the burden on the military to become more involved in the work traditionally done by others.

INTRODUCTION

Some of the knowledge, attitudes and skills normally found in civilian personnel are required by military staff so that they can better support – and when it is appropriate carry out – these essential functions of peace and stability campaigns. Tactical-level activity needs to be guided by relevant doctrine grounded in appropriate concepts and methods at the operational and strategic levels. This is a major challenge facing military operations in Afghanistan and other parts of the world.

The field of international development is one of the most complex areas of practice there is – it encompasses a broad range of social, cultural, psychological, spiritual, economic, political, physical, environmental, administrative and other factors that go into making a society function.

Although development workers and military personnel have not traditionally considered each other to have much in common and there are indeed important differences in their work, there are also many similarities in what they both do.

A common feature of international development and the military's activity is that they both intervene in a system to alter its trajectory to achieve a desired effect. Where development and military planners differ is in the role of the inhabitants of that system in this process. In development, the intervention is done with the invitation, permission and active participation of the system's inhabitants, with a view to having them take ownership of the innovation and carry it forward on their own well into the future – this is one way of looking at "sustainable development". In most traditional conflicts, military planners do not invite the target to help design, carry out and take ownership of their initiatives.

Each uses their own tools to achieve their own objectives, and they work in systems that have quite different internal conditions: they have been accustomed to working at different stages of the nation-building sequence. Traditionally, the military secures an area and establishes some stability before significant development work begins. This role definition is a core feature of the culture and administrative machinery of both systems.

One of the difficulties with this arrangement is that peace and stability operations are often seen as purely military activities, and when military objectives have been met the troops withdraw, sometimes before the host country is able to adequately manage its own affairs: East Timor is an example. All too often the result has been a resurgence of violence requiring a reintroduction of foreign forces, sometimes in situations that have worsened in the interim, as in Haiti.

In conflicts such as in Afghanistan where an enemy moves within, and in some cases is actively supported by segments of the population, an orderly sequencing of different actors doing their respective jobs in environments of progressively higher levels of stability no longer applies. If we consider an ad hoc 10-level scale from total chaos and violence to total harmony and well-being, it can be said that the military usually works at levels 1 through 3 or so – beyond that level community norms supported by police and justice systems are the main elements in maintaining security and order in a healthy and open society. Most civilian development agencies are accustomed to working in these relatively stable contexts, say from levels 3 to about 5 – from that point on the society should be able to look after its own progress.

While the traditional view is that the military's main function is to help establish security, it has become increasingly evident that sustainable antidotes to insurgency and insecurity include good governance, adequate services to the public and a healthy economy that provides gainful employment and benefits the poor. These elements – which are usually considered as being squarely in the civilian development workers' domain – combine with local culture and belief systems to shape community norms linked to order, trust in government, and stability. Without security, effective government services and a healthy economy, insurgents will continue to find relatively accessible bases from which to operate, and peace-building will not take solid root in the population.

In this type of conflict it is clear that development work needs to begin earlier in the peace-building sequence, about level 1.5 onward. Development efforts must take place in the midst of overt conflict so community norms will shift away from supporting or passively accepting agents of the insurgency and toward increased trust in government.

The US military has recognized this need and its role in providing some of these services:

While security is essential to setting the stage for overall progress, lasting victory comes from a vibrant economy, political participation, and restored hope.... Depending on the state of the insurgency, therefore, (soldiers)... should prepare to execute many non-military missions to support COIN [counter-insurgency] efforts. Everyone has a role in nation building, not just Department of State and civil affairs personnel.[3]

This more turbulent arena for development interventions raises at least two issues:

- If the military becomes more of a development agency it will expose itself to the risks of mission creep as it ventures further into a complex area for which it might not be well equipped.

- If civilian development agencies place their personnel in high-risk environments they must be prepared to deal with casualties.

These issues have significant human, political and strategic-operational-tactical implications that can be addressed in part by answering the following questions:

- What kind of development work is required?

- Where should it take place?

- Who will do it?

There are no easy answers to these questions: what is clear is that all the major actors need to work together and share their knowledge and methods to achieve desired results. Canada's "Whole of Government" approach which combines military, development, diplomatic and other agencies is a broad-based response to the need to integrate our international peace and security activities. While each operation will have its own requirements, the military is increasingly being called upon to become more engaged in activities traditionally carried out solely by civilian agencies. In some cases the military itself is providing development-like support to increase the capacity of host-country institutions (i.e.: strategic planning assistance provided to the Afghan government by SAT in Kabul and the support for local government provided by the Civil-Military Co-operation (CIMIC) unit in the Kandahar Provincial Reconstruction Team (PRT)), and in others, the military works closely with foreign and domestic civilian agencies and local governments to support their development efforts. In both cases there are requirements that fall outside the scope of most traditional military training, education and institutional systems.

This book is designed to fill some of that gap. It is broken down as follows:

Chapter 1 describes the purpose of this book, which is mainly to provide a set of navigational aids for military leaders to help them have some sense of what this field of development is all about. It introduces the notion of a need for a change in mindset to achieve desired effects – this theme is taken up in greater detail later in the book. Chapter 1 also summarizes a few of the major planning frameworks in the development field, several factors linked to coherence (or lack thereof) in the area, excerpts from project documents from typical development initiatives in Afghanistan and Angola, and concludes with a section on gender and development.

Chapter 2 is a brief summary of the origins of the "Whole of Government" or "Integrated Approach" and the role of development in asymmetric or Fourth Generation Warfare.

Chapter 3 describes the origins and activities of one of Canada's first collaborative development/military missions, the SAT in Afghanistan, summarizes my role as the development worker on the team, and raises a few concerns about SAT operations.

Chapter 4 summarizes the main features of capacity development, the current label for a multi-dimensional process to increase the performance of an organization, community or society.

Chapter 5 describes strategy and methods, the main features of how development activity is conceptualized and carried out. It is no simple matter and hopefully this section will give military readers sufficient insight into development workers' thinking and methods so they can build bridges between their own strategies and the approaches used by their Birkenstock-wearing collaborators in this common enterprise.

INTRODUCTION

Chapter 6 is a summary description of who's who, the main local and foreign non-military actors who are likely to have some influence in a country where a peace and stability mission is being carried out. It also indicates some of the benefits and challenges that may be encountered in working with them.

Chapter 7 summarizes a few of the key factors in finding out how a society or region works and what is involved in designing and carrying out a series of activities to foster its development.

Chapter 8 discusses the mission of counter-insurgency campaigns and defines a number of areas where development-military collaboration calls for fundamental changes in approaches and identities of the actors in these joint enterprises.

Chapter 9 describes a few readily-available tools and approaches the military can use to select appropriate personnel for these joint missions, and to analyze and work with the environments in which they will be operating.

Chapter 10 summarizes the main lessons and recommendations implicit in other parts of this book and indicates the global issues that need to be addressed as an integrated civilian-military approach becomes a permanent feature in our international peace and security missions.

Each chapter is written largely as a stand-alone unit, with the view that readers may be more interested in some issues than in others. While repetition is hopefully kept to a minimum, this modular format makes it difficult to eliminate entirely.

Standardization and Skill Sets In Development Work

A note is in order on the variety of approaches and training processes in the development field. Unlike the military, which has a relatively consistent set of processes and structures from one country to another, there is little, if any, such standardization in international development. People become "development experts" through a wide variety of processes and there are ideologically opposed camps and associated debates within the field on many aspects of this work.

Skill sets are key elements in an intervention process. Not only do collaborating organizations such as CIDA and the CF normally operate in different environments, their talented human resources are produced by quite different educational systems: while the military has a relatively well-organized training program for virtually all its occupations, there is no equivalent in the development community. CIDA, for example, does not train its own development workers; there is no widely-accepted or well-organized route along which aspiring practitioners can move through progressively more complex levels of work, and learn processes to increase their expertise in the field. Although CIDA staff might think otherwise, the agency does not actually do development: it plans and administers it. Most of the actual field-level development work is done by a variety of Non-Governmental Organizations (NGOs) and consulting firms, each of which has their own way of operating and defining competence in the field.

While there are a number of universities offering degrees in something called "development" these vary widely in curriculum and philosophy, and most pay little attention to the basic organizational analysis and cross-cultural human relations skills which form the core of a practitioner's tool kit. Although some have fieldwork components which expose students to actual development projects, most teach *about* development rather than *how to do it*, and much of the curriculum focuses on theory and issues such as the evils of western imperialism and what has gone wrong rather than on what works.

This disorder is partially due to fundamental challenges facing the whole development field, which is in a constant state of redefinition at the core of its purpose and methodology. It is also due to the age and formative experience of most academics, many of whom draw from personal experience gained in their early years with agencies such as the Peace Corps or CUSO [Canadian University Services Overseas], which operated in a very different world.

An example of this challenge is the part of the field called "capacity development" that will be discussed in greater detail later in this book. Years of global debate searching for acceptable definitions, categorizations, methods and performance indicators have not yet produced a widely-accepted operational framework that can be clearly linked to an established hierarchy such as the strategic-operational-tactical planning system used by the military. This incoherent system produces a wide variety of professionals who can call themselves development practitioners, only some of who may be well-suited to collaborating with the military in theatres such as Afghanistan.

The information in this book is based on my views of development, many of which I hope are generally shared by my colleagues. Other practitioners may have quite different views on the topics in this monograph and may be able to support their opinions with information based on their own experience or on sources different from those I chose to include. There is little that can be done to assure the reader that mine is the "right" view of development – it is what I have thought or selected from the literature that is consistent with what I have seen and experienced and what seems to work, and that is about as solid as it gets in this business.

The implications of these comments are that military personnel who are collaborating with people in the development field should be prepared to encounter a variety of views and even contradictory perceptions of what is going on and how things ought to be done. This makes a complex area even more complicated – not only are there considerable challenges in the relationships between military actors and the local people, communities and administrative environments, there is also room for uncertainty in relating to potential co-workers in the development agencies with which the military needs to interact to help a society improve its circumstances.

Common factors in all these encounters are the need for high-quality human relations, and flexibility in applying best principles of development to the practical needs of the population being served. These process-related factors will contribute to achievement of optimum results. This monograph provides a number of navigation aids to support these efforts.

CHAPTER 1

Purpose of this Book and an Introduction to Development

Navigation Aids For Missions Like Afghanistan

As noted earlier, the changing nature of warfare is altering the roles and skill sets required of the military. Since the end of the Cold War, most conflicts have been based on asymmetric power relationships, or what Thomas Hammes describes as Fourth Generation Warfare[4], and have involved a number of new actors such as communities and religious groups in the fray. This new context combines a range of requirements formerly outside the scope of most military training, such as diplomacy, humanitarian aid and development, each of which is a field of practice at least as complex and challenging as military activity. Having some understanding of these previously distinct domains is a requirement for success in contemporary peace and stability missions.

The primary purpose of this book is therefore to provide a number of development-related "navigation aids" for senior officers to support their efforts on missions such as Afghanistan and other similar campaigns which they may be called upon to undertake in the future.

Increase Effectiveness of Development-Military Collaboration

The military is not alone in needing to better understand how another intervention-oriented group thinks and operates. The numerous development agency personnel who are operating in regions where there are active peace and security missions need to work with the military to help local actors strengthen their systems of government and improve their economies. While this monograph is focused primarily on helping the military better understand development, it is far from being a comprehensive guidebook to help the development community and the military better understand each others' ways of thinking and operating. It illustrates several of the many areas where military and development concepts and approaches differ and other areas where they resemble each other, and should help improve the effectiveness of the collaboration that is essential in helping host societies improve their circumstances.

A Continuum of Inputs: Kinetic, Stability, Humanitarian, Development

A variety of inputs are made in an environment which is the focus of international peace and security operations. As indicated in the concept of the Three Block War, these vary from intense combat at one end of the continuum, to the provision of humanitarian aid, development, and ultimately, as conditions near the other end of the continuum improve, the withdrawal of foreign actors as the society begins to provide its own stability and manage its own self-generated growth. In the parts of the continuum where international aid agencies and military forces are active, there are several important distinctions in their inputs, described as Kinetic Operations, Stability Operations, Humanitarian Aid, and Development.

This book deals mainly with the latter two – it touches on humanitarian aid, but focuses mainly on development, which is one component of the third block of the Three Block War, and on what follows as a people are helped to build up a fully-functional society.

Because security conditions are likely to vary in different parts of a country or region, the same central command group is likely to be leading intense kinetic operations in one area while helping strengthen local government or support the private sector in another. Military actors play a major role – direct or indirect – in all these contexts and they need to know enough about the overall development process so the long-term impact of their input can be as constructive as possible.

Change of Mindset: Thinking About Two Things at the Same Time

While kinetic operations play a major role in Fourth Generation Warfare, conflicts such as in Afghanistan are not resolved using weapons alone. The broad range of supports needed to build a sustainable society are the inputs that create the conditions for a lasting peace. As noted earlier, due to security problems most civilian development specialists – foreigners and locals – who know how to provide the range of required inputs often cannot work in non-permissive environments. However, without some of those support mechanisms, the society is likely to continue to be an unstable environment in which insurgents can operate: somebody has to do the work needed to bring stability and development to an environment.

When discussing this situation with Brigadier-General (BGen) Daniel Pepin he spoke of discovering the need for a change of mindset as he worked at ISAF headquarters in Afghanistan.

> I am of the view that the military is able to adapt itself, whether it is to respond to a threat or an enemy and to find ways to win when confronted with this threat, and they are also able to adjust themselves to a development environment (as they did successfully in Bosnia, for example).
>
> The challenge that is relatively new is to be able to do both at the same time. From my experience in Afghanistan I have observed that the military (both Canadian and American) has a tendency to be more comfortable with kinetic than non-kinetic activities such as development. That is why when a situation arises where both types of interventions are necessary, kinetic operations receive more attention.
>
> This being said, my comments on changing the "mindset" referred to the capacity to develop an ability to act in both roles at the same time.[5]

When given a choice of tasks to accomplish it is natural that most people will focus on those they feel they are able to handle relatively easily and attach lower priority to those for which they feel less prepared – this is human nature. BGen Pepin's comments indicate that this is not good enough in modern peace and stability campaigns.

It is not surprising that some may want to shy away from becoming fully immersed in the development side of a campaign – it is complicated stuff. The field includes all the elements required for a stable, prosperous and sustainable society – governance, justice, education, health, agriculture, a vibrant private sector that provides employment for the poor, and more. The essence of "development" is to support a country's efforts to increase the capacity of all of these elements to serve the society: no easy task.

This monograph provides a number of "navigation aids" to help military leaders make sense of the sometimes bewildering array of non-kinetic requirements and to have a better sense of what is needed, where to focus their energies, and who to work with to increase stability in the societies in which they are working. Its purpose is to help military leaders become more comfortable with development so they can better balance their support for kinetic and non-kinetic initiatives.

Development for what?

What is development for? This seemingly obvious question is far from simple and is a much-debated topic in some quarters. Is it just material development? Is it having access to the goods and services required for a good physical existence, or is there more to it than things one can purchase or construct?

Maslow's hierarchy of needs[6] identifies matters such as safety and physical functions as the foundational requirements – without them other higher-order social, psychological and emotional needs cannot be met. One of the primary objectives of Canada's engagement in Afghanistan or other fragile states is to support the achievement of basic safety and stability as well as broader objectives in the development of a sustainable society. The following sections summarize and discuss the merits of the main types of plans that are usually found in one form or another at the core of development initiatives.

Millennium Development Goals

The "Millennium Development Goals" (MDG), which are often cited as objectives of development, are described in a 2004 paper prepared by the North-South Institute for the then-incoming Prime Minister (Paul Martin):

> In September 2000, 147 world leaders gathered in New York and agreed on the Millennium Declaration, outlining their collective commitment to sustainable development and poverty reduction. In December 2000, the UN General Assembly asked the Secretary-General to prepare a road map for the implementation of the declaration. Building upon previous work undertaken by the OECD [Organization for Economic Co-operation and Development], the annex to this road map sets out 8 Millennium Development Goals, along with 18 targets and 48 indicators to measure progress toward them. A powerful momentum is building behind these goals. They are becoming a measure of the commitment of donor countries and a measure of the success, or failure, of development assistance.[7]

The Goals and Targets are summarized as follows:

Goals	Targets
1. Eradicate extreme poverty and hunger	1. Halve, between 1990 and 2015, the proportion of people whose income is less than $1 per day.
	2. Halve, between 1990 and 2015, the proportion of people who suffer from hunger.
2. Achieve universal primary education	3. Ensure that by 2015 children everywhere—boys and girls alike—will be able to complete a full course of primary schooling.
3. Promote gender equality and empower women	4. Eliminate gender disparity in primary and secondary education preferably by 2005 and to all levels of education no later than 2015.
4. Reduce child mortality	5. Reduce by two thirds, between 1990 and 2015, the under-5 mortality rate.
5. Improve maternal health	6. Reduce by three fourths, between 1990 and 2015, the maternal mortality ratio.
6. Combat HIV/AIDS, malaria, and other diseases	7. Have halted by 2015, and begun to reverse, the spread of HIV/AIDS.
	8. Have halted by 2015, and begun to reverse, the incidence of malaria and other major diseases.

cont...

Goals	Targets
7. Ensure environmental sustainability	9. Integrate the principles of sustainable development into country policies and programs and reverse the loss of environmental resources.
	10. Halve by 2015 the proportion of people without sustainable access to safe drinking water.
	11. By 2020, to have achieved a significant improvement in the lives of at least 100 million slum dwellers.
8. Develop a global partnership for development	12. Develop further an open, rule-based, predictable, non-discriminatory trading and financial system (includes a commitment to good governance, development, and poverty reduction, both nationally and internationally).
	13. Address the special needs of the LDCs [Least Developed Countries]. This includes tariff- and quota-free access for their exports, enhanced debt relief for heavily indebted poor countries, cancellation of official bilateral debt, and more generous official development assistance for countries committed to poverty reduction.
	14. Address the special needs of landlocked countries and small island developing states.
	15. Deal comprehensively with the debt problems of developing countries through national and international measures in order to make debt sustainable in the long term.
	16. In cooperation with developing countries, develop and implement strategies for decent and productive work for youth.
	17. In co-operation with pharmaceutical companies, provide access to affordable, essential drugs in developing countries.
	18. In co-operation with the private sector, make available the benefits of new technologies, especially information and communication.

TABLE 1 – MILLENNIUM GOALS AND TARGETS[8]

Most international development activities make reference to the MDGs when they describe their objectives. However, the Goals are the subject of considerable debate (as is much of what goes on in the development field). One form of critique is based on charges that the MDGs are the product of a northern neo-liberal view of the world and do not adequately reflect the views and priorities of the south.

Another line of critique is based on a concern that the Goals are set unrealistically high and do not take into account the lack of capacity in recipient countries that limits their ability to absorb and properly utilize development funds. An example is a paper by Clemens, Kenny and Moss, which offers a critique of the MDGs and argues that the current emphasis on universal goals and donor aid flow could undermine development efforts in two ways:

- most countries will fail to achieve the MDGs because they have been set at a level which is unrealistically high for most countries, requiring unprecedented levels of growth and development within a very short time-frame. Consequently, the authors argue, the specific targets of the MDGs have set up many countries for unavoidable 'failure'. The risk, they suggest, is that some governments pursuing wise policies and making historically encouraging progress on development indicators could be weakened or de-legitimized by the label of 'failure' in 2015.

- calls for increases in aid to achieve the MDGs tend to assume a straightforward relationship between the volume of aid and the rate of development. However, the paper cites evidence that suggests that there is a weak link between the volume of aid and the rate of development, and highlights the often overlooked assumptions upon which costings of the MDGs are based. The authors argue that the relationship between aid and development is complex, and is dependent on factors such as national capacity to productively utilize additional funds.[9]

The authors warn that the MDGs may run the risk of creating an unwarranted climate of pessimism about development and aid and lead to reductions in aid. They suggest that future international development goals should:

- be country-specific and flexible, using country-specific benchmarks;

- take countries' historical performance into account;

- focus more on intermediate targets than outcomes; and

C H A P T E R 1

- be considered benchmarks to spur action in cases where assistance is not working, rather than technically feasible goals.[10]

There are other critiques as well, dealing with issues such as gender equity, the needs of people with disabilities, and the lack of attention to security, political processes and other underlying factors which make real change possible. Military members working with development agencies in the field are likely to encounter staff of NGOs and other organizations who are highly critical of the MDGs as a suitable framework for development activity – this is part of the diversity within the field.

Even though there may be problems with the MDGs, they have a broad base of international support and have become established as high-level strategic goals and major categories for planning development activity. With varying degrees of success, each donor country tries to incorporate them into their development initiatives, and recipient countries reflect them in their national development plans, which are usually based on what is known as a Poverty Reduction Strategy Paper (PRSP).

Poverty Reduction Strategy Papers (also called National Development Plans) – and what often actually happens

Most countries seeking international assistance are required by the International Monetary Fund (IMF) to prepare a PRSP that describes their recent history, current situation and how they want to improve in a variety of categories. PRSPs are usually defined for a specific time frame, typically five years. The international financial institutes (IFIs) provide guidelines on how the poverty reduction plans are to be prepared:

> ... all low-income countries... have been required to prepare a PRSP to be eligible for any World Bank borrowing. A dramatic innovation introduced with the PRSP was the requirement that governments engage in "broad-based consultations" with civil society and the private sector in order to affirm that the PRSP has public support. The rationale of such a process relates to the widely-recognized need for "ownership" of development policies by governments and their publics, if those policies are to be implemented.[11]

8

In most post-conflict states during the early stages of reconstruction there are limited means to carry out broad-based consultations, and civil society and private sector organizations are not well developed. The first PRSPs therefore rarely have the public ownership and support desired by the IFIs. These shortcomings are apparently accepted by the World Bank (WB) and other donors who recognize the country's PRSP as part of an evolving framework for their inputs.

In keeping with this arrangement, by early 2006, Afghanistan had prepared the Interim Afghan National Development Strategy (I-ANDS) and major donors accepted the related UN-sanctioned Afghanistan Compact as the framework for supporting the reconstruction of that country. CIDA has a development plan to guide its expenditures in Afghanistan; a framework that evolves as conditions in the country change and as CIDA also undergoes changes in how it wishes to support development in Afghanistan and elsewhere.

Other recipient countries have their own equivalent PRSPs, and donor countries and international development agencies (such as the WB and UNDP) that work in these countries have designed programs that usually match these plans in a manner consistent with their own foreign policy priorities or development mandates.

There are questions in some quarters about the use of PRSPs in a country in conflict. Alison Scott of the IMF wrote:

> The general principles of the PRSP assume that it is a national strategy built on consensus and social inclusion. This may be a difficult assumption in conflict-affected countries because those in power are often a party to the conflict and may feel that it requires a military solution. Inter-group hostility may impede consensus, and marginalized groups may lack voice and representation. Conflict resolution and peace building may be important for poverty reduction, but this may be difficult to bring about in a situation of ongoing tension and hostility.
>
> In general, PRSPs also need to be technically sound, contextually relevant and realistic. They should provide an appropriate diagnosis of poverty, and a set of policies that are relevant to it and

capable of being resourced and implemented. In conflict-affected countries, the PRSP should include an analysis of both conflict-related and structural poverty, and would have to adjust the scope of policy interventions to local resource and capacity constraints. In some cases a twin-pronged or phased strategy may be appropriate, initially concentrating on short-term needs and priorities.

Depending on the scale of conflict involved and especially if the conflict is still ongoing, there may be very considerable constraints on a PRSP process. However, the PRSP also offers an important opportunity for addressing some of the more serious problems of conflict-related poverty, as well as for reforming the wider social, economic and political problems. The PRSP could provide a framework for improved coordination on humanitarian assistance; lay the basis for short-term reconstruction and reconciliation, as well as longer-term development; strengthen democratic processes and help to build technical capacity amongst government and civil society groups. All these changes would be gradual, and would most likely be effective where the focus of the PRSP was limited to the areas where real progress could be made, even within the conflict environment. Within this narrower remit, capacity could be built and lessons learned that could be scaled up when the conflict subsided.[12]

In post-conflict societies the first PRSPs are usually prepared with input from a relatively small group of senior bureaucrats, foreign consultants and politicians. Other parts of these countries' governing and administrative systems are not aware of its provisions and operate in ways that are not influenced by the framework. This is not surprising in a recovering fragile state that does not have a well-developed communications system or a smoothly-running, well-coordinated public service.

In a parallel and largely unrelated activity, the international development ministries in the many donor countries have implementation plans for the countries in which they want to work. These donor countries' programs reflect their own foreign policy priorities and these may (or may not) be consistent with the recipient countries' development priorities.

While development funds are usually allocated for initiatives consistent with the host country's PRSP and the donors' development and foreign policy priorities, the actual picture can be quite different and far from being as clear as this sounds. Sometimes a recipient country is in such a position that it will take whatever help it can get and will accept donor input regardless of consistency with its own priorities as defined in its PRSP. This is called donor-driven aid and is a problem in many parts of the world.

Donors sometimes fund initiatives that fall outside their official development strategy framework. Even though some in the donor network might be familiar with their own policies and priorities, they may not exert control over the various agencies supported by their country's development funds. International NGOs that receive support from a variety of governments, like Médecins Sans Frontières (MSF), CARE or Oxfam, have their own development priorities that may or may not reflect the strategies of the countries from which they receive their funds. Their priorities may also be quite different than the goals in the PRSPs of the countries in which they operate.

To make things even more interesting, there can be considerable variety in the development strategies of the many donor agencies and countries, resulting in a rather uncoordinated set of inputs. These and other related problems have long been recognized by donor countries and agencies, and they are taking steps to remedy the situation. One such effort resulted in what has been called the Paris Declaration on Aid Effectiveness, an international agreement endorsed on 2 March 2005, to which over 100 Ministers, Heads of Agencies and other Senior Officials have ascribed, committing their countries and organisations to continue to increase efforts in harmonisation, alignment and managing aid for results with a set of monitorable actions and indicators.

Although the Declaration is seen as a positive step in coordinating the flow of development assistance to a country in need, the situation in most recipient countries does not yet match the aspirations of the many heads of state who signed the document. The Declaration is often mentioned as a desirable but unrealized ideal when observers complain about the lack of coordination of aid activity in a country.

Competition among aid agencies is one of the obstacles to full coordination. NGOs can find themselves vying with each other for limited funds, so they try to present themselves as unique and better than their rivals in

CHAPTER 1

important ways; this contributes to a reluctance to collaborate. Donors sometimes compete with each other for "good" projects that are often seen as places to "invest" their funds where there will be "good return", in terms of clear measurable improvements in some aspect of the country's operations. In fragile states there can be relatively few of these good places to invest. Donor agencies that do not spend sufficient funds, especially in some of the more publicized troubled regions of the world, are therefore at risk of having their budgets reduced, resulting in loss of personnel and a host of other problems they prefer to avoid. This is part of what goes on in the background in what some cynically call Aid Incorporated, a self-perpetuating industry. This is a large topic that is beyond the scope of this monograph.

Donors also have their own priorities and funding mechanisms, each with their own time frames and procedures. Some are not able or willing to channel their funds through the host country government in keeping with a provision of the Paris Declaration that was designed to strengthen local administrative capacity. Recipient countries are faced with a major challenge in attempting to harmonize, coordinate and absorb these inputs in support of their own development strategies.

The link between the need to coordinate Canadian and other countries' international development activities to improve the performance of government in fragile post-conflict states was clearly described in the paper by the North-South Institute:

> This (coordination) seems particularly important in order to include, in the purview of the new framework, countries which are on the periphery of the international system because they are failed states, or mired in protracted conflict, or for other reasons have become regarded as "poor performers". If such countries are ignored, or if attempts are not made to engage them and address their particular issues, there is a serious danger that they will become havens for conflict, terrorism, disease and other problems that do not respect international borders. Multilateral organizations (the UN, international financial institutions) and regional groups (the African Union, OAS) are better placed (than Canada) to deal with failed states or poor performers. However, there is currently no accepted approach to such countries—no

CHAPTER 1

acknowledged or proven way of helping "poor performers" turn into "good performers." Canada should take a leadership role in the multilateral organizations and in working with regional groups such as the AU to spearhead initiatives to deal with such countries satisfactorily.[13]

These comments on the challenges of PRSPs indicate that the military notion of a broadly-accepted campaign plan that aligns everyone's activities around a common mission is a much-discussed ideal that does not really exist in international development. Simply reading the PRSP and the donor countries' plans will not provide sufficient information to predict or define where development activity is taking place and what kinds of initiatives are being supported. There are many actors who have influence on what goes on in a country, a number of whom are likely to be doing things outside the planning frameworks described here. Coordinating these (or even keeping track of who is doing what in various parts of a country) is an ongoing challenge in this field.

There is also some question as to whether elaborate national development plans are at all realistic or useful – in the section on "Planning as Public Relations" in his acclaimed book, *The Rise and Fall of Strategic Planning*, Henry Mintzberg, a respected management scholar, states:

> ... national leaders who wish to be thought modern ... have a document with which to dazzle their visitors, one that no one who matters attends to. In fact, it need not be a means to surmount a nation's difficulties, but rather a mode of covering them up. And why shouldn't they do this? After all, capitalist America insisted upon a plan in return for its foreign aid to poor countries. It did not matter whether the plan worked; what did count was the ability to produce a document which looked like a plan ... Presumably to be able to plan is tantamount to being able to spend money wisely.[14]

This seems to be confirmed by the experience of a member of the SAT-A who read an early draft of this monograph. He reported several areas where senior Afghan government ministry staff did not demonstrate ownership of a number of initiatives, including not paying much attention to the Afghan National Development Strategy (ANDS), Afghanistan's PRSP:

I have numerous other examples I could mention as well – one of them being the Afghan National Development Strategy. As you mention in your book, the fact that the international community demands a PRSP as a condition to release development funds is somewhat flawed. One of the responsibilities I inherited was acting as the ministry's focal point for the ANDS as it relates to the Air Transport benchmarks. The main difficulty I have realized over the last month or so with this responsibility is that the ANDS is hardly a blip on the radar for any of the ministry staff, including the Deputy Ministers and Minister. In reality, the ones bearing the torch of the ANDS within the Ministry are the international advisors (all 3 of us). With what I know about how the ANDS secretariat is staffed and structured, and what I know now about the composition of the average line ministries (i.e., I strongly suspect the situation in MoTCA [Ministry of Transport and Civil Aviation] is the same elsewhere), I find it hard to believe that implementation of the ANDS can be achieved – there appears to be a large disconnect between what the international community wants, and what the current Afghan government is actually capable of and willing to do.[15]

So, while it is necessary to have a way to align inputs around clearly defined lines of action, and for some systematic method of determining priorities and assessing performance, one should not consider that a country's PRSP is the only thing to consider in defining what happens or deciding how to support a country's progress – it may play a much smaller role than some in the development field would like to admit. There are many other factors at play.

Development activity is often influenced by the personal characteristics of key individuals in the network of participating agencies (senior UN agency personnel, ambassadors, Heads of Aid, program managers and others) as well as formal and informal leaders in the host country's government and other systems. These personality-based factors can cause major divergences and changes in activity from one year to the next. It is far from being a stable, predictable affair in which everyone's priorities are consistent with stated goals and remain relatively clear and consistent over time.

These comments on the limitations and public relations aspects of PRSPs do not mean they are worthless and should be ignored. Far from it: in spite of their shortcomings they can act as a coordinating framework for inputs to help selected parts of a country's system move forward. Some coordination is better than none. The military can play a significant role in fostering coherence in these circumstances by becoming informed about the host country's PRSP and doing whatever possible to align military and civilian development activity with the main features of the plan. This alignment can support the host government's efforts to improve conditions in the country, and increase the consistency of the messages received by the population. Even if the people have no information about the PRSP, when they see similar types of high-priority activities being carried out in a rather consistent manner across the country they will gradually receive the message that their government has a strategy and is doing what it can to build a society that works, and that the donor community is supporting these efforts.

This broad topic will surface again at several points in Chapters 6 and 8, where there are more detailed descriptions of the many players in the development arena, and a discussion of the effects one wants to achieve in a peace and security mission.

Whose Vision Of Development?

A contentious issue in international development is the broad question of what constitutes a "developed" society and what sorts of things a development process should support. The overall purpose of development, which is to strengthen societies' abilities to provide opportunities for all members to realize their potential and to make their contributions to the advancement of the human family, can be approached in a wide variety of ways that are suited to the various contexts in question. While most development is based on western models of society, there are other visions that are rooted in the cultures and traditions of the countries receiving international assistance. Some address this issue by considering a social order as being "developed" when it is relatively stable and where international norms are respected, even if the indigenous patterns (which may be linked to forms of Islamic, Buddhist or Hindu principles, for example) are based on beliefs that are at odds with those at the root of the development agencies' own norms and cultures.

This variety of concepts of what development actually *is* requires practitioners (many of whom have been shaped by western concepts) to know

CHAPTER 1

how to identify and build on the patterns embedded in the host society, a process which can present a significant challenge. The difficulty cannot be reliably addressed by simply hiring professional host-country nationals to design and manage the development process. Many of them have been trained in the western model and their work-related thinking may well have been de-coupled from the patterns of thought in their cultures of origin. Most live in two worlds – the cultures of their families and home communities, and of academia and the development agency they work for – and when carrying out a development project they can be as culturally insensitive as an ethnocentric foreigner.

Sustainable development requires building on existing patterns of thought and collective behaviour, patterns which are rooted in a people's culture and beliefs. There are limits to the extent to which a project can be compatible with local culture – in trying to do so it may become incompatible with the implicit cultural patterns of the donor agency. A development initiative that is significantly at odds with the often unstated cultural patterns of the funding agency is not likely to survive: it is likely to be seen as incompetent development and be terminated by the donor. This fundamental contradiction is one of several major struggles in international development, and is a much bigger issue than can be dealt with in this monograph.

The issue of different conceptualizations of development was clearly articulated in Bjorn Hettne's 1982 report, *Development Theory and the Third World,* in which he traces the evolution of the underpinnings of development theory and practice. He identified two emergent trends in his work: concern for the environment, and what he called the indigenization of development theory. The latter theme acknowledges that the very foundation of what is considered to be development, and as a consequence how inputs should be designed and activities carried out, needs to be solidly rooted in the cultures and priorities of the recipient countries.

Many seasoned practitioners know there is a need for culturally-appropriate development design, but this awareness does not always find its way into action: what often actually happens, unfortunately, is that development inputs are designed and delivered with inadequate consideration of the compatibility of their underlying concepts with the patterns in local cultures. Where they are compatible with local cultures, the development agents managing them often need to go to extraordinary lengths to make them also appear compatible with the donor's underlying and largely invisible cultural patterns, and this is not always possible. This is a major contributor to ineffective development initiatives.

Culture And Criteria For Assessing Aid Effectiveness

Culture plays a big part in evaluating the impacts of development activity. The notion of "increasing aid effectiveness" is often discussed, and a variety of elaborate mechanisms are used to determine whether aid funds are achieving worthy results. Most projects use some sort of a results-based planning and monitoring framework to link inputs to measurable changes in the society receiving assistance (see sample project template on page 18).

As noted earlier, the conceptual framework used to plan, carry out and evaluate a development initiative is almost always rooted in the culture of the donor society and the professional groups involved. Although sustainable development requires that host country systems take over the initiative once external inputs cease, this usually involves discussions with officials of the government agencies in the sectors involved (water, agriculture, justice, etc.) who have learned how to negotiate with donor representatives. While there may be some contact with the ultimate recipients of the aid inputs, rarely are the intended beneficiaries of these inputs meaningfully involved in designing the project and in evaluating its results. The lack of an indigenous perspective in project design and evaluation contributes to the challenges described in the previous section.

While seasoned aid workers often know how to help beneficiaries express their needs and do what they can to incorporate them in project design, many inexperienced development agents, such as members of a recently-formed CIMIC unit, for example, may not yet have learned how this is done. Their lack of knowledge of the population may prompt them to use only industrialized-country criteria to assess aid effectiveness. These criteria may be focused on measuring factors of interest to the donors and might miss key elements that are of concern to the recipient population, and as such, may not be addressing what is of greatest importance to the people. Consequently, the inputs might miss the mark as far as the host society is concerned.

CHAPTER 1

PROGRAM-PROJECT PLANNING SHEET

Results-Based Management (RBM) Performance Framework – Canadian International Development Agency (CIDA)

Program-Project Title: (Name of the program or project) **Program-Project #:** (S # or K #) **Division & Section:** (e.g. ICD, EIP)
CPB [Contracts and Procurement Partner] Partner: (Name of Canadian partner – NGO etc.) **CIDA Officer:** (Name of responsible officer)

START: (Expected start date of the program or project, i.e. month & year) **END:** (Expected end date of the program or project, i.e. month & year)	**PRIORITY(IES):** (Main ODA priority(ies) addressed by the program or project)	**BRANCH RESULT(S):** (Branch Results addressed by the program or project)	**COUNTRY(IES):** (in which program or project will be implemented)
Total Budget: (The total amount of all contributions for the overall program or project) **CIDA Contribution:** (The amount of CPB's contribution only to the overall program or project)		**OBJECTIVES:** (Short-term "statements of intent" or purpose to be achieved within the life of a specific project or a period of a specific program. Linked to program or project outcome results)	**GOAL(S):** (Broad, long-term strategic "statements of intent" of the program or project. Linked to the impact results)
ACTIVITIES (The coordination, technical assistance, training and other project related actions organized and executed by project personnel. **Tip:** Answer the question "how" will we achieve the expected results – see definition of "result" below – of the program or project, i.e. what do we want to achieve?) **A result** is a describable or measurable change of state that is derived from a cause and effect relationship; at the output, outcome and impact level.	**OUTPUTS** (Expected outputs are the immediate, visible, concrete, tangible and logical consequences of a program or project inputs & activities)	**OUTCOMES** (Expected outcomes are the short-term effect of the program or project which are linked to the objectives. Corresponds to developmental results that are the logical consequence of achieving a combination of outputs. This is generally the level where the beneficiaries or end-users take ownership of the project and CIDA funding comes to an end. **Tip:** Results at the outcome level should answer the question:"What" is the observable, measurable change occurring in the program or project?)	**IMPACT(S)** (The broader, higher level, long-term effect or consequences linked to the goal(s) or vision of the program or project. Impact results are developmental results at the societal level that are the logical consequences of a combination of outcomes. **Tip:** Answer the question "why" are we doing this program or project?)

PERFORMANCE INDICATORS		
(Specific performance measures chosen because they provide valid, useful, practical, and comparable measures of progress towards achieving expected results. They can be quantitative: measures of quantity, including statistical statements and/or qualitative: judgments and perceptions derived from subjective analysis)		
(Performance indicators necessary to measure the progress towards achieving expected outputs)	(Performance indicators necessary to measure the progress towards achieving expected outcomes. **Tip:** Select indicators that are realistic and for which it is cost effective to collect the required data!)	(Performance indicators necessary to measure the progress towards achieving the expected impacts)
REACH		
(For "whom" will the program or project make a difference? The users, participants and direct beneficiaries – at the outcome level – or main clients of the program or project in terms of scope including WID/GE [Women in Development/Gender Equity] targets when appropriate. Can also include key stakeholders and delivery agents)		
RISKS & ASSUMPTIONS		
(The probability that a critical assumption required to attain the expected results is not met. Should be in direct link to the program or project and include both internal and external risks)		

TABLE 2 – PROGRAM-PROJECT PLANNING SHEET

However, it is not a simple matter of asking the recipients what they want and using their criteria as the only measure of assessing development effectiveness. Some aspects of indigenous culture may be obsolete, such as societies that have entrenched culturally-based patterns of gender inequality. In these societies, local people may not attach much importance to fostering the full participation of women in all aspects of life, and will not spontaneously include this in the criteria used to assess aid effectiveness. Also, traditional cultural factors may be at the root of the conflict that brought soldiers to the country in the first place – one of the desired effects of the peace and security mission is to help the society change this part of its long-established patterns of belief and behaviour.

While local or indigenous criteria are important to include in an assessment of aid effectiveness, international criteria are also important in development project design and evaluation. Practitioners need to know enough to make an appropriate blending of these sometimes quite different perspectives on development practice. This is one of the major challenges in the field, and is discussed in greater detail in Chapter 8.

Results-Based Management Performance Framework

To provide military readers with an indication of how a development agency designs its activities, an excerpt from CIDA's program planning documentation is shown above. Ideally, an entire development project or program can be described in summary form using this Results-Based Management (RBM) Performance Framework.

TABLE 2 – PROGRAM-PROJECT PLANNING SHEET (SEE PAGES 18 & 19)

Sample Public Sector Reform Projects – Afghanistan and Angola

As noted earlier, in a fragile post-conflict state the preparation of the first few PRSPs is often done by a relatively small group within a central ministry, often with considerable input from foreign consultants. Although they obtain information from other ministries to write the country's plan, this often also involves only a few people in each of those ministries. The departments rarely have the capacity to extend this consultative and goal-setting process to the working level, which often continues to operate much as in the past. It is a major challenge to build capacity and reorient public sector personnel so they clearly understand and know how to support the PRSP.

Donors such as UNDP, the WB and others are well aware of this and focus considerable effort on strengthening government operations, with an emphasis on public sector reform. The following excerpts from typical projects in Afghanistan and Angola provide an indication of what some of these projects are addressing.

Afghanistan: Request for Proposals for a Public Administration Reform Project

Project title: Consultancy Services to support the Independent Administrative Reform and Civil Service Commission to develop human resources policies and procedures and provide human resource training to ministries and agencies.

1. Background

1.1 Years of conflict in Afghanistan resulted in government with a deeply fragmented administration, poor policy management capacity, outdated administrative and financial management systems, a serious disconnect between provinces and the centre, and enduring capacity constraints. While many of the formal structures and some of the traditional practices of public administration remained in place, they lacked the human, financial and physical resources to do their job, particularly in a modern context.

...

2. Objectives

2.1 For the government to carry out its functions efficiently and provide effective delivery of basic services to its citizens, it will require appropriately skilled, experienced and motivated staff (with improved gender and ethnic balance) in better defined civil service positions with clear duties and outputs. The human resource management component of the Civil Service Reform project seeks to establish an effective system for managing human resources throughout government through establishing

CHAPTER 1

clear rules and procedures and supporting their implementation across government...

This excerpt of a 57-page document is part of a Request for Proposals (RFP) for a WB-funded project. The RFP is usually prepared by a WB staffer or a consultant who writes it after some discussion with senior government personnel. Very few regular Afghan public servants are capable of writing such a document on their own. Once the RFP has been written, it is reviewed by a few senior members of the relevant department in the host government who are strongly encouraged to approve it so the work can get underway. The extent to which senior officials fully understand the project documents and the entire process behind them is open to question.

Angola: Terms of Reference (TOR) for a Capacity Development Adviser

1. Background:
Angola suffered a period of 30 years of civil war, which ended in April 2002. The war had a severe impact in all aspects, causing thousands of deaths, millions of IDPs [internally displaced persons]; widespread existence of land mines; destruction of social and economic infrastructures and services; explosive population growth in the main cities, interruption of the economic life and macro-economic instability.

Both from the Colonial system and the socialist regime, Angola inherited a highly centralized system of governance, with institutional fragilities which undermines its capacity to create the enabling governance environment for development.

Consequently, Angola faces several constraints to its development, such as: a weak and centralized governance system, low Human Capital, low capacity for effective service delivery, a low incentive system, low statistics and Budgeting & Monitoring and Evaluation, limited civil society participation, and a constrained private sector. All of these constraints are hindering an enabling environment for development, which would include an efficient and effective public administration, rule of law, decentralization, existence of regulatory systems, civil participation and transparency and accountability.

2. Areas of Intervention

Against this background, UNDP Angola developed a Capacity Development Concept Paper which outlines major areas for capacity development interventions. However, final and specific areas of intervention would be determined by the CD Strategy Programme.

At this stage, possible areas of intervention would focus on both functional (cross-cutting or generic capacities) and technical (associated with particular field of professional expertise) capacities.

A medium and long-term CD strategy plan would focus on essentially strengthening the government and civil society functional capacities as described below and ensuring partnerships, co-ordination and involvement of the private sector in the process. The CS strategy plan will tackle:

Policy dialogue & partnership...

Mobilize & analyze, information and knowledge...

Monitoring & Accountability...

Implementation & Management...

The TOR describe the position's tasks and required qualifications in considerable detail – for a six- to eight-week assignment to work with the Angolan government and Civil Society Organizations (CSOs) to design a capacity development program to strengthen CSOs and enhance their role in improving governance in the country.

These two project document samples are for central ministry-level interventions that usually extend over several years and have long-term benefits for a population. In a counter-insurgency situation there are often also a number of shorter-term "Quick-Impact Projects" that attempt to rapidly improve conditions in communities and districts in which the military is operating. Factors related to these short-term smaller-scale activities are discussed later in this book.

In post-conflict, fragile states donors exert considerable influence on the focus, scope and depth of development initiatives largely because of two factors: the lack of capacity in the host country's systems, and the fact that they control the funds. This is particularly evident with the larger donors such as USAID and the WB that are sometimes viewed by local government officials as exerting a new kind of colonialist influence on the recipient country.

Gender And Development

Sustainable and equitable development requires the full participation of both genders, and until improvements occur in this aspect of a society the population will fail to realize its full potential. This has increasingly been recognized as a major challenge facing humanity, especially in conflict zones, and is the focus of a number of international conventions. One of these, UN Resolution 1325 (2000), is the first resolution ever passed by the Security Council (SC) that specifically addresses the impact of war on women, and women's contributions to conflict resolution and sustainable peace.[16]

This relatively short (less than 4 pages) and powerful UN resolution, available for download from the Security Council's website, is well worth a read:

> Reaffirming the important role of women in the prevention and resolution of conflicts and in peace-building, and stressing the importance of their equal participation and full involvement in all efforts for the maintenance and promotion of peace and security, and the need to increase their role in decision-making with regard to conflict prevention and resolution ... [17]

While gender equity and the full participation of women is widely recognized and often discussed as a major issue, it is frequently overlooked in planning development programs. In a recent communication with a professor of conflict studies at St. Paul University in Ottawa, her frustration was evident:

> ... it's amazing that women ... a vital element in Afghanistan's peace building (are) often missing in discussions about Afghanistan.

> Nothing, nada! They have much to contribute, many of them very empowered and in the middle of this all, working very hard but not included as they should be.
>
> I really don't believe peace and development will come to Afghanistan until this element is front and centre with so many others. Women have traditionally been very involved in development, especially in the rural areas where their labour was seen as necessary for the family's economic well-being. These sorts of historical/contextual issues need to be incorporated and exploited much more effectively.[18]

The challenge of gender equity is present in virtually all sectors of development, and can be a difficult area in which to accomplish positive results. An example can be seen in one of the rarely-heard criticisms of much-publicized women-focused microfinance projects in places like Bangladesh, where the women's increased wealth simply gives the men more to exploit. Many microfinance projects are recognizing this and are focusing their attention on widows and single mothers to avoid this problem. While this might be a short-term solution, it does not produce a permanent change in the balance of power and the quality of gender relations in the society.

Other initiatives have been more successful in changing gender-related patterns in communities. Some development projects, for example, stipulate that the distribution of development funds for community-level projects require both men and women to participate in community consultations on determining priorities and deciding what should be done. The perspectives and energies that women bring to the decision-making process enrich the consultation and contribute to higher-quality results that benefit the entire community. Some communities have experienced the benefits of higher-quality decisions from these mixed-gender consultations and decide to keep that process going. The new inclusive consultation process has become part of how these communities operate and continues after the projects have run their course.

The National Solidarity Program (NSP) in Afghanistan began as a women-centred co-operative movement facilitated by UN (Habitat) in Mazar-e-Sharif in the mid-1990s. Originally called the Community Fora Program, as it expanded to other communities such as Kabul and Bamiyan, it was successful in providing social and economic development services to thousands of people in the areas they served. The model was adapted by the new Karzai government as a means to foster village-level development, and although the women-centred focus was not maintained, the NSP is active in over 20,000 villages in the country. Without the ownership and full participation of women at the outset, this model would never have demonstrated its value and become one of the most successful development initiatives in the country.

The promotion of gender equity is as important in so-called developed societies as in the countries that are the focus of international assistance. There is still much to be done: the lack of women's voices in places of power is a global problem, and the fuss that is made when a woman becomes leader of a country, such as has occurred in Chile, Argentina and Germany, indicates how much further there is yet to go before the ideal is realized and gender equity becomes an established norm rather than an exception.

Achievement of gender equity requires concerted attention especially from men. It is not just a women's issue: until men assume responsibility for helping establish women's equality, the progress of the human family will be retarded. It is a security issue as well: patterns of male domination and oppression in the family foster attitudes that can surface in broader conflicts in the workplace, the community and ultimately in international affairs.

While development needs to be culturally-sensitive, there are some aspects of traditional culture that are simply obsolete, and those that perpetuate the inequality of women and men are clearly among the practices that need to change. A society cannot progress without the full participation of all its members, and overcoming the marginalization of women is one of the major requirements for growth.

It is usually the women (and their children) who bear a disproportionately heavy burden in zones of conflict, and their perspective provides information from sectors of the society that are hardest hit by the unrest. They often generate some of the best solutions to address the problems associated with the conflict.

All military and development initiatives in peace and security missions should make special efforts to become well informed of gender equity issues and any resources available in their areas of operation, and do whatever they can to shift existing patterns of belief and behaviour in the direction called for by UN Resolution 1325.

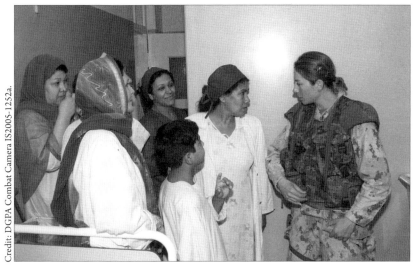

Credit: DGPA Combat Camera IS2005-1252a.

PHOTO 1: WOMEN, POTENTIAL CATALYSTS FOR AFGHAN TRANS-FORMATION, MAKING CONTACT WITH A CANADIAN FEMALE SOLDIER. IS THIS THE HOPE FOR THE FUTURE?

Specific actions that can be undertaken by military actors wanting to operate in a gender-aware mode include:

- When considering any community development initiative ask whether both men and women are involved in the planning and operation of the project, and do whatever possible to get women's views and active participation in the initiative.

- Ask community contacts how a planned initiative will differentially effect men and women, boys and girls, and encourage them to get disaggregated impact data wherever possible – simply asking the question and gathering the data promotes awareness of gender equity in the community.

- Wherever possible demonstrate gender equity in operations, for example as shown in the above photo of a female Canadian soldier talking with Afghan women.

- Create opportunities for the women in an area of operation (AO) to express their views to external agents and to their local leadership so their opinions and suggestions can be incorporated in the design of any intervention.

Additional resources may be available from host country agencies and development organizations working in the AO. Gender equity is a major theme in development in most parts of the world, and it is likely there are a number of government organizations and NGOs working in the field wherever there are peace and security operations. Many are likely to have connections with formal and informal women's groups in areas where the military operates. Most will welcome being sought out by military actors seeking information on ways to support their efforts and will provide relevant information on gender equity issues and strategies in the AO that the military can include in the development dimension of its operations.

Conclusion

This chapter has summarized a few of the major themes and issues in international development to provide a general overview of this large, complex and sometimes contradictory area of practice. What actually happens in the field is usually shaped by the personalities of the people involved and the frameworks of the projects and organizations that are active in the area; these can vary significantly from one agency or region to another. Most will reflect some version of the major elements highlighted here.

Further information on how development is actually done is described in Chapters 4 and 5, which summarize the main features of capacity development and describe other intervention strategies and methods.

CHAPTER 2

Background and Context

Origins And Description Of 3D Or The "Whole of Government" Approach

The "Whole of Government" approach is a recent example of various forms of civilian-military collaboration with a long history that includes the Marshall Plan in Europe and the reconstruction of Japan following WWII. These were essentially development operations that involved considerable civilian and military cooperation and were carefully designed to meet social, political and military objectives – to build viable and sustainable democratic capitalist states and reduce the likelihood that Germany and Japan would return to conditions that could result in further war.

There was a reduction in civilian-military collaboration during the decades of the Cold War, with the exception of counter-insurgency campaigns in countries such as Malaya, Oman and Vietnam. Field Marshal Sir Gerald Templer, who led the British response to the Malayan emergency of 1948-1960, coined the famous phrase 'hearts and minds', and expressed his view on the nature of counter-insurgency operations like this: "...the shooting side of the business is only 25 per cent of the trouble and the other 75 per cent lies in getting the people of this country behind us."[19]

Development activity focuses on that "other 75 per cent".

Most of the agencies providing international development assistance established their roots in reconstruction during the postwar era as well as in the preceding colonial period. That colonial legacy continues to exert its influence: as noted earlier, development is seen as beneficial and fostering emancipation and self-reliance and at the same time as an extension of colonialism, with major agencies such as the WB, USAID and UNDP as the new agents of western imperialism. This is a major theme in the critique of what has been called Aid Incorporated and is a factor in the thinking of many of the leaders of host country systems that are the focus of most stabilization and development efforts. They welcome international assistance and know they are dependent on these powerful entities for resources to increase the capacity of their systems to serve their people.

A full exploration of this complex and contentious issue is beyond the scope of this monograph – it is sufficient to note that in addition to the predominantly benevolent and altruistic intent there is a directive, value-laden and control-oriented dimension in the efforts of the military and most development actors who are working in Afghanistan and other similar fragile states, and that officials in these countries are well aware of this dynamic.

Canada's 3D or "Whole of Government" approach is rooted in this rich and complex history, the more recent versions of which have emerged since 2000. The term '3D' originated within the Department of Foreign Affairs and International Trade (DFAIT) in the fall of 2002 when it appeared in an official document related to International Security Policy. It entered into popular usage in the department within the 2003/04 period and became a more common part of official government discourse in the period following the release of Canada's International Policy Statement in 2005. In July of 2005, CIDA was invited by the military to assign a development worker to be part of the first deployment of the Canadian Forces' SAT in Kabul (described in the next chapter). I was hired by CIDA to be the capacity development specialist on that team for a year beginning in September 2005, as an experiment in field-level coordination of development and military resources to foster stability and security in a fragile state.

Canada is not the only country that has seen a need for better coordination of development, diplomacy and military efforts in its international development, peace and security activities. The United Kingdom (UK) is one of several countries that have also been moving forward in this area, as indicated to me by a former military attaché to the British High Commission:

> Around 2000, a small experiment was started in UK government, allocating a special funding pool to be managed jointly by the Department for International Development (DFID), the Ministry of Defense (MOD) and the Foreign Ministry. The idea was that the three would agree what proportion of military support and aid was appropriate to a situation: they would then allocate funds accordingly. Those involved seemed to think it worked; where the program is today, I don't know.

> Some bright spark invented the term 3D to explain the approach
> – from which has grown the proliferation in use and interpreta-
> tion that we see around today! (I claim personal responsibility for
> introducing the term to Canada).[20]

Australia has instituted a "Whole of Government" approach in its international development efforts. An example is their Regional Assistance Mission to Solomon Islands (RAMSI) project. Their contribution to RAMSI
was a "Whole of Government" initiative that involved a broad range of
Australian Government expertise, including deployment of certain agency
officials to Solomon Islands. These agencies included the Australia Federal
Police (AFP), the Treasury, the Australian Office of Financial Management, Department of Finance and Administration (DOFA), and Australian Customs Service (ACS).

Both the UK and the US have long had DEVADs working at various levels in Afghanistan, as have most of the other nations' PRTs in the country.
While the extent of integration varies (most development personnel are
adjuncts to military-led activity) this is an indication that development-
military collaboration is seen as key to the success of the North Atlantic
Treaty Organization (NATO)-led mission.

What Exactly Is "Whole of Government"?

A variety of terms have been used to describe the collaboration or integration of the efforts of several government departments in a more coherent
multi-party intervention in a foreign country. The current discourse in
Canada began with 3D (Diplomacy, Defence and Development), then
added a "T" (3D+T) to denote the powerful role of trade and the private sector in improving conditions in a country. After the 2006 election
and the change in government, the terminology shifted from 3D (which
was seen as a concept linked to the defeated Liberal party) to "Whole of
Government".

Although the literature continues to use 3D to mean essentially the same
thing, the broader term more accurately describes Canada's international
efforts which in Afghanistan, at one time or another, have included personnel from the military, the Royal Canadian Mounted Police (RCMP),
the Department of Justice, Elections Canada, Corrections Canada and

a number of other ministries supporting a variety of counterparts in the host country's systems. Some work relatively independently on specific projects, while others engage in more collaborative activities that call for an integrated approach in projects that combine expertise from several disciplines.

For example, in early 2007 the Canadian operations in Kandahar had personnel from CIDA, DFAIT, the RCMP and occasionally from other government departments working individually and/or together with the military to strengthen governance and improve conditions in the region. The overall Canadian effort in the region was coordinated by the military commander who provided a venue and conducted regular meetings where all actors shared information on their activities and requirements. In some cases staffs of other departments were led by the military commander, while in others they worked relatively independently, keeping each other and the commander informed of their work so coordination and security issues could be properly addressed. This is what "Whole of Government" was in Kandahar in early 2007; however, this tactical-level configuration can expect to change over time due to rotation of personnel and the need to adjust to new circumstances in the AO. Another "Whole of Government" initiative in Afghanistan, the SAT-A based in Kabul, was a quite different operation. Team members were providing a variety of inputs to increase the capacity of a broad range of Government of Afghanistan operations – this is described in the next chapter.

Just as "Whole of Government" encompasses a broad range of resources and skills that can be provided by Canada to a country (the "supply" side), helping with the reconstruction of a fragile post-conflict state is a full-spectrum capacity development operation with requests for assistance likely to come from a range of organizations with an array of needs (the "demand" side). Opportunities to be of service are everywhere and are of massive scope. Strengthening the education sector is a good example: it requires curriculum design, teacher training, production of materials, administration skills, construction and facilities maintenance, community participation, and more, and it needs these at four levels (primary, secondary, post-secondary and technical). The justice and security sectors are at least as complex, as is the health sector. The private sector provides most of the employment and produces the consumer goods the population needs. Transportation, energy, construction, agriculture and communications are essential. In a viable state the institutions of civil society have a major role to play, as do other agencies outside of government such as religious and cultural organizations and the foundation of the whole thing, the institution of the family. Parliament or its equivalent is of course a major and complex component of the system. Men and women need to fully participate in all these sectors. The list goes on and on. A well-functioning society has adequate capacity in all these and other areas, and each is a potential point for development assistance. While a country like Canada wants to make its inputs where they can make the most difference, it has to be strategic and selective to achieve optimum results. There are limits to what "Whole of Government" can actually do, and there is considerable confusion about what the term actually means.

In operationalizing "Whole of Government" there is no doubt that inter-agency collaboration is required and that, where it is appropriate, activities of Canadian personnel should be aligned around common objectives and operate in a coherent manner. Using military terms, this coherence is required at all three levels: strategic, operational and tactical. While most collaboration is taking place at the tactical level and there is considerable discussion at senior levels of government ministries (regular meetings at the ADM level in Ottawa), the strategic and operational levels need greater definition and the CF requires relevant doctrine that provides a framework for military and other actors working in fragile states. It is likely to be a challenge for the military to develop this doctrine, partly because there is lack of clarity around what 3D or "Whole of Government" actually is, whether it is an approach, a strategy or a management tool, or possibly something else:

> The few academics who have attempted to analyze 3D security come from various disciplines and employ different methodologies. The confusion this results in leads to a variety of social scientific opinions, but little strategic analysis. For example, in a recent article, 3D security is presented simultaneously as a strategy and an approach. "The '3D' approach is a comprehensive strategy by the Canadian government to coordinate departmental and agency cooperation of its foreign policy." The same document argues, not much later, that 3D security can best be understood as a management tool for foreign policy. This somewhat careless use of language is an example of the confusion of how to interpret

CHAPTER 2

the 3D construct. Indeed, if 3D security is simultaneously an approach, a strategy and a management tool, then what exactly is it, how can it be used, and what is it not?[21]

Achieving clarity is difficult for a number of reasons, not least of which is the sheer complexity of what is (or can be) involved. In the section titled, "An Agenda for the Next Prime Minister" the North-South Institute's 2004 paper called for a more integrated and focused approach in Canada's global development efforts, and identified a number of the many entities that are active on the international stage. It also noted several important limitations in using the MDGs as a framework for development programming:

> *Policy Framework.* To be effective, Canada's policy on international development must henceforth be interdepartmental in scope and execution. No longer can "development" be the exclusive domain of CIDA. Neither are the Departments of Foreign Affairs and International Trade, Finance, Agriculture, Health, Environment, Human Resources Development, Natural Resources, Industry Canada, and Defence the only ones involved with developing countries. Many other departments and agencies, such as Export Development Canada, the Wheat Board, and the Canadian Commercial Corporation, to name a few, also have responsibilities and mandates in the developing world. Moreover, in two crucial sectors – education and health – the provincial governments have lead responsibility, not the federal government. The involvement of all these departments and agencies, at both the federal and provincial level, in development activities may mean that Canada's overall ODA [Official Development Assistance] effort is underestimated by the official figures.

> It is crucial that Canada's next Prime Minister bring all these departments and agencies, including the provincial governments, under a single and coherent national development policy umbrella. This will not happen without strong and clear direction from the Prime Minister as head of government; the natural tendency is for Departments and Agencies to pursue their own distinct mandates, whether or not they support what they perceive as the specific objectives of others.

Not only will the Prime Minister have to exercise leadership to ensure policy coherence. It is equally crucial that development policy is coherent around a clear objective, or set of objectives, related to the needs of developing countries first and foremost. That is precisely why, in its recent study, The North-South Institute framed the issue in terms of "Poverty and Policy Coherence." In other words, since poverty reduction and its eventual eradication are the overarching objectives of development, the policies and programs of all departments, agencies and organizations dealing with developing countries must cohere around these central objectives (rather than Canada's commercial or political interests and objectives).

The Millennium Development Goals, endorsed by world leaders and most international organizations, now provide a more comprehensive, time-bound set of objectives and targets around which to organize a coherent development policy. The first goal, for example, calls for reducing by half the proportion of people living in poverty (i.e. less than one dollar a day income-equivalent) by the year 2015. In Canada, the MDGs are certainly integral to CIDA's current policy framework. However, they should also form part of the policy and operational mandate of other departments or agencies with programs in or dealings (for example, through the Canadian private sector) with developing countries. The eighth goal, in particular, calls upon developed countries to form partnerships with developing countries, through the trade and financial system, debt relief, and co-operation with the private sector.

While the MDGs provide a framework under which a coherent development policy can be organized, it is important to recognize they fall short in certain respects. For example, there is no reference to the need to resolve and prevent conflicts, which are widespread in much of Africa and elsewhere (e.g. Colombia and Sri Lanka) and gravely undermine the possibility of achieving the MDGs. There is also no reference to the importance of basic human rights and freedoms, which a number of experts, including Amartya Sen…, consider fundamental to any holistic notion of development. Therefore, if it adopts the MDGs as an organizing framework for a coherent, interdepartmental development policy, Canada should integrate into that framework other elements, such as conflict resolution and prevention, and the protection and strengthening of fundamental human rights and freedoms. Other principles stressed in this paper should also inform this policy framework – including the twin principles of supporting *diversity* and *ownership* in the development strategies and policies that developing countries choose to adopt.

To achieve policy coherence around the MDGs, involving the full spectrum of federal departments and agencies, will require unambiguous commitment from the Prime Minister, as head of government, and will require embodying this commitment in a legislative mandate and organizational machinery, to ensure consistent follow-through by departments, agencies and officials. The North-South Institute recommended in its study, "Poverty and Policy Coherence," initiating the process with a White Paper, which could serve as a vehicle to re-energize public engagement on international development in Canada, which is imperative. The Prime Minister and the Government as a whole must com-municate to the Canadian public their vision and inject a sense of passion and urgency to their commitment, and obtain public buy-in. Subsequently, legislation could give statutory authority to the government's new policy framework and create the organiza-tional machinery to implement and monitor it.

The approach suggested here has at least two precedents in Eur-ope – the U.K., under the Blair Government, which released two White Papers pointing toward greater policy coherence…, and Sweden, which has introduced legislation. It would be useful, if Canada were to adopt a similar course, to take stock of achieve-ments and shortcomings in those and other countries.

Organizational Machinery. There are a number of ways in which organizational machinery could be configured to ensure that the new policy framework is implemented. We recommend a Cabinet Committee on international development (or at least a subcom-mittee of the Foreign Affairs and Defence Committee) chaired by the International Cooperation Minister and comprising key

Ministers whose responsibilities involve extensive dealings with developing countries. A parallel recommendation is interdepartmental coordination on country strategies, so that at a minimum, Departments and Agencies would exchange information on their activities and programs in developing countries to strengthen synergies around the policy framework, and remedy inconsistencies or conflicts. More ambitiously, coordination could aim at a unified set of country strategies in which the roles and interrelationships of various departments and agencies in particular countries could be spelled out, in the context of the overarching policy framework. The process of coordination and consultation should, as much as possible, engage civil society and private sector actors in Canada and developing countries, along with governments in those countries.[22]

This lengthy excerpt serves to illustrate some of the complexities of international development and the challenges involved in achieving more coherence in Canada's many activities in the world. "Whole of Government" can involve all of this, or only a part of the many items on the list. Although the government has moved in the direction suggested by the North-South Institute, the level of coherence suggested in their paper has not been achieved.

This level of integration is unlikely to become a reality, and Canada will have to content itself with much less policy coherence than the North-South Institute is proposing and proceed without a comprehensive legislative framework and detailed plan. The prevailing level of political will, operational constraints and bureaucratic inertia are likely to produce a more diffuse form of institutional networking that will require the ability to figure out what is needed in a given situation and decide what actions to take to meet the goals of the mission at any particular point in time.

Ideally, the concept of integration should be applied at all levels of an intervention, from the policy formulation and conceptual phase through all steps to the application of Canadian resources and expertise in the field. The concept implies that personnel at all levels of CIDA, DND and Foreign Affairs staff (and possibly members of other agencies) should form collaborative units at the strategic, operational and tactical levels that enable their diverse contributions to be fully expressed and merged into a single integrated output. Whether this seamless multi-level collaboration is practical is open to question – it might well be that representatives of these various agencies work in an integrated fashion at some levels, while they operate in parallel or sequential modes in others. This is not new: distribution of humanitarian assistance has long been part of military operations, and in some peace-building initiatives such as the Balkans, CIDA's development initiatives may have been collaboratively planned but the allocation of development resources was done primarily by military personnel who had direct access to the communities.

This calls for a flexible operational framework that can adapt to conditions in any particular situation and design interventions that suit rapidly changing and unpredictable circumstances. Although high-level goals might be clearly defined, the steps required to reach them may not be as evident and it is likely that an exploratory strategy of "management by groping along" will prevail. This strategy is described as follows:

> An excellent manager has a very good sense of the objectives but lacks a precise idea about how to realize them. Nevertheless, the manager does possess some ideas – some deduced from theory, some adapted from past experiences, some based strictly on hunches – about how to achieve their goals. Unfortunately, neither the general theories nor the specific techniques in any manager's repertoire are derived from situations precisely like the current one. From the numerous "lessons" that the manager has learned from the past, they must not only choose those that appear to be the most appropriate, but they must also adapt them to the unique characteristics of the new task they face.

> Thus, despite years of experience and study, even the best manager must grope along. They test different ideas and gauge their results. Then they try different combinations and permutations of the more productive ideas. Rather than develop a detailed strategy to be followed unswervingly, a good manager establishes a specific direction – a very clear objective – and then gropes his/her way towards it. He/she knows where he/she are trying to go but is not sure how to get there. So he/she tries numerous things. Some work, some do not. Some are partially productive and are modified to see if they can be improved. Finally, what works best takes hold. That is "Management by Groping Along."[23]

The situation is made even more complex and difficult to address in a policy framework by the realization that a "Whole of Government" approach in peace and security missions can apply to a range of situations that may or may not be in the midst of overt conflict. As Willemijn Keizer postulates:

> It is important to realize that 3D security does not constrain itself to periods of overt violent conflict. Rather, it requires integrated programs in pre-conflict, conflict, and post-conflict situations, resulting in a shift in emphasis between the Ds. In the first case, the focus will likely be on development and diplomatic efforts to prevent conflict. In the second, the focus will mainly be on ending the conflict through military and diplomatic means, combined with humanitarian aid. In the third, the focus will be on recovering from the conflict through the co-operation of military and development efforts. Thus, traditional state security institutions (like the armed forces) will continue to play a key role under a 3D paradigm. However, they will need to co-operate, coordinate, and at times, integrate with other instruments of power under the direction of Canadian civil authority. Separating various governmental agencies has proved to be an ineffective and inefficient response to today's threats.
>
> A 3D approach internationally and "Whole of Government" abroad, demand a fully integrated and unified effort on the part of all the instruments of contemporary national power. An approach that only employs the military in order to ensure that 'peace breaks out' is no longer sufficient, as conflict actors are frequently not under the command of a state-structure. Simply put, military victory in contemporary conflicts, if this even can be achieved, has little value. Rather, conflicts revolve around societal, political, ethnic and cultural tensions that need to be resolved. Success therefore cannot be a matter of the military alone, but needs a different framework, with different benchmarks, different values and different approaches.
>
> [Achieving] the goal of integration requires not only rigorous conceptual analysis on the part of each agency; it also demands an organizational structure to implement the idea. Thus, bureaucratic support, integrated policy development and coordination

are of key importance if 3D security is to succeed. Moreover, as Canada is unlikely to intervene in a conflict without the help of other states, it also requires operational support internationally. That is, to succeed in practice, 3D must shift from a "Whole of Government" approach to a "Whole of Alliance Approach". [24]

It is noteworthy that while Canada is experiencing difficulty in achieving a strategy for coherence and integration in its international efforts, the comprehensive government-wide plans or PRSPs – described earlier – which are required of countries by the IMF and the WB before development assistance can be distributed, expect fragile recovering post-conflict countries to demonstrate even higher levels of goal congruence and coordination in their government operations than are found in most donor countries' domestic administrative systems. It is doubtful that even our country's smallest province, Prince Edward Island, has a comprehensive development plan similar to that in the I-ANDS or the PRSPs of other countries that are receiving international development assistance. This matter is rarely discussed among development agencies.

These challenges raise the question of how much planning, integration and coordination it is reasonable to expect on either side of the developer-developee relationship. Are we asking too much? If so, what is reasonable, or at best what is sufficient to do what is needed, and how should this be done? What implications do these questions have for 3D or "Whole of Government" missions? These are difficult and as yet unresolved issues.

These questions and many more are all part of the reality of implementing a "Whole of Government" approach in development-military collaboration to help strengthen fragile post-conflict states. Whatever doctrine is developed to guide strategic, operational and tactical activity in these contexts must recognize the difficulties in attempting to be fully comprehensive and integrated in these efforts and provide a framework in which intelligent and mission-driven, process-based "groping along" leads to high quality results.

The next chapter describes the origins and early activities of the SAT-A, an excellent example of intelligent groping along with the framework of a general objective: helping strengthen the Karzai government in Afghanistan.

CHAPTER 3

Strategic Advisory Team
In Afghanistan

Introduction

One of the first deployments under Canada's 3D or "Whole of Government" approach was the SAT-A. This section begins with a description of its origins and a summary of the team's main activities in 2005-2006, followed by a description of my work while on the team, a few comments on SAT's second and third Rotos and on the planning process used to guide SAT, and ends with a few concerns about how SAT was operating.

Origins Of SAT-A

When General (Gen) Rick Hillier was commander of NATO's International Security Assistance Force (ISAF) in Kabul in 2003, he became acutely aware of the Afghan government's inadequate planning capacity and saw this deficit as having serious security implications. According to Col Capstick, while Afghanistan had visionary leadership, the machinery of government and the civil service had been crippled by three decades of conflict. Taking steps to remedy the situation, Gen Hillier provided military planners to assist the Afghan Minister of Finance in the creation of a long-term framework for development and the first post-Taliban national budget. This work was greatly appreciated by senior Afghan officials including the President. Unfortunately, Hillier's replacement at ISAF HQ did not see it as a priority and the military's planning support to the central agencies of the Afghan government stopped in 2004.

The termination of support at the end of the tour of duty is an example of an inability to ensure the continuation of an effective operation from one leader to the next, a characteristic of military operations that does not lend itself to sustainable development. The way SAT operated helped to counter (but does not eliminate) this all too common problem in civilian-military operations in supporting the recovery of failed states.

When General Hillier visited Kabul as Chief of the Defence Staff in the spring of 2005, he was asked by President Karzai to provide another group of planners similar to those that had helped his government in 2003-2004, and the General committed to having a team in place that autumn. On his return to Canada he asked Col Mike Capstick to assemble a team and go to Kabul to help President Karzai build a democratic and stable government. In August, 2006, Col Capstick described the process as follows:

> In June 2005, I was tasked by the Chief of the Defence Staff to setup and deploy a "Strategic Advisory Team" to Afghanistan to assist the Government of the Islamic Republic of Afghanistan. In his usual "mission command" style, General Hillier told me to get to Kabul, conduct the doctrinal mission reconnaissance and speak with the Canadian Ambassador to determine the needs. The team would consist of around a dozen people and we would work for the Government. A unique mission – to say the least![25]

As this initial direction was being given, links with DFAIT and CIDA were being pursued in an effort to make this an integrated multi-agency initiative. Securing representation from the latter and aligning efforts with the former, however, presented some challenges to Col Capstick, and mounting such a team for the first time proved to be a significant test that required flexibility and patience with regards to the intricacies of departmental and intra-governmental politics. As part of this process, I was contacted by CIDA in August and travelled to Afghanistan with members of the group in mid-September 2005 – there was no member from DFAIT on the team. Ultimately, the ability of the DND to field elements on short notice enabled the team to be assembled and eventually deploy as directed. The group began working in Kabul within a few days of our arrival.

The team's purpose was consistent with international and national concerns about global threats associated with fragile and failed states as established by the UN Security Council in 1992, which concluded that:

> Failed, failing, and rogue states are havens for international criminals and terrorists, and although international norms of state

sovereignty prohibit intervention by one state in the domestic affairs of another, the international community can no longer ignore these internal conflicts.[26]

In light of that danger, the Government of Canada mandated DND, in the Defence Policy Statement, to maintain combat-capable Canadian forces focused on the challenge of restoring peace and stability to failed and fragile states. In his Master's thesis on this topic, Major Michel-Henri St-Louis makes a direct link between SAT and this DND policy:

> In today's and tomorrow's security environment, this paper suggests that the department will need to add the capabilities that SAT brings in order to respond to this mandated focus. If it is accepted that state building is and will continue to be at the center of Canada's international interventions, then a capability specifically involved in enabling good governance would facilitate strategic success.[27]

SAT-A Roto 0 Membership And Sample Activities

Major St-Louis describes the first SAT as follows:

> The original SAT was made up of fifteen members. Twelve were military, two were civilian public servants of DND and one was a co-operant from the CIDA. The military members were a mix from the three components air-naval-land, as well as regular and reserves. One of the public servants was an operational research scientist, whereas the other was a strategic planner from the central staff.[28]

One of the military members was a strategic communications specialist; the others were planners or support personnel. Most members were on one-year assignments, although there were a number of personnel changes throughout the year, most significantly at the six-month point when several members ended their tour and were replaced. Handovers were done in a manner that maintained continuity with the Afghans with whom SAT had begun establishing relationships during the previous months. These handovers were not carried beyond the term of Roto 0 – apart from sharing reports there seemed to be no structured way to maintain continuity with the arrival of the next team. This will be discussed further in the section on issues and concerns about SAT later in this chapter.

As SAT made contacts with Afghan government officials (a key process described in greater detail below) work got underway. Small teams and individuals were assigned to engage with various parts of the Afghan government and the donor community as suitable opportunities were developed. Brief and partial summaries of these activities follow to provide a general indication of the work done by members of SAT.

Support for the Afghan National Development Strategy

On his arrival in Kabul Col Capstick met with Canadian Ambassador Chris Alexander and CIDA's Head of Aid, Nipa Banerjee, two seasoned and well-respected officials who introduced him to a number of key officers in the Afghan government. One such meeting was with the President's chief financial advisor who was responsible for the team preparing the government's strategic plan, or PRSP. He was eager to receive SAT's support for this effort. This early entry into the government system made it possible for one three-member team of planners to immediately begin working with the group preparing the ANDS, mainly by providing support for the operations of the office and helping to categorize and organize the array of information received from across the government.

This support was instrumental in helping the Afghan government present the I-ANDS at a major donor's meeting in London in January 2006, and secure ratification of the Afghanistan Compact, a UN-sanctioned plan for global support for security and other measures to strengthen the Afghan government. Later in 2006, the team working with the I-ANDS helped Afghan officials bring this framework to the attention of ISAF, the US's Enduring Freedom leadership and the PRTs, and these government planning documents subsequently began to act as an organizing framework for the efforts of most major military and development agencies in the country.

Assisting with donor coordination

Donor coordination is one of the major challenges in international development assistance, and in most countries in which the aid community is active the various agencies attempt to institute some form of coordinating mechanism. This is consistent with the Paris Declaration described earlier, and the senior UN representative in the country often takes a lead in this effort. In this case Canada's Head of Aid, Ms. Banerjee, had been requested by the donor community to help coordinate their efforts – a difficult task. Early in SAT's work a small team was assigned to assist her with this challenge, mainly by helping define the purpose of the process, proposing a structure and indicating possible lines of action for the group's consideration. These efforts met with limited success due to a number of factors, one of which was the significant difference between the relatively orderly chain of command and planning process to which the military is accustomed and the diverse culture(s) and much fuzzier decision-making systems of the various actors in the donor and diplomatic organizations. SAT members found it a frustrating exercise and ultimately sought other places to apply their skills.

Support for the Civil Service Commission and public sector reform

As SAT began its operations the Afghan government was in the early stages of a major public sector reform process that needed a great deal of help. With some 300,000 public servants – a figure which included teachers and health system workers but not the security and military sectors – and 30 years of war and neglect, strengthening the public sector was a major focus of many development agencies including UNDP and the WB.

In early October 2005, I was invited to accompany one of the Canadian embassy's CIDA officers to a meeting where a draft of the government's first Training and Development Strategy was presented to the donor community for review and comment. My suggestions for improvement of the strategy resulted in an invitation to work with the Director of the Training and Development Department (TDD) in the Independent Administrative Reform and Civil Service Commission (IARCSC). This became the focus of my work for the rest of my term with SAT, which will be summarized below. I provided a similar commentary on the Public Administration Reform (PAR) strategy, which was well received by the head of that unit of IARCSC. By the end of October this work had opened the door for other members of the team to become engaged in supporting the Commission and its public sector reform process. In early November, a second 3-member SAT planning team began working with the upper levels of the

IARCSC. Over the next two months, the team became progressively more engaged in providing strategic planning and organizational development support for several IARCSC units and helped the Commission strengthen its operations. This work consisted mainly of helping Afghan counterparts clarify objectives and develop work plans, improve their management and planning skills; identifying and bridging gaps in inter-unit coordination; increasing the capacity of the Monitoring and Evaluation (M&E) unit; helping with gender-related programming; and contributing to an overall plan to strengthen IARCSC's internal functions and thus improve its services to the rest of the government.

One of the reasons the Chairman of IARCSC permitted his unit managers to begin receiving support from SAT was that the team was a Canadian effort and he considered Canadians acceptable to work with "because they had no agenda".[29] This is interesting in light of the fact (as noted earlier) that many recipients of international aid see most donor agencies such as USAID, UNDP and the WB as neo-colonial agents of a new form of imperialism and they are regarded with some suspicion by host country officials who depend on their support. Apparently Canada has not been tarred with that same brush.

SAT members also worked with Technical Advisors (TAs) of other agencies such as the British Council and the WB who were also supporting public sector reform. More will be said about this below.

One of the team's main points of contact with IARCSC was the office of the Special Advisor to the Commissioner, a capable but overworked woman with considerable energy and enthusiasm but with essentially no line authority. Over several months this lack of line authority, coupled with internal conflicts and a reluctance by the Commissioner to make politically unpopular decisions that would increase the Commission's effectiveness, contributed to a sense among team members that they were not making as much of a contribution to improving the government as they would have liked and in June 2006, they began looking for more fertile ground in which to work. They felt the Commission was not moving forward as quickly as it could, and they wanted to apply their skills where they could see more results from their efforts.

This more fertile ground was found in other parts of the government, including the Ministry of Rural Rehabilitation and Development (MRRD)–

described below – and over a two-month period in mid-2006 most of the team's members shifted their focus to that key ministry. The strategic role of IARCSC was considered important enough to merit an ongoing presence, however, and one team member was kept in place supporting the Special Advisor's office. This support (which took the form of acting as her Chief of Staff or Executive Assistant) continued over the term of Roto 0 and was carried forward into Roto 1 after our replacements arrived in August 2006.

Strengthening strategic communications in government

It was clear to SAT and to many in the diplomatic and donor communities as well as within the Afghan civil service that the government did not have an effective public communications system, with the result that the population was not receiving sufficient accurate information about the government's plans and its achievements. This had a negative effect on public opinion and the credibility of the Karzai government. The strategic importance of good public communications in a counter-insurgency was evident to all major actors and it was also a concern that the insurgents seemed to be making better use of this "weapon" than the government or the international community.

One of a number of examples of inadequate communication was linked to news (in 2005) about much-anticipated increases in public service pay levels, part of public sector reform. When the raises finally did come through they were a tiny fraction of what the public servants had anticipated, resulting in angry demonstrations outside several government buildings. This public anger and loss of credibility were mainly because the government did not have an effective public communications mechanism and the few communications units that were in existence were poorly supported and understaffed.

SAT's strategic communications specialist began addressing this challenge at the outset of the mission, and over the following months succeeded in establishing relationships with a number of communications units within the government and in the network of donor agencies, particularly with those in the UN system. He helped several of the government's units develop communications strategies and worked with their personnel to increase the effectiveness of their operations. He also helped establish an informal network of communications specialists in the donor and diplomatic agencies, and shared information on the ANDS with the members of this network so their efforts could be consistent with the country's development strategy. His work also addressed the military's domestic Canadian communications needs, and he had a role in organizing several visits to Canada of high-level Afghans who were in a position to accurately and persuasively inform the public on the situation in Afghanistan. In addition, he increased the scope and effectiveness of SAT's strategic planners: his linkages with communications specialists in a number of ministries helped open doors for other members of SAT to provide planning and capacity development services in at least two other areas of the government: the MRRD and the Centre of Government, the office of the President's Chief of Staff. This resulted in the team gaining access to these two significant parts of the government system (summary descriptions follow).

Support for Minister of Rural Rehabilitation and Development's office

After establishing a good relationship with the newly-appointed Minister of Rural Rehabilitation and Development – a process which is described later in the section on intervention strategy and methods – SAT personnel were invited to move into a space near the Minister's office and begin providing strategic planning services to the ministry's senior management group. Considerable work had been done developing a high-level plan covering most of MRRD's many operations and SAT was able to quickly become engaged in helping implement this plan in various parts of the ministry.

The team made major contributions to MRRD's planning process, beginning late in the term of the first SAT group. This was continued by our replacements after our departure in August 2006. The second team's CIDA development specialist spent much of his time with this team, focusing his energies on helping with a variety of projects in the ministry.

Support to Centre of Government

As a result of initial contacts made by SAT's strategic communications specialist in mid-2006, two members of the team were invited to work with the Chief of Staff of the Office of the President. Although the office had been operating for some time and was receiving assistance from other TAs, there were ongoing challenges in managing the flow of information and in establishing clear delegation and decision-making processes. Our members helped the staff analyze their operations and identify areas that could be strengthened, and provided several examples of centre of government administrative structures for their consideration. Receiving an invitation to assist in this manner was an indication of the high level of credibility and trust established by SAT-A personnel in the relatively short time the team had been in the field.

Analysis and research

SAT's operational research scientist produced a number of pertinent studies and reports over the term of the project. These included an analysis of the National Assembly and Provincial Council elections held in September 2005, and preparing a draft document that helped lend order to the donor and diplomatic coordination challenge noted above (a straw man for the Afghanistan Compact, done for then-Canadian Ambassador Chris Alexander). During our support for public sector reform she produced several well-received documents, including a clear summary of public administration reform in six developing countries (Malaysia, Jordan, Kazakhstan, Mongolia, Tanzania and Chile) with possible lessons for Afghanistan. The paper was translated into Dari and provided to senior IARCSC officials. It helped greatly in placing their efforts in a broader context, and with other documents that she produced these resources helped the Commission clearly map its path toward a more effective public service. The other documents for IARCSC included a comparative PAR matrix (Malaysia, Morocco and India/Rajasthan) and a comparative paper on Civil Service Laws that was useful in developing the legislative base for operation of the Afghan public service. She also prepared a major report for senior US and NATO military commanders (JTF-A [Joint Task Force – Afghanistan], CFC-A [Combined Forces Command – Afghanistan] and ISAF) on how to link PRT activities to the ANDS.

My Role On SAT-A

As noted earlier, my primary role in SAT-A's support for the Afghan government was through a linkage with the Training and Development Department of IARCSC, following an invitation from the unit's

Director, Dr. Wali Hamidzada, after he reviewed my comments on their draft training and development strategy. By the end of October I had been assigned a desk in an area across the hall from his office, and began working with him to help clarify and document his ideas for the development of this part of the public service.

Dr. Hamidzada had become a physics professor in the US after emigrating from Afghanistan in the 1970s, and had been in IARCSC for about 18 months on the Afghan Expatriate Program, a WB-funded initiative that brought skilled Afghans from the diaspora back to help with the reconstruction of their country. Although he had a well-trained mind and knew a lot about higher education and the background politics of Afghanistan, he had no prior experience being a senior manager in a large organization or setting up and running a public service training program, and welcomed assistance in fulfilling his responsibilities.

After working with him for several weeks on an informal basis to document a number of key elements of the organization he wanted to build, he requested my full-time support for his unit, and I became the Senior Advisor to the Director of the TDD. My work with him covered a broad range of activities found in the start-up phase of a developing country's public service training system. SAT members working elsewhere in the Commission provided support by preparing a strategic plan for the TDD as one of several parts of IARCSC. My work focused on activities such as reviewing the legislative and policy framework, helping prepare the unit's human resource plan and budget, designing training programs, drafting proposals for support from donors, increasing the capacity of the TDD's M&E unit, working with TDD staff to design and deliver management training and organizational development supports, and acting as a sounding board for Dr. Hamidzada as required.

Subsequent SAT-A Operations (After August 2006)

Our team was replaced by SAT Roto 1 in August 2006. I returned to Kabul in December 2006 to work for three months with UNDP in IARCSC's newly-formed Capacity Development Secretariat and later in 2007 to help draft a strategic plan for the Civil Service Institute. During these missions

I had several contacts with our replacements and with CIDA's Head of Aid at the Canadian embassy. I had been told before going back that the next SAT operation was quite different than ours, and my encounters confirmed that information. Being "different" is not necessarily better or worse, and I could not determine which because I did not have access to enough information (nor the mandate) to make a judgment as to the relative effectiveness of the two groups in terms of the purpose of the mission, strengthening the Afghan government. Two areas in which it was evident that the second group differed from the first were in social networking and in their capacity development strategy. The third group's operations seemed to differ somewhat from either of the others.

The first team had consciously established an open and welcoming social climate to facilitate networking with members of other development organizations and with Afghans in the government. This included well-attended weekly social gatherings to which SAT members invited friends and contacts and provided food and refreshments – these were not continued by the second group, which had a quite different and much less open social climate. The third group had reinstituted the weekly social gatherings that were a central part of the team's networking strategy.

The second team's approach to capacity development differed from the first. In our group, Col Capstick made it clear that our job was to "lead from behind" or to do whatever possible to make sure that our team was not doing the work but helping the Afghans learn how to do what was required on their own. This was consistent with a capacity development approach rather than capacity replacement (to be discussed in the next chapter on capacity development). His replacement said that this distinction was not a central feature of how the second team operated. Members were placed in situations where they were expected to do what was necessary to help Government of Afghanistan units function, and this could include doing the actual work as well as helping Afghans learn to do it for themselves. The second team saw their job as doing capacity replacement as well as development.

There were other differences as well, in terms of the range of ministries served (the second group worked in far more ministries than the first) and the linkages between SAT and the Canadian embassy. After Chris Alexander's term as ambassador ended and he went to work with the United

Nations Assistance Mission in Afghanistan (UNAMA), our team's primary link to the embassy was CIDA's Head of Aid. The relationships became more structured as time progressed: during the second roto the new ambassador became more involved and required SAT and CIDA's Head of Aid to meet regularly to exchange information on activities in their respective areas of responsibility. The communications were formal and more clearly defined, making social issues less critical to the working environment.

The tone and feel of the third group was quite different than either of the two previous teams, and their activities seemed to be more broadly diffused across the government. It was interesting to note that the same mission operating in the same environment and presumably with the same orders appeared to operate quite differently from one roto to the next.

Relations With Other Donors And Technical Advisors

SAT members frequently found themselves working in areas that were also being served by TAs funded by a variety of donors. These were often highly paid professionals who had varying levels of expertise in the areas in which they were working.

Nonetheless, the team faced a number of challenges. For example, some of the international community's representatives in Kabul "were suspicious as to what a group of military planners could bring to the nation building effort. Some benign rivalries with other agencies were also felt at the mid-manager level. Thirdly, there was always the concern that someone else was already doing the same work. With the high number of TAs, international agencies and personnel from ISAF and the US HQ (CFC-A) in Kabul, it was common to meet someone working on exactly the same issues as the SAT."[30]

In some cases the relationships between SAT personnel and the TAs were complementary and mutually supportive, and in others they were not. An example of a supportive relationship in the TDD was when a UNDP-funded evaluation specialist arrived shortly before the end of my term with SAT. Part of my work there was building up the TDD's M&E system, and I was providing basic training to the head of the M&E unit. When the UNDP consultant arrived, he validated the work I was doing and built upon it to increase the unit's capacity even further. We shared information on other areas I had worked on, and I provided him with the materials I had been developing so there would be continuity in the services being received by the department. I also introduced him to the Afghans with whom I had been working and we collaborated in a way which demonstrated our complementary skills to the benefit of the client. When I returned to Kabul a few months later to work on another project the Afghans on the M&E team reported that they had benefited from the inputs of both TAs and were independently conducting a variety of evaluations across the government.

In another more problematic case, I worked with TAs funded by another major donor who had been tasked with preparing an employee performance evaluation process for the government. They were handing this work off to me shortly before the end of their contract and their departure from Kabul in the hopes that somebody would carry it on. I had considerable experience in this field and found that their models were not consistent with best practices in management, and was in the position of having to maintain an effective relationship with these advisors while informing the Afghan officials they were serving that their work was not consistent with current approaches in the field. It was difficult to avoid being seen by the Afghan officials as competing with the other group of TAs – a challenge that was compounded by the fact the Afghan official who was being served by these TAs did not know enough about the topic to make an informed judgment on his own. These challenges were resolved when I prepared a basic performance management framework based on current best practices and the Afghans could see the differences between the two approaches. The other TAs had left Kabul by that time so an overt confrontation was avoided.

There were a number of other situations in which SAT personnel worked in areas that were being served by TAs, and while many of these were constructive and mutually beneficial, there were several in which the encounters were troublesome and the TAs reacted negatively to the presence of SAT members in their work areas. One such example was within MRRD, where the Minister invited the SAT to occupy space near his office that had previously been allocated to a high-priced consulting firm whose members were rather upset that they were being asked to relocate. Managing these complex relationships was one of the major challenges in our service to the Afghan government. These TAs were part of the complex array of elements exerting influence (for better or worse) on the progress of the government's operations and had to be taken into account in SAT's strategy as we proceeded with our mission.

This general issue will be discussed later in this monograph, in the section on development strategy: it is necessary to have some sense of all the players who are active in a system so their influence can be taken into account in the intervention and in influencing the course of the system's trajectory.

SAT-A's Own Strategic Planning Process

Although SAT was encouraging Afghans to use a typical military strategic planning approach that has a number of well-defined and sequenced categories of information and processes, it used a less-structured method in its own planning to guide SAT itself as it sought ways to serve the Afghan government. This process seemed more akin to a development worker's model than a military campaign. As noted earlier, a goal-oriented "management by groping along" strategy is often what is actually used in most situations where methods that worked in previous practice cannot be directly applied to new situations.

As will be described in greater detail later in this monograph, a development strategy usually has the following components:

- Define the overall purpose of your intervention and obtain a general mandate to act.

- Begin to establish relationships with members of the host (not "target") system and identify areas which are likely to permit entry.

- Enter the system and begin providing services while further assessing visible characteristics to more clearly understand the components and operations of the system.

- Systematically broaden or focus your input to serve the purpose of the mission

- Help members of the host system carry on with the inputs and activities until they are able to carry the process further on their own.

All of this requires a lot of "groping along" – having a clear idea of the purpose of the mission but not knowing exactly what is needed to achieve the desired effect. Col Capstick mentioned this in his comments on the early stages of the first team's activities in Kabul:

> In his usual "mission command" style, General Hillier told me to get to Kabul, conduct the doctrinal mission reconnaissance and speak with the Canadian Ambassador to determine the needs. ... When we left Canada we still had no firm idea as to where we would be employed or which Afghan agencies we would work with. The Ambassador of the day, Chris Alexander and the Head of Aid, Nipa Banerjee essentially "shopped" me around town and together we identified the office developing Afghanistan's National Development Strategy as the main effort. This resulted in the Senior Economic Advisor to the President becoming our main point of contact within the Government and that after close consultation with both the Canadian Ambassador and Head of Aid, our operational focus would be squarely in the development and governance realms. Our basic concept of operations is to embed planners with Afghan staff with a view to passing on our basic military staff planning skills.[31]

It was interesting that an ambiguity-tolerant, mission-driven and exploratory method was used to open doors, establish relationships and begin serving the Afghan government, while the main skill being imparted to the Afghans seemed to be a rather traditionally structured linear approach to strategic planning. SAT's situation required the more unstructured approach to guide its own operations. Some development workers collaborating with the military on such missions in fragile states may raise questions about this difference, and suggest that the vision-driven and rather open-ended method might be more appropriate than the somewhat formally-scripted linear approach for an organization trying to grapple with the host of unpredictable factors on the ground. Many in the military might be tempted to apply a tightly-structured linear approach to guide SAT-like operations, and would likely be unsuccessful as a result. This is addressed further in the following discussion of the model of planning used by SAT.

Issues Or Concerns About SAT

While SAT-A has received solidly positive feedback from senior officials in the Afghan government and from the civil servants with whom SAT personnel worked, there have been several concerns voiced by people who were in a position to comment. My own observations and others' concerns are related to the scope of SAT operations and to the implications of the relatively low level of development-related knowledge and skills of SAT's military personnel.

Spread too thin, too fast?

The rapid spread of SAT services to a number of additional ministries during the early stages of the second team's activities was a cause for concern in the development community and in ISAF. This was clearly stated in an email in October 2005 from a DEVAD working in ISAF HQ:

> The new SAT guys are really making waves in the development community. They've moved into RRD [Rural Rehabilitation and Development] and are heading into Finance and Education. Really out of control. ISAF is trying to reign (sic) them in.[32]

Although I did not receive further information to clarify the factors that were the basis of this concern and why this would be seen as a problem, the comment and its tone were in marked contrast to the collegial quality and content of communication from the same DEVAD and her colleagues at ISAF during the first team's work in Kabul.

Pushing too hard? Frustration and backlash

An area I observed and was concerned about was the directive approach taken by a number of SAT members and their impatience and frustration when things did not go how they wanted. One of the things that is learned early in most development workers' careers is that one cannot push a system and expect it to progress any faster than the slowest member with influence is willing to move. The military mindset seems to have difficulty with this fact of development life. A classic indicator of this problem occurred one afternoon at the SAT residence when I came into the common room to find one of the team members sitting there in an obviously agitated state.

When I asked him what was up his response was an outburst: "I am a military officer! I have been trained to act and achieve results! These guys just won't move!" He was talking about the Afghan civil servants with whom he was working and who had not done the seemingly straightforward things they all said they would do to improve their operations.

A number of team members (mainly the younger ones) regularly expressed frustration at how slowly the Afghan system moved, and tried whatever they could to get the Afghans to remove what seemed to be obvious roadblocks to progress and increase their units' effectiveness. This is common in many parts of the world: while recipients of aid are accustomed to receiving advice and encouragement from foreign technical specialists, and know their presence is necessary to maintain donor interest in supporting their operations, many have created subtle methods of not changing things in the way the advisors want and thus preserving the integrity of their existing systems, however dysfunctional they may be. Often there are valid reasons and powerful motives for this "resistance to change" that the foreign advisors do not understand and the locals cannot (or choose not to) adequately explain.

SAT members did not seem to sufficiently appreciate the full implications of the fact that all behaviour is intentional and appears rational to the person or group at the time. To help a system move it is essential to figure out the motivation structure behind what is being observed and seeing what can be done to help shift internal patterns so the system progresses on its own. This can be difficult, and expectations of achievement often have to be scaled back considerably and occasionally redirected entirely as one becomes familiar with the internal workings of a system. One of the consequences of not grasping this dynamic is that the advisor's well-intentioned encouragement might be seen as pushing too hard and will result in the advisor being shut out of the system, sometimes by subtle measures that are not always obvious to the advisor, who might not even be aware that they are no longer able to exert influence on the system with which they are working.

These often frustrating aspects of development work will be dealt with in greater detail later in the section on intervention strategy and methods.

Unintended consequences from inappropriate models of planning

I was also concerned about signs that SAT's military planners did not have an adequate grasp of a whole-system approach where activities in one part of an organization can have problematic impacts on other sectors that may seem unrelated to the primary area of input. In some areas they also did not seem to know what a contextually-appropriate approach to planning was and how to selectively apply the type of planning principles and procedures that were suited to the carrying capacity of the system.

An example of this was seen in the introduction of a structured planning process at the upper levels of IARCSC that required staff at intermediate levels of the system to spend a great deal of time writing reports and making up activity plans and measurable objectives when their part of the system was not ready for that level of organization and did not have sufficient skilled human resources or the management structures to do it properly. While the plan might have looked really good at the upper levels, the frequency of reporting and level of detail that was required overwhelmed the few people in the middle of the system who had the necessary skills and were asked to generate the information required by the overall plan. In the area in which I worked it was seen as a frustrating and time consuming paper exercise that would not amount to much. (This could describe strategic planning exercises in many organizations, not just the Afghan public service.)

Due to the high levels of unpredictability and scarcity of human and material resources in the environment a less elaborate vision-driven process-based model would have been easier to implement and would have been of greater benefit to the people in the system. Henry Mintzberg makes a similar point in an article in *Harvard Business Review*:

> Managers don't always need to program their strategies formally. Sometimes they must leave their strategies flexible, as broad visions, to adapt to a changing environment. Only when an organization is sure of the relative stability of its environment and is in need of the tight coordination of a myriad of intricate operations (as is typically the case of airlines with their needs for complicated scheduling) does such strategic programming make sense.[33]

Even though the planning strategy seemed to be more detailed and elaborate than was suited to the context it did have some benefits, and with SAT's other inputs on issues such as organizational linkages, management practices, information flow and goal congruence, it considerably strengthened the Commission. A more open-ended approach to strategic planning is described in Chapter 9.

A year later, senior IARCSC officials reported they were not using the plan prepared with SAT's assistance. They did, however, have a better grasp of strategic planning concepts than before SAT personnel began working with them.

Getting in over their heads

Another area of concern was that the ability of SAT personnel to establish good relationships with officials in the government might in some cases have opened doors and brought them into situations where they were asked to do work for which they were not sufficiently qualified. These invitations could come on the basis of quality of relationship more than on the Afghan officials' ability to accurately assess the competencies required for the work they needed done. Because of their lack of experience in some domains, both parties would not know how complex the field actually was, but team members would do their best to provide the requested services nonetheless.

The support provided for preparation of the ANDS was largely technical, with no requirement for SAT members to have subject matter expertise in public sector operations or in drafting PRSPs – there seemed to be no problems in that situation. Also, when in-depth analysis was required in some areas SAT's research scientist was a tremendous resource and produced valuable material to guide some of these efforts. In some other areas, however, I had concerns about the team's ability to adequately address the questions they were being asked.

An example of this was the advice the team provided on the optimum structure and decision-making processes for the office of the Chief of Staff of the President. This was essentially providing advice on the design of a Privy Council Office (PCO) level operation, which is a highly specialized area of governance and capacity building, particularly in an Islamic state emerging from 30 years of war. I observed (and assisted) the team that was drafting organizational charts and was suggesting decision-making processes for consideration by the President's staff and wondered to what extent they were aware of the depth and complexity of the issues they were addressing.

Although my concerns on this general issue were shared by other members of the international development community in Kabul, I don't think this means it was wrong for SAT to provide this sort of advice when the opportunity arose. Much of what development workers do takes place at the edges of their competency, or just over that line, especially when working in post-conflict fragile states. It is not an area in which people have had a long history of service, so that much of what is done requires an exploratory or "management by groping along" coping strategy.

It is easy to get in over your head in this work, and to not even know that this has happened, and to forge on regardless. There are few specialists available who have the expertise or broader base of experience in these situations so there are few options other than to do as competent a job as possible and hope for the best. What's important is for operations like SAT to make this feeling-our-way exploratory process overt and to not pretend things are otherwise, to adopt a learning organization way of operating, to become institutionally highly tolerant of ambiguity, and to establish open and structured ways of doing as much as possible to get the best guidance available when it is needed.

Insufficient integration of development and military expertise

Another concern was the lack of genuine integration of development and military approaches in SAT operations. On the first SAT mission, development and military co-existed, they were not integrated. The term "integration" implies a fusion of inputs to create something new, where both parties change to achieve a synthesis, a type of hybrid vigour in the output of an operation. This did not happen except in a few isolated cases where military members sought advice from the team's development specialist and other professionals and used this information in their work.

This problem was a factor in the second as well as the first SAT mission: on both teams the development specialist lived with the military members but in the professional realm he operated in a relatively isolated enclave and did not significantly contribute to the design of the work of other parts of the team. There was no systematic way of collectively reviewing team activity and having development perspectives fully engaged in analysis and planning the work of each group. As a result the exploratory planning process described earlier did not fully benefit from inputs from the development specialists on the team. This isolation was less evident in the third team where the CIDA member had regular consultations with the various teams working in the ministries.

CF operations in Kandahar apparently did not have that problem: the commander held daily meetings at which all players in the "Whole of Government" approach could freely express their views and exchange insights on how best to fulfill the objectives of their mission. This involvement was confirmed in discussions with the CIDA DEVAD who worked there at the time.[34] The commander regularly took her into his confidence and clearly incorporated her recommendations in his planning and decision-making processes. This delivered a message to other military members on the mission and they frequently sought her out for input in their mission planning work. This strategy, which was more a consequence of the commander's personality than of something built into the CF's operating structure for the Afghanistan campaign, was not evident with SAT in Kabul. The fact the Kandahar DEVAD had full colonel equivalent rank also helped – the lack of equivalent rank for the development specialist on SAT contributed to role ambiguity and had a negative impact on the extent to which development inputs were incorporated in the team's activities.

The first SAT team held daily meetings to discuss important but rather superficial issues such as transportation requirements and other organizational matters. There was no real substantive discussion of the work the smaller teams were doing except among team members themselves, and there was no structured way to share views on what they were finding, discover how this might be useful for other teams, and decide where they could go next.

Thus, while SAT was indeed a 3D or "Whole of Government" operation, the presence of a development specialist did not have as much impact on the first team's operations as it could have, resulting in lower levels of achievement than if things had been managed otherwise. The second team was much the same. It would have been relatively easy to establish regular shared briefing sessions in which the activities and concerns of each team could be reviewed and thus benefit from analysis and comment from all available talent. The third team operated considerably better in this respect. Hopefully subsequent SAT missions will be structured to ensure optimum contribution of all relevant voices on the team.

Inadequate handovers and lessons learned

There seemed to be no systematic way of ensuring handovers and continuity from one team to the next. While the military presumably shared Roto 0 reports with incoming staff of Roto 1, apparently there was no structured debriefing and exchange of lessons learned process between the first and second group.[35]

CIDA also had no systematic debriefing and lessons learned process. Apart from a one-hour information session shortly after my return in August 2006, the Afghanistan desk did not set up any mechanism to extract relevant information and incorporate this in guidance in plans for the next group of CIDA specialists going to Afghanistan. This applied to other CIDA personnel as well – at the time this was written there had been about a half-dozen CIDA personnel working in Afghanistan and the department had not systematically sought out key elements of their experience to incorporate in their planning process. Any exchanges that did take place were at the personal initiative of individual CIDA staff who sought out their replacements and arranged meetings to brief them on what they could expect when they were deployed.

Summary

In spite of the concerns and areas for improvement listed above it is clear that SAT-A did a great job. It is well known that the best antidote for an insurgency is an effective government that is working with the population to create the conditions for a functioning society, and the SAT clearly had – and with its subsequent deployments continues to have – a major role in supporting this process. According to St-Louis:

> The Chairman of the IARCSC, Dr. A. Mushahed, supported the use of military planners in an advisory role for purely civilian

governance issues. In his view, "…concentration on security operations is not the only way to defeat the terrorists. Service delivery of the government, when it is efficient, is another way."[36] Military campaigns and the personnel waging them need to be as concerned with security as they are with the strengthening of the country in which they are deployed. Military skills enabled the SAT to do that. Col Capstick, who had experienced stability and peacekeeping operations as a commander in Cyprus and Bosnia, reinforced that idea: "Planning Afghanistan's national economic development strategy or civil service is not a heck of a lot different than planning General Fraser's campaign in terms of the skills needed and the steps."[37] While military planners are not expected to know the answer to a governance problem, they can act as enablers in the weak national institutions of the host nation. By facilitating the developments of strategies, ensuring capacity transfer and the adherence to rigorous processes, the skills brought to bear by military planners can play a role in creating the conditions for success.[38]

In spite of SAT-A Commander, Col Mike Capstick's frequent emphatic assertions that "the military does not do development!" the whole SAT operation was essentially a cross-cultural organization development and capacity building exercise in which military planning and management skills were being applied to support a complex and challenging public sector reform process. The team was fulfilling General Hillier's intent – to strengthen the Afghan government – and learned a great deal in the process that will help Canada and its partner countries in the Afghanistan campaign and with any subsequent peace and security missions conducted in fragile post-conflict states.

Most of the issues described in this section have also been found in the operations of PRTs and are reported in considerable detail in a study carried out by a team from Princeton University.[39]

CHAPTER 4

What is "Capacity Development"?

Introduction

This chapter is a summary of what is meant by the term "capacity development" in relation to a fragile post-conflict state and provides navigation aids to help analyze situations, understand some of the moral, structural and skill issues involved, and to focus inputs where they are likely to have the greatest beneficial effects.

Capacity development has many definitions. A good example is the following, taken from the Australian Agency for International Development (AusAID):

> The process of developing competencies and capabilities in individuals, groups, organisations, sectors or countries which will lead to sustained and self-generating performance improvement.[40]

While most development agencies say they are doing something called capacity development, it is a complex and ill-defined field of practice. Barakat and Chard describe it as follows:

> A core concept of recent and ongoing recovery programmes, both for war-torn societies and those devastated by poverty and recurring natural disaster, is the need to establish local and national good governance based on developing institutions for collaboration between the state, civil society and the market through capacity building. The terms 'institutional development' and 'capacity building' have been discussed in an extensive literature over several decades. However, a review of these writings gives the impression of constantly shifting, unclear and contested definitions of these key terms. The recent inclusion of 'governance'

and 'civil society' in the debate, as the current means of describing the institutional development and capacity-building aims of the international financial institutions, donor governments and humanitarian agencies in respect of their assistance to devastated countries and communities, seems simply to have added to the confusion by masking contradictory aims under the banner of a common rhetoric.[41]

There is also some question about terminology – whether it is capacity *building* or capacity *development*. The latter is used in this monograph for the reasons described in a study by Femke Gordijn:

> Some organisations make a distinction between Capacity Building and Capacity Development, others use both expressions for the same meaning. The difference is that building could implicitly mean that you start from nothing to build up capacities, whereas development starts from what is already there and strengthens that. Nomvula Dlamini, (of the Community Development Resource Association, Zambia): "Good that you are not talking about Capacity Building but Capacity Development. Because we are enhancing and strengthening what is already there, we focus on what is already present in an organisation or person. How to enhance what is there, to help finding the power, to help change other people's environment. But often organisations don't spend enough time to see what is already there.[42]

While some who work in the capacity development field insist that it is a new form of international development practice, others see it as an extension or broadening of previous approaches to this work. One way to describe it is as a whole-system, integrated approach to helping a society increase its performance. Although the literature is extensive there are few readily-available overviews of the broad range of elements and approaches that fall within this general label. The following Capacity Development Analysis Framework is an attempt to put many of the parts of this field in a concise and comprehensive format.

Capacity Development Analysis Framework

The purpose of a development effort is to influence a system to alter its trajectory and achieve a desired effect, usually in terms of increasing performance in some relevant manner. Actors can use this framework to analyze a complex environment and select appropriate points and types of interventions to achieve their objectives, and/or to assess the results of an initiative. It can be used to provide clarity in designing or assessing international development projects as well as organizational or community development activities in any environment.

Capacity development is a multi-dimensional activity that can address a variety of components in a development initiative taking place in an environment (government, region, company, NGO, community, etc.). The following chart illustrates these various levels and dimensions, any of which can be the focus of an analysis process or intervention to increase system performance. These components are described more fully below:

Level of Activity	Dimension of Analysis or Intervention					
	Values	Structure	Skills	Resources	Operations	Performance
Context						
Organization(s)						
Sub-Unit						
Group/Team						
Individual						

TABLE 3 – THE LEVELS AND DIMENSIONS OF CAPACITY DEVELOPMENT[43]

Strengths in any of these dimensions or levels indicate potential areas to reinforce to improve system effectiveness and performance. Weaknesses in any of these components will negatively impact on the ability of an organization or country to address its development objectives. Both strengths and weaknesses are potential points for capacity development inputs.

In addition, capacity development inputs can be made at each stage of a development initiative. Most international development projects have the following steps:

- initial scoping and conceptualization;

- project planning, design and approval;

- drafting requests for proposals and awarding contracts;

- project operations and management;

- project monitoring and evaluation; and

- applying lessons learned and feedback for subsequent initiatives, etc.

The earlier in the cycle that capacity development inputs are made, the more likely the initiative will be effective in increasing performance and fostering the sustainability of desired changes.

The tools used by capacity development practitioners – legislation and policy development, organizational analysis and restructuring, change management processes, mentoring and training, etc. – can be applied as appropriate in any of the levels or dimensions in the framework, and at the various stages in a project cycle.

Levels and dimensions of capacity development activity

Capacity development analysis and inputs can focus on any level of a system – from the distant environment of which the system is unaware to the visible context (such as global markets, monetary policies or political structures) through to complex multi-agency administrative systems or single organizations, their sub-units, teams and individual staff, and to the unseen internal environments deep within the consciousness of the individuals populating a system.

The various dimensions of capacity development in Table 3 (p. 67) can be described as follows:

- *Values*: the beliefs, cultures, attitudes, incentives and motivations of the people in the system.

- *Structure*: the system's structure – its legislation, governance and policy frameworks and power relationships. This is sometimes called the institutional framework: roles and relationships and the formal and informal rules determining the interaction of a system's members.

- *Skills*: the capabilities and competencies of the system's members defined on at least three levels: cognitive (knowledge), affective (volition or attitudes) and behavioural (action).

- *Resources*: the tools and assets available to the system.

- *Operations*: how a system actually works – its formal and informal leadership, decision-making and management methods, business processes, accountabilities, and other aspects of its functions.

- *Performance*: what the system actually accomplishes – the results of its activities.

The nature of a capacity development initiative will be determined by factors such as the types of influence actors can bring to bear on a system; their priorities, points of entry and impact; their relationships with members of the system; and the desired duration of the intended effect. Sustainable change in a system's trajectory requires ownership and perpetuation of the intervention by the system's members.

This analysis framework is intended to help actors better understand the complex environments in which they are working and to focus their attention on areas which are most likely to bring about desired changes in these systems.

Capacity Development In A Recovering Post-Conflict State: What Needs To Be Done?

Capacity development in a fragile post-conflict state is a daunting multi-faceted task. What needs to be done, where to begin, when, and how to do it? These questions are at the core of the design of any peace and security mission.

Just about everything needs to be done, as soon as possible. One example of the scope of work that is required is the opening paragraph of the TOR of a Request for Proposals for a public sector reform project in Afghanistan:

Years of conflict in Afghanistan resulted in government with a deeply fragmented administration, poor policy management capacity, outdated administrative and financial management systems, a serious disconnect between provinces and the centre, and enduring capacity constraints. While many of the formal structures and some of the traditional practices of public administration remained in place, they lacked the human, financial and physical resources to do their job, particularly in a modern context.[44]

This example is from but one of dozens of projects focused on strengthening the public service, which is an essential but relatively small part of any society. A broader and more detailed indication of the many elements that require attention is the "Table of Contents" of an April 2005 US State Department publication, *Post-Conflict Reconstruction: Essential Tasks*:

I   SECURITY
- Disposition of Armed and Other Security Forces, Intelligence Services and Belligerents
- Territorial Security
- Public Order and Safety
- Protection of Indigenous Individuals, Infrastructure and Institutions
- Protection of Reconstruction and Stabilization Personnel and Institutions
- Security Coordination
- Public Information and Communications

II   GOVERNANCE and PARTICIPATION
Governance
- National Constituting Processes
- Transitional Governance
- Executive Authority
- Legislative Strengthening
- Local Governance
- Transparency and Anti-Corruption

Participation
- Elections
- Political Parties
- Civil Society and Media
- Public Information and Communications

III HUMANITARIAN ASSISTANCE and SOCIAL WELL-BEING
- Refugees and Internally Displaced Persons
- Trafficking in Persons
- Food Security
- Shelter and Non-Food Relief
- Humanitarian Demining
- Public Health
- Education
- Social Protection
- Assessment, Analysis and Reporting
- Public Information and Communications

IV ECONOMIC STABILIZATION and INFRASTRUCTURE
Economic Stabilization
- Employment Generation
- Monetary Policy
- Fiscal Policy and Governance
- General Economic Policy
- Financial Sector
- Debt
- Trade
- Market Economy
- Legal and Regulatory Reform
- Agricultural Development
- Social Safety Net

Infrastructure
- Transportation
- Telecommunications
- Energy
- General Infrastructure
- Public Information and Communications

V JUSTICE and RECONCILIATION
- Interim Criminal Justice System
- Indigenous Police
- Judicial Personnel and Infrastructure
- Property
- Legal System Reform

- Human Rights
- Corrections
- War Crime Courts and Tribunals
- Truth Commissions and Remembrance
- Community Rebuilding
- Public Information and Communications[45]

Each of these items is a major area in itself – to address them all seems impossible. However, each country or society requires attention in all these areas and more if it is to establish order and sustainable peace.

The main task of capacity development is to work with the legitimate elements of the host society to increase their ability to build solid institutions and organizations to address these issues. The Capacity Development Analysis Framework (above), or some other similar organizing template, can be used to analyze, plan, implement and evaluate interventions in each of the areas requiring attention. The not-so-simple matter of identifying which of these many areas should be the focus of attention at any given time is addressed in the following chapter on intervention strategy and methods.

Capacity Development Or Capacity Replacement? A Continuum

External parties intervening to help the reconstruction of a fragile post-conflict state are faced with the urgent need to get systems up and running so the society can function at an acceptable level. "Capacity replacement" denotes a process that fills the many gaps with outsiders who will sooner or later leave to return home. While there is a tendency to fill key vacancies in the local system with foreigners who presumably know how to do the required jobs, this is an expensive and temporary solution that might be culturally and contextually inappropriate as well as counter-productive in the long run. Capacity replacement is a short-term fix and has its limits.

There may well be situations in which time-limited capacity replacement is appropriate – foreign technicians operating a country's electrical or communications infrastructure, running its main airports, managing parts of its financial systems, and so on – services required for basic functions of the society. Sustainable development, however, requires that locals be in charge of the instruments of state. Any capacity replacement process should function in a manner that strengthens the ability of host country nationals to provide those services.

Ultimately, capacity replacement needs to become capacity development, an intervention process in which outsiders collaborate with locals to help them do the work required to perform the services the public needs. It is similar to the well-known expression "Teach a man to fish and he will have food for a lifetime." For obvious reasons most in the assistance community see development as more desirable than replacement. However, many in the military may tend to favour the former, due to the urgency of the need and also due to their short-term orientation based on fixed-term deployments and other factors in how the military operates. In many cases there are several intermediate stages as locals are gradually helped to acquire the capacity to manage their own affairs without external support.

AusAID has defined a "staged capacity building model" which describes several types of relationships in a situation where an advisor is working with a group of local employees:

> The model requires the work group and adviser to work together, through one or a series of short workshops or meetings, to identify the main work functions of the group and decide the current stage (or level) of capacity for each function. In order to keep the model simple, four stages are proposed which reflect the degree of reliance on and involvement of the adviser, and the degree of 'ownership' or responsibility by counterparts.

The four stages of the model are described below:

> In the *Development Stage,* the adviser controls the particular work function and may do most of the work, takes the decisions or is highly influential in the decision-making process. This is typically the case when an adviser is appointed to an in-line position, or where capacity for particular functions is very low.

> In the *Guided Stage,* the adviser still has a high level of control, but counterparts can undertake the straightforward elements of the function under supervision or guidance. Staff may not be fully

aware of the full function – they 'may not know what they don't know' – and may not be aware of the need to follow through and take responsibility for ensuring the process or function is fully completed.

In the *Assisted Stage*, counterparts are now taking prime responsibility for the function, can handle most of the complex aspects and know when they need to ask for assistance. The adviser's role is more one of support, with occasional reminders and prompts to follow through, and occasional higher levels of support for new situations or for infrequent events (such as preparing an annual budget).

In the *Independent Stage*, counterparts are now fully competent to do the whole function. They may still use an external adviser for highly technical work that occurs only once a year or on an ad hoc basis. This is similar to bringing in external consultants as needed, a common practice in developed countries if it is more cost-effective to 'buy in' the capacity rather than develop it in-house.[46]

This major dimension of how an external intervener works with locals to increase the capacity of their systems is discussed more completely in the next chapter on intervention strategies and methods.

Lessons Learned From The Experience Of Rebuilding War-Torn Societies

Rebuilding a war-torn society has multiple dimensions that extend well beyond the material elements such as paving roads or reconstructing buildings – there is a deeper psychological dynamic that needs to be taken into consideration. My Afghan colleagues often alluded to this factor as a profound damage of the entire population's mental or psychological state, a type of collective post-traumatic stress disorder arising from 30 years of war. Part of this has been described by Barakat and Chard as follows:

> The circumstances of a war-torn society are only 'special' (Stiefel, 1999), compared with those of countries devastated and impoverished by economic crisis or natural disasters, in one

key aspect: the extent of the damage done to social relations by the violence and therefore the fragility and fragmentation of its institutions, from the family, the traditional organisation of local communities, to the institutions of government. One immediately obvious aspect of the breakdown of organised activities is of course the fact that transfer of knowledge and organisational culture (informal and formal education) between the generations has broken down, leaving a human resource deficit. The other less tangible but more significant aspect is the breakdown of trust in human relations and confidence in planning for the future. The fixed-term pre-planned project culture that ... characterize most donor-funded interventions, is particularly unsuited to these circumstances, since it allows no space for solutions to evolve as people recover their confidence, understand their changed circumstances, identify possible courses of action, and thus become able to make choices about what they need to know and learn in order to pursue their goals. Usually the cart is put before the horse: organisational structures are imposed and skills training is delivered in measurable packages of 'person hours' long before the real institutional and capacity building needs can be understood. It is, however, never the case that no social institutions or capacities survive, although often it is the 'rule-based' institutions of non-formal collaboration in civil society that are strengthened by the struggle to survive a war, while formal organisational structures may indeed have broken down. The donor haste to see recognisable organisations in place often ignores these institutional capacities instead of building on them but, as Stiefel suggests, the lessons learned about best practice for development are applicable and indeed even more necessary in recovery from war.[47]

Barakat and Chard further state that years of analysis of case studies have produced "...a consensus among practitioners and implementing agencies on what they ought to be doing in development work. That is, transforming practice from a top-down 'blueprint' to a participatory 'learning-process' approach building on existing institutions and capacities."[48] The best practices in development include flexible, community-centred projects, full participation of locals in project planning and operations, and channelling resources through host country institutions so they can increase their capacity to handle the fiscal and management aspects of these operations.

While Barakat and Chard address the interveners' strategies and projects, there are conditions within the "recipient" population they have mentioned that need to be better understood and taken into account as initiatives are designed and implemented. The psychologically complex factors noted above have significant impacts on how people relate to each other – whether they see themselves as members of a nation or primarily as members of large family networks, tribal groups or other affiliations – they directly affect their priorities and decision-making processes. These need to be understood and noted as part of the values-related factors in the capacity development analysis framework above and taken into account in providing effective support for the reconstruction of fragile post-conflict states.

Values Dimension In Capacity Development: The Moral Horizon

The values dimension of capacity development needs to be well understood in designing interventions in peace and stability campaigns in post-conflict states. This can be a challenge for actors from countries such as Canada where a relatively high level of trust and civic-mindedness amongst government officials and others is taken as a given.

The lower the level of security and order in a society, the smaller the administrative unit with which one can work – survival needs force people to be concerned about the well being of their immediate family and kin or clan groups and to treat others quite differently.

An African analyst of the situation in Darfur recently described one of the underlying factors in that conflict as a problem with the "narrow moral horizon" of some of the primary actors. He said the militias that were wreaking havoc in the region thought only of the benefit to their immediate kin group or extended families, and cared little for the well-being of the broader population.[49] Similar comments have been made about the values underlying problems in troubled areas such as Somalia, Afghanistan and elsewhere. This narrow moral horizon made it possible for aggressors in Darfur to "do unto others things that they would not do unto themselves." Even being members of the same faith (Islam) seemed to make little difference: the people under attack remarked that both groups were Muslims and yet the attackers would chant "Allah-u-Akbar" as they killed and pillaged in the refugee camps inhabited by their fellow Muslims. This is not an exclusively African or Muslim challenge: in the European theatre in both World Wars soldiers on both sides prayed to the same Christ for help as they did whatever they could to eliminate each other.

A narrow moral horizon can also be seen in other less-violent situations such as the operation of the civil service in many so-called developing countries, where it becomes evident to most observers that the notion that the civil service exists to serve the public is not universally shared. When trying to understand the behaviour of public servants in Bangladesh, for example, it became clear that the purpose of the civil service seemed to be mainly to serve the public servant rather than the public as a whole. The higher the level of insecurity and mistrust in a country, the more likely this motive will be active in the decision-making processes of government employees.

While there are exceptions and there are many high-minded individuals in leadership and administrative positions in fragile states such as Afghanistan and others, it cannot be assumed that the values that one hopes are present in the Canadian public service are active in the decision-making processes of officials in the countries where peace and security missions operate. People often seek positions that will give them access to state resources (or development funds) that can be shared with others in their affinity groups rather than distributed equitably across the entire population they are supposed to be serving. It is something that needs considerable attention: according to Francis Fukuyama, trust is "a prerequisite for development of a prosperous, stable state".[50]

What some call corruption others can view as a normal way of doing business. An Egyptian medical colleague who came to study in Canada and subsequently worked in a Toronto hospital reported that when he arrived he was perplexed at the notion of "conflict of interest" – he did not know what it meant. When he finally understood the idea he was surprised that it was seen as a problem that should be avoided: it was an unknown concept for a professional who came from a country where nepotism and favouritism are considered natural and necessary in dealing with everyday life. He has since adopted Canadian values on this and many other issues, but his earlier experience helps him understand what some might be quick to call unethical behaviour in people from many other parts of the world.[51]

CHAPTER 4

This presents external actors with a complex challenge as they try to work with local officials to strengthen their systems. The benefits provided by technical assistance programs can be seen by locals as ripe fruit that are ready to be picked and taken home to one's family and friends. It is difficult for an outsider to see whether this is indeed taking place and how to limit abuse of well-intentioned inputs. If left unchecked, this tendency can significantly distort the local power structure and exacerbate the problems the foreigners have been mandated to resolve.

It is possible to limit the potential for abuse of access to resources by people who have a narrow moral horizon by establishing effective relationships with people who know the background patterns of affiliations in the AO, and who can advise how to structure the design and distribution of benefits in ways that can more equitably serve the populations in question. These issues are discussed further in the following chapters.

Focusing Inputs For Greatest Effect

The challenging matter of where to focus development inputs in a peace and security campaign is helped by considering the AusAID definition of capacity development cited earlier:

> The process of developing competencies and capabilities in individuals, groups, organisations, sectors or countries which will lead to sustained and self-generating performance improvement.

With this definition in mind, long-term and short-term inputs to a recipient's system should be designed on the basis of several factors – the capacity development analysis framework described above can provide categories to guide these decisions:

- What is the intervener's mandate to interact with the recipients' system?

- What effect or result does the intervener want to achieve, and at what level of the system?

- Who are the potential recipients, what is their current condition, and what do they say they need?

- What are the capacity-related strengths and weaknesses in the recipient's system?

- What does the intervener have to offer?

- What points of contact exist between the intervener and the recipients?

- What mechanisms exist to connect interveners' resources to recipients' needs?

- Which of the available interveners' resources will likely produce the greatest beneficial short term and long term effect in the recipient's system?

- Which intervention(s) will generate the most valuable information for the intervener and act as a basis for further support?

Another analysis method uses a medical model to diagnose and define an intervention strategy:

- What problems are observed? Consider these as symptoms of a deeper issue.

- What are the underlying causes of these observed symptoms?

- What are the possible treatments for these causes?

- Which of these treatments are feasible?

The selected intervention strategy is based on the findings of the last item on both of these lists. As discussed in greater detail in the next chapter, an active feedback process should be used to monitor progress and adjust course as required.

CHAPTER 5

Intervention Strategy and Methods

Introduction

This chapter summarizes a few of the concepts and strategies used by development specialists in their work, and describes an analytical tool, General Systems Theory, that helps analyze patterns, define relationships and select intervention strategies in this complex area of practice. This is followed by examples of development activities that illustrate these concepts at work.

As noted earlier, the approaches used by military and development actors have a number of things in common and several important areas where they differ. One of the commonalities is that they both intervene in a system to achieve an effect by applying influence (resources) with the intention of altering the system's trajectory in a desirable direction. Differences in approach include the role of the system's inhabitants in carrying out the intervention, the primary sources of power or influence for change, and the time required to achieve the desired effect.

When considering making input to strengthen a system an obvious question is, "what should we work on?" In the previous chapter, the US State Department's list, *Post-Conflict Reconstruction: Essential Tasks*, describes the array of elements that need to be functioning at an adequate level in an effective society: it is a huge list, and external agents with limited time and resources can address only a few of these items in any given period. If everything needs to be built, fixed or strengthened, and we can only help with a few bits of this massive job, which ones should we focus on, how should this be done and who will do it? The answers depend on a number of factors, primarily the context in which work is taking place, the capacities of the intervener and of the local population, and conditions in the area that is the focus of attention.

CHAPTER 5

A moving target

One of the main factors that development workers consider as they plan and carry out an intervention is that the entire field of operation is in a constant state of flux – while the host society has existed for centuries, in most post-conflict fragile states conditions are changing rapidly, as are the external parties (donors, etc.) who want to help strengthen the country's systems. Development inputs are relatively short-term applications of resources from a changing source that are aimed at a moving target – and they need to be focused on the optimum point(s) in that target to achieve the desired effect as the whole environment moves through time. It is important to remember that the desired effect is not an end state, it is "a process … which will lead to sustained and self-generating performance improvement." The development process never really ends: at some point external parties may disengage, but work goes on as long as the society exists. This is a very fluid business. Not only is the entire system moving through time, there are a multiplicity of forces that can have an impact on its trajectory – the development project's inputs are only one of many. Other factors well outside the control of the external parties, such as the history of relationships in the area, economic forces, the weather, the media, religious leaders and more, can affect the course of events in the system. This makes targeting inputs to achieve particular effects a challenging matter indeed.

A number of terms used in this section, such as "system," "influence" and "trajectory" are found in General System Theory, a conceptual framework that helps lend order to complex and fluid multidimensional processes such as development: this analysis and planning tool, which may be similar to some used in the military, is briefly described in the following pages.

System Theory In Development

General System Theory, which was developed by Ludwig von Bertalanffy and others, provides an analytical framework that can be used to describe some of the many factors involved in development.[52] It helps define some of key issues such as assessing patterns of power and influence, deciding where to intervene, understanding the dynamics of inter-group relation-ships, and designing and carrying out development activities. System Theory concepts, such as the description of various environments related to a system and the key notion of entropy can also be used in capacity development. Some terms such as systems and sub-systems, closed and open boundaries, the transfer of energy or influence across boundaries and system balance (or homeostasis) as a system moves through time are used to clarify what can seem to be a bewildering array of information involved in development work. These terms are defined as follows:

System

A system is defined by von Bertalanffy as "a set of elements standing in interaction" – in other words, a group of things which have something in common. This includes any grouping with any sort of relationship – a collection of people, a forest, the planets, rabbits on a hillside, a pile of rocks, etc. – if it is possible to identify a group of things, this cluster can be seen as a "system".

There can be smaller systems (sub-systems) within other, larger systems – a clear example of this would be a single household in a village (see illustration below). The activities inside that house would be seen as taking place within a system (the family group involved in that household), which in turn exists within the larger system of the village itself. The village can also be seen as a sub-system, one of a number of communities which together comprise an even greater system, the region or territory in which they all are located.

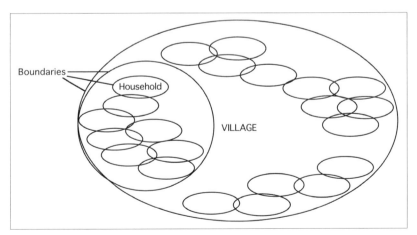

FIGURE 1 – SYSTEM, SUB-SYSTEMS AND BOUNDARIES.

System boundary

Each system is defined by some sort of boundary, which can be thought of as an imaginary line that determines what is inside and what is outside of a system.

In the example given above there is a boundary around the small system of the single household, and there could be another boundary which includes several households in that part of the village. There could also be a boundary around the whole community or area in which these people live.

System boundaries can be "drawn" wherever any observer wishes, and for any purpose. In a village, for example, it may be convenient to see the community as a cluster of different households or family groups. In this case boundaries would be imagined which marked out these families. At other times, it may be useful to show the various age groups, levels of education or degree of economic well-being, affinity groups, gender distribution in leadership positions, and so forth: boundaries can be drawn in whatever manner suits the purpose of the analysis.

Open and closed systems

The boundary around any system can be said to be "open" or "closed". A closed system is one that is completely sealed off from its environment by its boundary, such as a candle burning in an air-tight jar. The activity within such a closed system will continue until all the needed resources are consumed, at which point activity will cease (i.e. the candle flame will consume all the oxygen in the jar and then it will go out).

There are relatively few completely closed systems in our world. All "organic" systems, a term which includes human beings and their communities, are open systems: that is, each has a boundary which is open to some extent and which makes it possible for energy or influence (in various forms, such as information or other resources) to pass into and out of its system.

One of the factors determining the "openness" of the system boundary between a community and its environment would be the ease of communication. If there were roads or television and telephone links that permitted free exchange of goods and information across the boundary between the village and the rest of the world, that system boundary could be said to be very open. If, on the other hand, there was less ease of communication, if there were no roads, or the phone system did not work, the boundary could be said to be relatively closed.

The same openness would apply if the people were co-operative and worked together in harmony: they would share things across their respective boundaries. If there were tensions in the community, however, and people did not communicate and share things easily with each other, boundaries would be relatively closed. A lack of trust among families in a community, for example, would contribute to making boundaries between these groups seem rather closed.

Energy in system theory

The various things that pass across the boundaries of systems can be called energy or influence. There are different forms of this influence. A human being requires physical energy in the form of food in order to survive. We also use other forms of influence which can be termed social power or psychological energy. This "social energy", which is often in the form of information, is usually the main product of human relationships and is a necessary element in the functioning of social systems. There are usually various kinds of social energy, and different people in a community hold varying amounts of these types of power. Some energy is able to help communities progress in a beneficial direction, while other forms can be unhelpful. Understanding how to help communities acquire and control beneficial types of energy to further their own progress is one of the main aims of sustainable development.

Entropy in system theory

The term "entropy" describes a force or tendency that is present in all systems: they all tend to "run down", and to progress to a stage of reduced coherence and eventually to completely random disorder. Especially in relatively closed systems: they consume all the energy they have available and eventually stop functioning or "fall apart". An example is organic systems that receive insufficient food: they die and their bodies eventually decompose. A lack of affection has a similar destructive effect on a child's psychological development.

CHAPTER 5

The tendency toward entropy in organic or social systems needs to be constantly countered through the generation of constructive energy from within or the exchange of influence across boundaries from one system to another. This reverse tendency, which has been called "negative entropy", maintains or increases the order or harmony within systems.

Examples of constructive energy or influence that can act as negative entropy are food, affection, education, medicine, or anything else that helps sustain or improve the circumstances and cohesiveness of the members of a community. Destructive forms of energy that will reduce the well-being of social systems, and as such tend toward disunity and disorder, are oppression, injustice, violence, back-biting, malnutrition, poverty, and any other forces which prevent people from working together to achieve mutually-acceptable goals for their collective betterment.

As noted in the previous chapter, these destructive forces (e.g. lack of trust) are frequently present in post-conflict war-torn societies, and it can be difficult to establish and maintain the highly-ordered forms of cooperation and social cohesiveness which foster collective action, harmony and well-being among people in these contexts.

"Homeostasis", or dynamic balance (and change) in system theory

"Homeostasis" is a term that is used to describe a condition inside a system. It is a "steady state" or a "dynamic balance" which occurs within a system when the relationship between its internal and external conditions stays essentially the same from one day to the next. The concept of homeostasis thus includes reference to the passage of time: a system will move through time in a state of dynamic equilibrium if it can continue to gain access to the resources it needs to keep itself in that condition. This is the system's trajectory.

If there is a desire to help shift a system's trajectory there is a need to alter its "steady state" by modifying some of the conditions in or around that system. Anything that alters the energy flow within or between parts of a system can bring about changes in trajectory.

For example, a community which has high levels of disunity among sub-groups and is not progressing as a result can be changed by giving influential members of each sub-group an important task to do which requires them to collaborate with their counterparts in other sub-groups. Working on this common task is likely to improve the relationships among sub-groups and foster a system-wide shift from conflict toward cooperation, and change the community's trajectory for the better. The system will move at the rate permitted by the most reluctant member who has any influence on how it will progress.

The core of development work is the process of analysis of a system's conditions and introduction of resources that strengthen forces that alter the system's trajectory and promote beneficial change. In the example above the resources that were introduced were the design of the shared activity and the ability to help key members of conflicting sub-systems see the benefit in working together for their common benefit.

The following figure illustrates some elements of the concept of homeostasis.

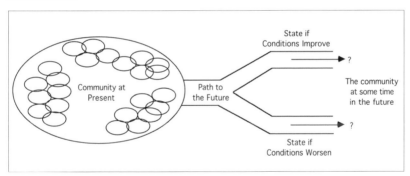

FIGURE 2 – STEADY STATE, OR DYNAMIC BALANCE AND CHANGES IN A COMMUNITY AS IT GOES THROUGH TIME.

Boundary management

As stated earlier, the condition within an open system is in a dynamic balance, or steady-state. The nature of that steady state is influenced by the energy or influence that crosses the system's boundary. If there is a need to achieve (or maintain) a desirable condition within a system, it is necessary to control or manage the flow of energy across its boundaries – to have them be open or closed as appropriate to maintain acceptable internal conditions as the system moves through time.

In the previous example of overcoming disunity among sub-groups in a community the boundaries were open enough to allow a shared exercise to be introduced, and sub-group boundaries that were previously closed due to inter-group conflict became more open as members worked together on the common task and combined their forces to achieve mutual benefit.

One of the main differences between military and development strategies is that for development workers the boundaries are usually controlled from within the recipient's system: as will be discussed later, in development the door opens (and closes) from the other side. In our work we don't kick in doors to get what we want.

System environments

There are several environments related to any system. These are illustrated in the following figure:

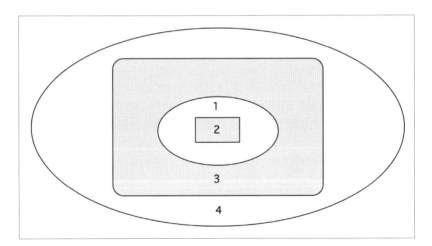

FIGURE 3 – SYSTEM ENVIRONMENTS.

1. The system under consideration, and the internal environment of which it is aware.
2. The deeper internal environment of which the system is not aware.
3. The system's external environment of which it is aware.
4. The system's distant external environment of which it is not aware.

Environments form the context within which any system exists, and energy or influence might be able to flow across the boundary from any environment to any other to alter the conditions in any part of the system.

These environments can be illustrated using the following example of a village in Afghanistan. If the system under consideration (#1) is the total population and geographical area of the village, examples of the dynamics of these environments could be as follows:

#2. *The Deeper Internal Environment of which the System is Unaware* – could be an internal struggle among senior clan leaders for control of the community and its attitudes toward the government and the insurgency. Although the population of the village may not know about the struggle, it is likely that any outcome of such a dispute will spill over into the public part of the system and cause changes in the way the community operates.

#3. *The External Environment* – changes in the visible environment, such as a firefight between insurgents and government forces on the edge of town, could make dramatic changes in the internal conditions of the system.

#4. *The Distant External Environment* – changes in environments which the villagers can't see, such as deliberations in member countries' foreign ministries prior to a meeting at NATO Headquarters to discuss commitments on troop deployments, would eventually create changes in the system. Another example could be a pharmaceutical laboratory's positive findings on the feasibility of using Afghan opium to produce medicinal products and a change in decisions on this matter among the board of directors of the multinational firm involved. This would likely bring about major changes throughout the entire environment and considerably alter conditions in the village.

Whole-System Approach

A "whole-system" approach is just what the term implies – that any change strategy must take into consideration as many elements as possible in its planning process so information is provided from a broad an array of inputs before decisions are taken. An example from the auto industry helps illustrate the point. One of the major Japanese firms wanted to explore the feasibility of making major changes in its operations. Before taking any specific actions they convened large gatherings of all the stakeholders they could assemble – those from within the organization, as well as from outside: car owners, private maintenance shops, parts suppliers, regulatory bodies, and more. In a relatively loosely-structured interaction they requested groups to spontaneously form and discuss several basic issues on which they wanted input. The result of these large free-form multi-party consultations were analyzed and incorporated into the company's plans. The information received was far richer than would have been produced by a narrower tightly-structured in-house planning session.

The same concept can be applied to peace and security missions: all actors with any influence on the environment must be accounted for in some way so their inputs can be appropriately considered in any intervention planning process.

Alignment

The concept of alignment is used in both community development and organizational development and is linked to the system's trajectory. It is based on the notion that all members of a system have resources and social energy and will direct that energy in ways that suit them. If they are aligned toward a common goal or guided by a shared vision of the purpose of their organization, their individual contributions will be mutually complementary and the system is likely to progress in the direction they want to go. If, however, their individual efforts are not aligned toward a common vision or goal, their energies will pull in various and conflicting directions and may tend to cancel each other out; the system will not move as hoped.

Anything which fosters alignment of the social energy of members of a system in a common direction will accelerate its movement along that trajectory.

Formal And Informal Influencers

Each social system has members who exert more influence than others, and the behaviours and attitudes of the rest of the system's members are affected by these leaders' priorities. Formal leaders are usually those who are elected or who otherwise occupy visible positions of leadership in the local administration. They may or may not have significant influence on their communities. Informal leaders are the people that community members seek out and heed when they want advice or guidance on matters of concern: they may or may not be formal leaders as well.

In Canadian Aboriginal communities, for example, the formal leadership may be the members of the Band Council who are readily visible to outsiders. Informal leaders, however, may be people who remain in the background and are unseen by external actors, but they are sought out by members of the Band Council and others for guidance before key decisions are taken. They may be more influential than the formal leadership.

Organizations have the same two-level pattern – the visible designated leadership in the formal hierarchy and the people the system's members turn to for advice on matters of concern. These informal influencers may not be the same people as the managers or supervisors on the organizational chart. They don't run the organization, but the organization will not run effectively if they don't support it.

A development intervention needs to take both types of influencers into account if it hopes to implement any changes in the system.

A System's Trajectory And Forces Of Globalization

The broader context within which development takes place needs to be taken into consideration in planning any intervention – community-level changes are linked to the external environment that exerts its influence even if it may not be clearly visible from the local level.

System Theory regards the entire world as a single system, with each country and region as sub-systems within this greater whole. Societies move through time on trajectories determined by the interplay of internal and external forces, and these effect systems at all levels from global to individual. One way of regarding international development is that it is supporting the trajectory of the entire human family toward a more equitable, ordered and unified world. Development is part of the multiple forces of globalization that are at work everywhere and all sub-systems are affected by this.

To place this in a historical context it is possible to say that we are part way through a complex process that began to move more quickly with the dawn of the industrialized era in the mid-1800s and will likely continue for another century or more before we have built the full range of institutions required to effectively manage a diverse and unified world. It is a long-term capacity development project that will continue to keep many people busy for decades to come.

While a full enumeration of the social and economic principles that are part of globalization is well beyond the scope of this monograph, naming a few will suffice to make the point. These include the equality of women and men, democratic constitutional governance, access to education, rule of law, respect for human rights, reduction of extremes of wealth and poverty, freedom of religion, and others which are reflected in the MDGs and various declarations of the UN and other international agencies.

Where there is alignment of forces within national and other sub-systems in a manner that is consistent with the general principles of globalization, those societies seem to do relatively well, and where there are forces which are not aligned in this direction societies do not perform as well.

This often contentious matter was clearly summarized in an article by Pranab Bardhan in a recent issue of *Scientific American*. He cited a number of examples of differences between countries that seem to have somewhat similar circumstances (such as Angola and Botswana) to illustrate that sub-systems which are moving in directions inconsistent with this global trajectory usually experience more problems than those that are in harmony with global processes.[53]

It should be noted here that the use of the term "globalization" as a factor in the world's trajectory does not imply that development workers support the Americanization of the planet – it is a far broader process that has dimensions we have yet to discover. A useful analysis of the challenges which lie ahead is Benjamin Barber's "Jihad vs. McWorld" which points out the difficulties with both religious fundamentalism and the spread of the multinationals – neither are democratic and the people have no voice in how they operate.[54]

Canadian foreign policy is increasingly focusing on this dimension of development. The conclusion of the government's recent response to a report from the Standing Committee on Foreign Affairs and International Development makes this clear:

> While half of the world's countries have made significant progress in establishing democratic systems of government, the path to a more democratic world is filled with obstacles and success cannot be taken for granted. The Government Response to the Report of the Standing Committee sets out a series of commitments and activities that will focus and maximize Canada's efforts in the field of international democracy support. In doing so, we can make a real difference in supporting democracy and improving the lives of citizens around the world.[55]

One of the factors fuelling the insurgency in Afghanistan is a resistance to globalization, a willingness by some to use brutal forms of violence to maintain an obsolete social order that is not compatible with the general principles at play in most of the world. This may apply to other conflicts as well. Any intervention that helps align community-level trajectories with global forces will counter the influences of the insurgency and foster the evolution of the society in a manner consistent with the patterns in the broader environment. Most effective development initiatives are consistent with this principle.

Project Design Within A Whole-System Approach

Effective development initiatives use a "whole-system approach" that takes into account as many contextual factors as possible as the intervention is being planned. This is done at the same time as a focused application of resources is being considered on a specific part of the system. An example from the security field is helpful in seeing what this entails – the following photo of a flip chart prepared by a group of staff officers at a training course offered by the Pearson Peacekeeping Centre illustrates the complexity of the issue.

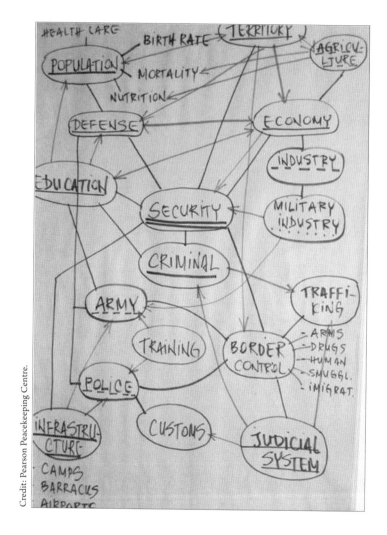

Credit: Pearson Peacekeeping Centre.

PHOTO 2: COMPONENTS OF SECURITY – PARTICIPANTS' WORKSHOP FLIP CHART. [56]

It is clear from this flip chart that establishing security in a region requires adequate capacity in an array of sectors: agriculture, health, education, industry, as well as those normally associated with security such as the justice system, police and the military. Other sectors such as transportation and communications could be added to the list. Most post-conflict reconstruction efforts attempt to address all these issues and more, but the job is too much for any one agency – a number of coordinated efforts are required which hopefully cover all the required sectors.

While taking into account the broad whole-system context, each participating agency will work with host-country partners and other collaborating agencies to design their intervention using some version of the following list.

1. The priorities and mandate of the mission.

2. The development plan (PRSP, etc) for that part of the host country's system (if any).

3. Existing level of performance and capacity development needs of the host country's systems.

4. The dynamics of the host environments (level of security, patterns of influence, trajectory, etc.).

5. Other agencies or actors with significant influence in the environment.

6. The resources available to the development agency.

7. The development agency's points of contact with the host country system (where the boundaries are most open).

8. The potential maximum direct and indirect benefits from the application of resources.

9. An assessment of risks and description of mitigating factors.

10. Specific activities to be undertaken by the development agency with host country partners.

11. The likely short-term, medium-term and long-term results (effects) of the intervention.

12. The likelihood that the intervention will become an integral part of the host system's operations and be carried forward by locals once external inputs cease (sustainability of effect).

13. Ability to monitor progress and results and generate lessons learned for subsequent interventions.

Project designs must be consistent with the realization that in sustainable
capacity development it is essential to build on the foundations of what
already exists, and to help local systems grow using strategies with which
the people are familiar so they can increase their effectiveness in serving
the population. Capacity development is an organic process that is rooted
in the soil of existing systems and capabilities and external actors need to
bear that in mind as they go about their business.

One of the criticisms of peace and security operations is that the military
seems to have difficulty adapting itself to this reality, with the result that
their inputs do not adequately strengthen host-country systems before the
mission ends and troops are withdrawn. This may be due in part to the
perception of power relations between military and host-country systems,
which influences how the military thinks about what it needs to do.

Power Relations: Acting On Or Acting With?

One of the challenges in international development is the perception of
ownership of the initiative and the quality of power relationships between
external actors and local systems. As noted earlier, development agencies
are often seen as neo-colonial agents of western imperialism, and although
host countries are dependent on inflows of foreign aid, they do not like
being in a powerless position: it is not conducive to fostering autonomous
and self-sustaining indigenous development. Although development agencies are in a control position, they usually try to work in a collaborative
and relatively egalitarian way with host country systems. The military is
not accustomed to acting in anything but the role of a powerful intervener
and controlling the field of action – they act *on* more often than act *with*
the focus of their attention. However, in a counter-insurgency campaign
where they address the 75 per cent of the intervention that is non-kinetic,
they need to learn new power relations and new language to describe what
they do.

A good example of the military's underlying assumptions of power and
control is in the terms used by a colleague describing NATO's whole-

system participatory strategy in designing interventions in a 3D environment – Effects Based Approach to Operations (EBAO):

> Effects Based Approach to Operations is key in the 3D environment. The idea of this approach is to determine what effects you want to have on the ground and in the end, find out who the players are that will help you achieve those effects, and then engage those players early in your planning to find out how to achieve those effects. If you don't engage all the players and coordinate, you may have unintended consequences.[57]

While he is describing a multi-party participatory process that is essential in an integrated peace and security operation, a development worker would say there is a difficulty with the role relationships implicit in the statement. The military strategy seems to presume it is NATO that will do the planning and achieve the effects, not the host country agencies with whom the intervener collaborates. While the military might well facilitate the process, they don't own the process, the local institutions do (or should). The vocabulary used indicates there is a substantive control orientation in perception of ownership of the intervention by the military, and this could be a problem.

While in practice the host country systems must become the main actors in establishing security, the choice of terminology indicates quite different perceptions of power and initiative in how development takes place. External actors should not act on the environment; they must work with the people and organizations in the host country to achieve stability. This may be part of the reason why a whole-system participatory approach to sustainable capacity development seems not to be part of the military's contribution in many peace and security missions, and why it is too often necessary for troops to return to places like East Timor and Haiti to help re-establish stability following their premature departure first time around.

Helping A System Move:
You Can't Push A Cat Upstairs

As noted earlier, a system will progress along its trajectory at the rate that its slowest member with influence wants to move. If people feel they are

CHAPTER 5

being asked to do something they don't really want to do (or can't do), or are pushed faster than they want to go, they will find ways to resist this pressure.

In cases where movement is not taking place in spite of repeated direct attempts to encourage change, alternate indirect strategies may be required. An example from BGen Pepin's work while he was in Afghanistan illustrates the point:

> In 2006 there were serious concerns within the command group at CJTF-76 [Coalition Joint Task Force 76] that a Governor of one of the eastern provinces had not yet prepared a provincial development plan, and the lack of this plan was hampering development efforts and contributing to insecurity in the area. BGen Pepin visited with the Governor more than once to encourage him to prepare a plan, and explained all the good reasons why this should be done. During each visit the Governor was warmly hospitable, fully engaged in the conversation and committed himself to having such a plan prepared. After the second visit there was still no sign of such a plan and BGen Pepin sensed the Governor was becoming irritated with these demands: knowing that escalating the matter within OEF/ISAF would not be productive, he decided to use a Afghan face and voice to try to convince the Governor. He discussed this problem with the Minister of MRRD, the ministry that was involved in coordinating the provincial development plans with the ANDS, and the Minister agreed to do what he could to encourage the Governor to prepare the plan. The Minister accepted the military's help with transportation to the province where he spent a full day meeting several key officials and providing advice and counsel to the Governor and his team of administrators. This event was a win/win situation both for the central and provincial governments. Within a short time the provincial development plan was initiated and a first draft produced.[58]

This is an example of an outsider having some access to a system but limited influence to change how it actually worked. The boundary between BGen Pepin and the Governor was open only to the extent necessary for polite conversation, but not open enough for the General's comments to effect a change in behaviour. BGen Pepin had a more open boundary with the Minister who saw the need for the plan and in turn exerted sufficient influence on the Governor to produce the desired effect. BGen Pepin could talk with the Governor but could not push him to act: the Minister could, and did. As a result of the Minister's input the Governor's behaviour was changed and progress was made.

In another situation, the SAT members working with IARCSC were well into helping the Commission improve its internal functioning, which included encouraging the Chairman's Special Advisor to establish regular senior management meetings where the heads of the various units in the Commission would meet to update each other on progress they were making on their units' strategy and work plans. SAT members had worked with each unit head to prepare work plans with measurable results, a process that was normal business practice for the advisors and was also espoused by several Afghan managers. The Afghans agreed that their work plans made good sense and that they would follow them and meet on a regular basis to report on progress and explore reasons for any problems they were having reaching anticipated objectives.

For reasons that were not made clear to SAT personnel, these meetings were rarely held on schedule, there were frequent absences and in one case a unit head went on a long unannounced road trip and did not do the work he had agreed to do to meet his work plan's objectives.

SAT had worked closely with these officials and they all had agreed to do what was required to improve the quality of management in the Commission, but they did not do what they said they would. It seemed they did not want to be pushed into something the advisors considered was good management practice, and found indirect ways of avoiding something they were uncomfortable doing. Although the reasons for non-involvement were not clear, it is likely that the avoidance was linked to a reluctance to admit there were problems they did not know how to resolve, and a desire to avoid the loss of face they would experience from a public admission of their problems. This is consistent with the lack of trust and other troublesome psychological traits associated with reconstruction of war-torn societies discussed earlier.

It is unlikely that the Afghans would have been able to articulate their reasons for avoidance, with the result that the SAT advisors were left with a clear awareness that something was not working but did not know why, and felt a deep sense of frustration rooted in not being able to pinpoint the reasons behind the lack of movement in the system.

Most seasoned development workers have experienced this challenge and can adjust their strategies to be more closely aligned with the ability of host nationals to absorb and apply new information and ways of operating, and can continue to help the system move forward, even if it is at a lower rate of progress than initially hoped.

Choosing An Intervention Strategy: The Best Or The Possible?

As noted earlier, in development work it is important to see the problems at the community or organizational level as symptoms which point to a cause or several causes, determine the possible remedies for those causes, consider which of those treatments are feasible or desirable and then to make a choice and apply the remedy, even if it is sub-optimal – in medicine sometimes the quickest cure for an illness does a lot of other damage and it is better to use a slower and less disruptive treatment to achieve something that comes close to the desired result.

An example from Afghanistan is associated with the realization that the head of one of the key government ministries was not able (or willing) to do his job properly and the most obvious solution was to get the President to replace him. Although this recommendation had been made several times no action was taken, much to the frustration of the advisors who were trying to help the ministry improve its performance.

A closer look at the situation shed some light on why this was the case. The minister was a former mujahadeen commander (like several others at that level) and had been given this high-placed post as part of an arrange-ment to keep him happy. He liked the status that came with the position, and had let it be known that he wanted yet a higher profile job for which he was even less qualified, so the appointment could not be made. If he were removed and suffered loss of face or status it would cause a great deal of trouble for the President, because he had a large number of friends in Parliament who would make life even more difficult than it already was. In the reality of the situation it was easier for the President to put up with a poorly functioning ministry than to suffer the consequences of applying the most obvious remedy – removal of the individual.

A less-disruptive but sub-optimal solution was found by encouraging the minister to appoint a competent assistant, who then became the main contact between the technical specialists and the ministry. However this less than ideal "treatment" brought with it a number of frustrations, because even though the assistant knew what was needed there was only so much that could be accomplished because of the minister's inability or unwillingness to do what was required to improve the functioning of the organization. A result was that much-needed organizational reforms that could have been done in a year or two took considerably longer; some did not happen at all and would have to wait until the minister moved out of the way.

The team of technical specialists had to reduce expectations of improvement in that part of the government's operations and to decide whether they wanted to keep on working with that ministry or to reassign their personnel to another part of government where conditions were more propitious. They opted for the latter, moving most of their resources to the more fertile environment, leaving a single member to continue working with the assistant to help accomplish what little could be achieved in spite of the blockage at the top of the system.

It is a difficult decision to make but there really was no other choice. The situation brings to mind the saying attributed to T.E. Lawrence in 1918:

> It is better to let them do it themselves imperfectly than to do it yourself perfectly. It is their country, their way, and our time is short.

Entering A System: The Door Opens From The Other Side

Gaining entry to a system is one of the more challenging aspects of development work. Sometimes an indirect approach brings great results – as in the case of how SAT was invited to work with the Minister's office at the MRRD.

Lieutenant-Colonel (LCol) Pierre St-Cyr was the leader of one of the SAT planning teams at the time of a Cabinet shuffle which saw an enthusiastic and capable Mr. Zia appointed to be Minister of Rural Rehabilitation and Development. The team had begun to establish relationships with the Ministry through the work of the strategic communications specialist, who had a good relationship with counterparts in the upper levels of MRRD. CIDA was also providing support to the Ministry. Shortly after the new Minister took office it came to CIDA's attention that he wanted to go to Kandahar to see conditions for himself, to check on the accuracy of the information he was receiving from his staff. With SAT's help the schedule of the Canadian C-130 Hercules (Herc) flight to Kandahar was adjusted to accommodate the Minister. LCol St-Cyr joined the group and accompanied the Minister on his first flight in a Herc, during which Zia was invited to sit in the cockpit, something he enjoyed immensely. All the way to Kandahar he let the Minister lead the discussion, and they talked a lot about flying (LCol St-Cyr is also a pilot) – by the time they landed the Minister was saying he wanted to be a pilot as well. They also discussed the Minister's vision and his ultimate goals for MRRD. In this conversation, LCol St-Cyr began to get some understanding of the Minister as a person. He said that he would accompany the Minister during the day, observe his interactions, and by the end of the day he would be in a better position to comment on potential advice and support from SAT.

Once in Kandahar, the Minister wanted to visit the Governor and his staff and do an assessment of his Ministry's operations in the area. The CIDA representative could not go outside the wire with the Minister, leaving the PRT Commander (who provided ground transportation) and LCol St-Cyr to accompany Zia to the Governor's palace. They found the Governor had left because of heightened security problems associated with the high-profile visit: he presented a major target. When it was time to return, Mr. Zia was in a pensive state, considerably disturbed by what he had seen: it was quite different and much worse than he had been led to believe at head office. LCol St-Cyr recalled the trip:

> On the return flight, it was obvious that Zia was exhausted… We discussed the events of the day, his perceptions, his intentions and his hopes. The (conversation during the) last part of the trip was oriented to his family, his country and on Canada. Before leaving the plane, I asked … to meet him for 15 minutes in his office, regarding a proposal to help him. He rapidly agreed, and at

that time, for some unknown reason, I knew we were on the path of building a solid relationship based on trust and confidence.[59]

Two days later, LCol St-Cyr, SAT Commander Col Capstick and the team's strategic communications specialist met the Minister in his office to propose SAT's support for his operations. LCol St-Cyr recalled: "The short discussion, basically due to his (established) confidence in us, led to an agreement of having the SAT-A working to support his Ministry."

The next day, the Minister announced to his senior staff that a group of offices adjacent to his own would be allocated to SAT, requiring the relocation of a group of advisors funded by a major development agency, and that his staff were to work closely with SAT members to improve the planning processes in the Ministry. This happened in July 2006: support continued to be provided by the second SAT Roto, and the third group of SAT planners were still working with MRRD in late 2007.

LCol St-Cyr's non-directive approach contributed to the door opening at the top of MRRD, a Ministry responsible for much of the government's activities in rural Afghanistan, including the NSP, which was present in over 20,000 villages across the country. It also contributed to keeping that door open.

Staying In A System: Keeping The Door Open

While gaining entry to a system is a first and necessary step in a development initiative, being permitted to remain in the system is another matter. SAT's successful entry into MRRD was sustained in large measure by the strategy used to keep their Afghan counterparts in the forefront of the work, and the high quality results of the team's efforts.

The first challenge Zia gave the team was to review the MRRD Strategic Plan – this was done in a way that reinforced Afghan ownership of the process and the results. LCol St-Cyr commented:

> Our credo was to ensure the Afghans would always have the (credit for) the work we were doing (with) them. Put an Afghan face on everything. This would lead to … capacity building with the Afghans. Results (were that) they were feeling more proud

and more responsible. ... Our office was decorated only with Afghan memorabilia. No Canadian items whatsoever. Zia was touched by that. Simple things like that (reinforced) our intent to (show) ... that we had no national hidden agenda.

The second challenge was to review and complement the MRRD Strategic Communication Plan. (Our strategic communications specialist) ... produced an excellent alternative enhancing their existing ... Plan.

The next step was to slightly modify the Strategic plan and to (develop) ... an Implementation plan. The implementation plan had to be agreed (to) by all stakeholders (tribes, provincial reps, area reps, ethnic groups etc.). This caused great concerns to Zia, thinking it would take months to get the inputs from all these stakeholders. We turned the problem into an efficient solution, (by) holding a mega conference with all these stakeholders, dividing them into groups (with mixed) reps from all parties. We trained ... Afghan facilitators and helped them in producing a work plan to validate, commonly, all 52 aims of the Strategic Plan. We then helped them ... turn the results into a coherent Implementation Plan that met each stakeholder's desires. This event took us one month to put together. We then left Afghanistan to be followed by no 2 SAT-A team.[60]

Two things contributed to the continued receptivity by the Minister: the SAT members' attitude and approach which put Afghans in the forefront and made it clear there was no ulterior motive or hidden agenda, and the team's ability to prepare useful products for the ministry. Sustainability of a worker's effectiveness is linked to appropriate values and a high quality relationship coupled with obvious technical competence that produces something of value for the host government agency.

The Door Also Closes – Examples

The door also closes from the other side, sometimes due to conditions in the recipient of assistance, and in others due to the behaviour of the providers of assistance. SAT encountered the first type of challenge, which led them to stop working with one of the Afghan government ministries. LCol St-Cyr commented:

A factor that we should have considered more deeply is the importance or the status of the individuals we were dealing with. The (Minister), a former Mujahadeen, wanted to keep a form of power, as he had in the past over his warriors. He was then clear that he would not accept advice from a foreigner that could affect his prestige over his subalterns. Also, he had to please his master (Karzai) in showing support in giving just enough attention to the SAT. This is a form of corruption, or hypocrisy.

There are some Afghans that (think they) do not need support from outsiders. These same Afghans firmly believe that they … have all the tools and knowledge to do what they have to do.

To avoid … these deceptions, we should analyze the opening, or the willingness of these individuals … (to see whether) they know if they need help or not. We should not force our way in. We have to understand the culture, the relationships they have (with) each other, the importance of their status and the desired end state.[61]

In some cases the providers' behaviour contributed to the closing of the door. In meetings with Afghans and development advisors from a number of agencies there were several situations in which the advisors' strong encouragement and insensitive enthusiasm, sometimes coupled with paternalism, contributed to their not being able to exert significant influence on the organizations they were trying to help. In some cases it may have been a function of incompatible or inappropriate communication styles or attitudes, and in others it was a matter of Afghans being expected to move faster than they wanted to go. The results were usually a shift in communication patterns coupled with extensive discussions among the Afghans, especially when the technical advisor was not present. These awkward situations affected not only foreigners – Afghan expatriates who returned to their home country to help the Karzai government could also find themselves being shut out and not being able to exert meaningful influence in the system.

Insensitive enthusiasm & paternalism

In one troublesome situation the representative of a major donor agency approached the Director of the Training and Development Department to discuss his plans and funding requirements for the next few years, to incorporate in their forecasts. The Director responded by reviewing the main features of the priority list his unit had prepared, complete with a work plan, draft timelines and priorities, to let the representative know where he wanted the organization to go. The donor representative glanced over the work plan and abruptly stated that the items on the list were not appropriate. She said she drew from her past experience in other countries and extensive academic work and overrode the client's wishes and prescribed the training and human resource development work she said they needed to build up the institutions of state. The tone of the meeting became much less cordial as she confronted the Director in a way that made it clear she thought that he did not know what he was doing and wanted to set him on what she saw as the right path. During this encounter he became steadily more angry and flustered, all the while feeling somewhat trapped because his operations depended on donor funds.

After the meeting ended he asked for feedback on what had happened. He was told there seemed to be problems with the representative's approach, which did not attempt to build on work done within the Afghan system. He agreed and said that her predecessor at the funding agency had a more collaborative approach and it was unfortunate he had been replaced. He said he was ready to tell the donor that they no longer wanted to do business with them, something that would have been a problem for the donor, since Afghanistan was one of their major clients and this Department's work was a key area in the donor's field of interest.

Unfortunately there are too many similar cases of technical advisors behaving in paternalistic and insensitive ways, resulting in increasing the distance between donors and their government clients.

Too much pressure and scapegoating

Some of the challenges SAT faced in working with IARCSC were in part the consequences of pressure from all sides on the Special Advisor to the Chairman, their main contact with the system. The Special Advisor was in a difficult position, caught between a Chairman who did not seem to know how to (or want to) improve his part of the organization, and the heads of the various units in the Commission, some of whom were not on good terms with the Special Advisor. Some of the inputs from SAT were based on the need to make a number of organizational changes that would affect the way the senior management team operated, its communications processes and other factors normally found in improvement of a senior management team.

SAT members were becoming increasingly frustrated in their work with IARCSC, largely because the Chairman did not seem to be responding to their organizational change suggestions by implementing them in a meaningful and timely manner. It became evident that things were getting worse when it was reported that the SAT member who had been working closely with the Special Advisor, and who was essentially her "right hand man" and sat in on almost everything she did, was being asked to wait outside her office while she had meetings in which he would previously have participated. At one point he was waiting outside her office over half an hour later than the time they had set for a meeting. This new more distant relationship was a sign of a deepening problem.

The advice SAT was providing was encouraging the Special Advisor to push the Chairman and heads of IARCSC units to implement measures to improve their operations. When it became clear that a number of these measures would not soon be translated into action, and the main blockages were the Chairman and several unit heads, SAT members began seriously considering shifting to MRRD (as noted earlier), a more receptive and fertile place to work.

The external pressure from SAT was making matters more difficult for the Advisor, who seemed to react by wanting to put some space between herself and the SAT team. Part of this distance was accompanied by comments to the effect that SAT had begun to be caught in internal IARCSC politics.

When things are going badly within a system, it often is easier to blame the outsiders for the problem rather than confront the internal actors and fix the dysfunctional dynamics at the source of the difficulty – to make the advisors be the scapegoats for challenges the host country system is not willing or able to address.

So not only did the SAT members' enthusiastic pressure have a negative effect on relations with the prime client contact (the Special Advisor), as part of the "closing of the door" with the Commission there were statements to the effect that the SAT team had become inappropriately involved in internal issues and conflicts. Once the Special Advisor began closing the door on SAT, the team had no option other than look for somewhere else to provide assistance to the government.

In the work of most seasoned development practitioners there are many examples of this closing of the door. Once it begins, it is next to impossible to reverse the process unless there are changes in who are the "point" people on both sides, and they are able to work in new ways to build the relationships afresh. The second SAT group assigned one member to work with the Advisor in an executive assistant capacity, a lower level of input than the previous team was attempting to make – this kept the door somewhat open but did not include the organizational change work the Commission required. It was a compromise that both parties could live with.

Where Does The Energy Come From For Social Progress?

One of the differences between military and development approaches is the source of energy they use to achieve a desired effect. While the military tends to think in terms of the power they bring from outside to achieve a result, development workers rely primarily on the energy that is already present in an environment to help a system move.

The origin of the NSP provides a good example. As noted earlier in the section on gender and development, in the mid-1990s UN (Habitat) staff in Mazar-e-Sherif began working with women living in the areas around several mosques, and after some experimentation several "Community Fora" were established. These women-led neighbourhood-based co-operatives started with relatively small grants as seed money to begin providing a range of services to the communities – some of their activities generated income that was used to help the organizations grow and operate on their own. By 1998 ten of these Fora were established in Mazar, Kabul and Bamyan and provided a model of grassroots governance that the Karzai government adopted and modified and subsequently spread as the NSP to over 20,000 villages across the country.

An indication of the extent of community support for the original Fora was that when the Taliban took Mazar in 1998 there was extensive looting and destruction of facilities linked to development agencies. The centres from which the Fora operated were protected by their neighbourhoods and remained undamaged throughout the turmoil.

In sustainable development it is clear that external resources are a temporary input to help a system reach the state that it can carry on with the initiative on its own after assistance ends. Care is required to avoid making inputs that create conditions that cannot be sustained when foreigners leave – the result can be disillusionment and disappointment which could fuel increased resentment and alienation toward external parties such as the government and the international community.

Quick Impact Projects (QIPs) And Sustainable Development

Another area where military and development practitioners differ is in the perception of how much time is required for a development initiative to achieve a desired sustainable effect. In a conflict zone where it is important to secure the support of local communities it is understandable that there will be a desire to find quick ways of achieving this result. Short-term projects with immediate impact are sought out, such as paving a road, repairing an irrigation canal or building a school. While these are often worthy efforts it is important to note that they may not make a significant long-term change in the area's trajectory – they may not increase the host environment's ability to fuel and manage its own growth.

The military operates on considerably shorter schedules than do most development agencies: they tend to think in terms of days, weeks and possibly months rather than in years. A community's norms and attitudes rarely change that quickly. While there may be a need for quick impact initiatives in an AO, wherever possible these should be designed as an integrated series of inputs that exert an on-going and sustainable influence on the living conditions and patterns of relationships in the community.

This is particularly important where the objective is to strengthen government operations at any level – most bureaucracies change relatively slowly. Fostering corporate culture change, strengthening management skills and providing staff development, for example, are long-term efforts in any country, and even more so when the organization is operating in

CHAPTER 5

an insecure environment and there is a long-standing history of corruption and cronyism, which is in turn linked to a people's perception of its government. It is unreasonable to expect most quick impact measures to have much of an effect on these fundamental contributors to the quality of a population's relationship with its government. Interventions of this type need to be carefully executed and expectations must be thoughtfully managed to avoid reinforcing disillusionment in a skeptical community. A group that has experienced a loss of hope is more difficult to work with than one in which hopes have not yet been raised and then dashed.

Conclusion

Unlike most military campaigns, development is a low-power intervention business – technical advisors are just that: advisors. There is no obvious equivalent of the military chain of command in the development field, and the local officials with whom we work are in essence the masters we serve. It is a challenging and contradiction-filled area of practice, partially because much of the servant's job is to help the master learn how to lead – to acquire the skills and exercise the authority required to properly manage the instruments of state – and also to direct the technical advisors who are there to help this happen.

In a recovering fragile state with an active counter-insurgency campaign a whole-system perspective is required to focus donors' temporary inputs on formal and informal leaders in sub-systems that have potential to align and accelerate the whole environment's movement along a desirable trajectory. The next two chapters summarize the cast of characters that need to be taken into account in these contexts, and provides some information on how host country systems work. These are part of the foundation on which capacity development specialists build to help societies move forward.

CHAPTER 6

The Cast of Characters – Who's Who?

Introduction

This chapter is an introduction to the wide variety of actors who may exert influence – positive or negative – in an AO. It's an attempt to deal with a need that several military officers expressed as wanting to know "who's who in the zoo."

In development work it is essential to take into account all major actors and to do whatever possible to encourage them to support the constructive movement of the society along its developmental path. In spite of the Paris Declaration on aid coordination described earlier, achieving this coherence is a major challenge in postwar reconstruction. As Paris and Sisk state:

> Organizational coherence involves the need for coordination among the myriad international actors involved in these (state building) operations, including national donors, regional organizations, international financial institutions, specialized international agencies, global bodies such as the UN and nongovernmental organizations. However, coordination is very difficult to achieve, due in part to the confusing or competing lines of authority and budgetary autonomy among these actors, including within the UN system itself. ...

> Beyond the coordination of international actors, there is also a need for organizational coherence among the legitimate representatives of the host society itself, so that international actors can engage effectively with national leaders. The danger, however, is that efforts to identify national-level interlocutors can result in an overemphasis on elites based in the capital, at the expense of regional and local institution-building.[62]

The various international and local actors who may exert influence in an environment can be placed in three broad categories:

1. Groups or forces that are already expending energy in a direction that is compatible with the society's reconstruction process, such as well-intentioned host country government and private sector organizations, families and social groups that want little more than a society that works, and most agencies of the international development community.

2. Entities that seem to be relatively neutral, in that their energies neither help nor hinder progress, such as community leaders in a conflict zone who are ambivalent about supporting either side – insurgents or the government.

3. Groups or forces that are expending energy in unconstructive ways and hindering the progress of the society along a beneficial trajectory, such as inept or corrupt officials, insurgents, members of the drug trade (local and international) and backroom man-oeuvring among powerful geopolitical and economic actors who are more interested furthering their own interests than in fostering the betterment of the people.

All three are active in fragile recovering states such as Afghanistan and need to be considered in a whole-system approach to the development and design of any intervention process:

- The first group's energies need to be reinforced and increased wherever possible.

- The second group – those who may be seen as neither helping nor hindering – should be clearly identified and carefully analyzed, since they have the potential to exert either positive or negative influences on the system. The negative potential needs to be ready to be countered in some way to maintain the system's progress, and measures are required to reinforce and productively engage any constructive energies that may emerge.

- The third group includes clearly destructive elements such as insurgents, warlords and corrupt leaders, as well as other negative influences such as parochialism, gender inequality, and illiteracy. These negative forces need to be regarded as impediments with influence that needs to be countered or neutralized, but which could also change to become supporters of constructive growth.

The second group is a key factor to engage in fostering healthy social progress and dealing with insurgents. In some parts of Iraq, for example, tribal leaders who were previously not actively supporting either side of the conflict began supporting government forces and contributed to driving foreign militants out of their areas of influence. The same has been seen in some areas of Afghanistan.

Some in the third group have been called "military entrepreneurs" – people for whom fighting is a business, and who can be influenced by seeing their interests being served by either being part of the conflict or by ceasing hostilities. Ideology plays less of a role in their behaviour than their desire for benefits and influence in their areas of operation. Financial or political measures are sometimes effective in reducing the disruptive influence of these actors. This is consistent with the well-known fact that wars against insurgencies are "won" primarily by political and economic incentives rather than kinetic means. Care must be taken, however, since some of these entrepreneurially-minded groups have been known to switch sides several times in a conflict, and some have taken money from both sides while pursuing their own agendas.

The military may consider some in the third group to be "the enemy" and be ready to plan campaigns to neutralize their influence. While there may well be members of a system whose influence needs to be forcefully countered, in the development world the concept of "enemy" is rarely used. As will be discussed in Chapter 8 on the need for a change in mindset, in development and also in business, the approach to dealing with groups who are seen as opponents to change is quite different than in the military.

This chapter provides basic descriptions of a number of the actors who have roles in post-conflict reconstruction, based largely on the situation in Afghanistan in late 2007. It begins with a description of the formal and informal dimensions of a society's structure and patterns of influence. Each AO will have its own cast of non-military characters who must be understood if the campaign is to succeed.

CHAPTER 6

Host-Country Systems – Formal And Informal

One way of regarding the recently-introduced government of a country like Afghanistan is as a relatively thin layer of new organizational patterns that has been spread over a much deeper layer of long-standing networks of relationships that really determine how the society operates. These two can be called the formal and informal levels of the host country's systems.

The persistence and importance of informal networks during and after a conflict was noted in an earlier comment by Barakat and Chard, and is repeated here for convenience:

> It is, however, never the case that no social institutions or capacities survive, although often it is the 'rule-based' institutions of non-formal collaboration in civil society that are strengthened by the struggle to survive a war, while formal organisational structures may indeed have broken down. The donor haste to see recognisable organisations in place often ignores these institutional capacities instead of building on them but ... the lessons learned about best practice for development are applicable and indeed even more necessary in recovery from war.[63]

Many organizations (including the military) have the same patterns: there is the formal organizational chart showing a tidy hierarchy of leaders, managers and subordinates, and then there is how the organization really operates and who has credibility, respect and influence in the system – these may not be the same people and groups as in the organizational chart. The second network is the informal web of relationships that is largely invisible to outsiders but which insiders know intimately: without support from the informal system the organization cannot function. Any effective capacity-development intervention needs to understand and incorporate both networks of influence in its strategy.

In places like Afghanistan the international community spends most of its time and energy engaging with the relatively thin formal layer, while what actually happens in the society is determined largely by the deeper informal network of relationships. Because of the short time that most military actors spend in the country, many fail to recognize the importance of the informal network, let alone discover how it operates.

People who occupy positions in both systems, such as host-country leaders and officials, are sometimes influenced more by the informal layer than the official formal level of their worlds. This is particularly true in societies which are ranked high on Geert Hofstede's collectivist dimension, where maintaining membership in one's group is more important than asserting one's individuality and acting independently.[64] An example of this is the reluctance of a finance official to disclose a supervisor's impropriety when the consequence of blowing the whistle would have been a strongly negative impact on the status and prestige of older members of his family and would have resulted in serious conflict and permanent damage to his relationship with his primary affinity and support group.

One of the truisms of psychology is that all behaviour is intentional and seems rational to the actor at the time. If the actions of a host-country official seem to make little sense to an observer who is a member of the international community and is expecting behaviour that is consistent with the patterns of the formal structure, it is likely that the largely invisible deeper dimension of the informal structure, which is that official's real psychological, social and economic home, is exerting its influence. In many cases these complex deeper patterns are not clearly evident even to the individuals themselves – they are largely transparent and difficult to explain to outsiders.

These informal networks are often deeply rooted in the individuals' histories. They may have been developed in childhood or while in school or even earlier, through kinship, social and business relationships extending back several generations. Discovering how they operate is a major challenge in development work – once some understanding is achieved, the deeper dimensions of the society's patterns of behaviour and belief become more evident and it is possible to apply appropriate influence with greater beneficial effect.

It can take some time to acquire this understanding: in community work in Aboriginal villages in northern Canada it takes a skilled practitioner at least six months of building relationships with members of several subgroups to begin to get a sense of how the informal dimension of the society operates. In a war-torn country where trust has been destroyed and where large-scale international development and military activity has had a major distorting effect on the society, achieving this understanding could take significantly longer.

CHAPTER 6

It is possible to link this discussion of formal and informal structures to the three groups mentioned earlier in this chapter – those who are in favour of the government's agenda, the ambivalent and those against. A host-country official's participation in government might seem to place him in the first group, while his informal allegiances might be rooted in one of the other groups. This is likely to result in marked differences between what he says and what he does, much to the consternation of external agents whose mission is to help the country move in a desirable direction.

Help is needed to gain sufficient clarity to make some headway in these situations: it is essential to work with "cultural brokers" – people who know something about the deeper dimensions of the society and how it operates, and who can effectively communicate this to outsiders. Their role is described in the following chapter.

Traditional, Local And Community-Based Organizations And Their Roles

Each local area or community has its own array of formal and informal organizations that need to be taken into account in a development effort. It can take some time to discover who these local groups are and how they work. The following information on community-level organizations was provided by Dr. Tooryalai Wesa, an Afghan-Canadian based in British Columbia who has worked for years in development in Kandahar, Helmand and other parts of Afghanistan. He begins by referring to the three categories of actors noted above.

> I believe the military needs people from all the mentioned categories for different occasions/deals/events. Religious and tribal leaders are the key players on both government as well as international sides. I think we should look for the following:
>
> 1. Rural (village political structure). There are some positions in the villages called *Malik* or *Arbab* in different part of the country. These are the positions selected by the rurals. People in these positions are dealing with the internal issues in the villages as well as with the district government.

2. Educational Institutions, rural schools, one-teacher schools. Mosques (imams) only take care of religious literacy. Usually an older lady (often a widow) teaches the holy book (Koran) to young girls and young boys. Certain hours in the morning and afternoon, children go to her house and read the holy book.

3. Irrigation. Each village has an assigned person, called *Mirawe*. He takes care of the irrigation system in the village. He is elected by the villagers. Since irrigation water is a problem, this person manages the time of the water. People get certain number of hours of irrigation water. The number of hours depends on the size of the farm. The more the size of the land is, the more hours he gets.

4. Agricultural. Co-ops, certain provinces in the country have scores of co-ops. The co-ops sell the products through the co-ops. Each co-op has a team (Administrator, treasurer, secretary and members). Kandahar, Helmand, and Parwan provinces were pretty famous for their co-ops in the good old days. Those co-ops were mostly grapes co-ops.

5. While I was working for UN in early 2006 in the provinces of Herat and Balkh, I introduced the idea of associations. I organized similar crop/livestock growers in one association. i.e. wheat growers, cotton growers, dairy, beef growers, etc. associations. The idea behind was to make it easy for the support of international NGOs. It means that when an NGO wants to support wheat, cotton or whatever growers, it knows who they are.

6. Village/community level NGOs. Numerous villages have (local) NGOs doing educational, construction, irrigation, etc. activities.

7. NSP, local *shuras*, are the very latest initiative.* Some of them are really helpful.

---

* The NSP is a successful Afghan government initiative providing a forum for community consultation on development priorities and activities. Local *shuras* (community consultation and decision-making gatherings) have been encouraged by the government.

CHAPTER 6

Any new idea, program, or action introduced to the villages must have certain characteristics to be adopted by the locals, otherwise, locals will resist it. Furthermore, the communication or dissemination of each program requires certain methods, media, etc.[65]

This list shows that rural communities have a multiplicity of local organizations and decision-making processes that deal with a variety of issues. Some address contentious matters such as determining access to a scarce resource such as water in an irrigation system – the person making these rulings is often selected by the community because of a high minded character and a history of fairness and justice in decision-making.

International actors wanting to work with communities need to recognize that a variety of decision-making systems already exist, and that if new forms are to be introduced they must be consistent with prevailing patterns of thought and communication if they are to be effective. In Afghanistan the NSP and local *shuras* built on existing processes and were successful as a result.

When a society is in the midst of conflict these indigenous systems can come under stress from a variety of sources. In some areas significant number of IDPs – who arrive seeking shelter and who are not part of local long-term social networks – can overwhelm the ability of traditional processes to manage community affairs.

In other areas the insurgents systematically assassinate community leaders who are not sympathetic to their cause and brutal means are used to secure the community's support for their efforts. The loss of respected leaders has a significant impact on the population's organizational ability. Without this leadership it is difficult for outsiders to gain a sense of how the community works, largely because its internal decision-making processes have been disrupted. A period of security and stability is required before the community selects new respected leaders to manage its affairs.

International Development, Financial And Humanitarian Agencies

This section is a brief summary of the major international organizations working in a country such as Afghanistan. A similar array of agencies is present in most countries where the military is carrying out UN-mandated peace and security missions.

Special Representative of the Secretary-General

When the United Nations Security Council authorizes peace and security missions the UN usually assigns a Special Representative of the Secretary-General (SRSG) whose office is a link between the UN and the host country's government and acts in a coordination role for international agencies working in the area. In Afghanistan this role is taken up by the head of UNAMA who leads an operation with about 1000 employees, the vast majority of whom are Afghans. The ability of the SRSG to exert meaningful influence on the many international actors working in a country varies widely – in some the office exerts a strong influence while in others the post is less effective in carrying out these duties.

The International Committee of the Red Cross

The International Committee of the Red Cross (ICRC) is not considered in the same category as most international development or humanitarian NGOs (described below) – it is a unique organization supported by a body of international law.

The ICRC describes itself as an independent, neutral organization ensuring humanitarian protection and assistance for victims of war and armed violence. It has a permanent mandate under international law to take impartial action for prisoners, the wounded and sick, and civilians affected by conflict. With its HQ in Geneva, the ICRC is based in around 80 countries and has a total of more than 12,000 staff. In situations of conflict, the ICRC coordinates the response by national Red Cross and Red Crescent societies and their International Federation. The ICRC is at the origin of both the International Red Cross/Red Crescent Movement and of international humanitarian law, notably the Geneva Conventions.

ICRC personnel are committed to principles of neutrality and impartiality and fiercely guard their independence so they can protect all victims of armed conflict, without interference by any of the parties to the conflict – this can be difficult to understand for military units that want to provide assistance. An example is an ICRC-operated health facility in Kandahar

CHAPTER 6

that prevented military personnel from coming onto the hospital grounds, a situation described by a former Afghanistan-based ICRC official as follows:

> Medical facilities should have a status under international law that makes them neutral establishments. By having a proliferation of weapon bearers in the hospital it brought this neutral status into question; it made more likely an attack at the hospital by parties to the conflict, it made victims reluctant to go to the hospital for fear of being caught up in fighting, and it increased the risk to both those doing humanitarian work at the hospital and those seeking relief. It was not a case of the parties to the conflict thinking that the ICRC (and others engaged in medical support) would be assumed to be sympathetic to one party or the other. This is simply not a place for weapons bearers to be conspicuous.[66]

The complex matter of relations between the military and humanitarian relief and development agencies is discussed later in this chapter.

International multilateral development agencies

Among the major multilateral international development agencies working in countries like Afghanistan are the UNDP and a host of other UN agencies including the World Health Organization (WHO), the World Food Program (WFP), the UN's main refugee organization, United Nations High Commission for Refugees (UNHCR), the Food and Agriculture Organization (FAO) of the United Nations, the United Nations Human Settlements Program (UN-Habitat), and others.

Although they are funded by contributions from member states of the UN, each of these organizations has its own headquarters and operating guidelines, and thousands of employees worldwide. However, they are all part of the UN system, coordinating their efforts is an ongoing challenge.

One of UNDP's largest and longest-running programs is in Afghanistan:

> UNDP has been present in Afghanistan for over 50 years and continued to operate from Islamabad during the Taliban régime. During that decade, UNDP delivered USD 200 million of

assistance to communities throughout the country. UNDP re-established its offices in Kabul in early 2002. UNDP supports the people of Afghanistan as they face new challenges and move their country from recovery to development towards the achievement of the Millennium Development Goals by 2020.

Since the Bonn Agreement was signed in December 2001, UNDP has delivered USD 1.1 billion of assistance to Afghanistan. In 2005, UNDP delivered USD 349 million of development assistance, mainly for elections, disarmament, reconstruction and institution building. In 2006, UNDP delivered USD 202 million focusing mainly on state building, security sector reform (police) and rural development.

UNDP operates within the framework of the Integrated United Nations Mission in Afghanistan (UNAMA) and within the United Nations Development Assistance Framework (UNDAF). In December 2005, UNDP signed a new country program with the Government that covers the areas of state-building, democracy and sustainable livelihoods, in line with the Interim Afghanistan National Development Strategy (I-ANDS). UNDP operates in all 34 provinces of Afghanistan.[67]

The money dispensed by UNDP is provided by member states of the UN as part of their multilateral ODA funds.

The European Union (EU) also supports international development activities through its executive agency, the European Commission (EC), which has a unit that provides funding for a variety of development projects worldwide. A significant portion of all humanitarian aid is provided by the EU.

International financial institutions

International financial institutions (IFIs) active in Afghanistan in 2008 include the WB, the Islamic Development Bank and the Asian Development Bank (ADB). These organizations provide funds to the host government, advise on fiscal policy reform, strengthen the host country's financial institutions, and fund and manage a variety of development projects. They are likely to be active in most similar recovering fragile states.

Most of the projects funded by the IFIs are carried out by large consult-ing firms such as Bearing Point, Chemonics International, Adam Smith International, and a host of others who are contracted to help increase the capacity of host governments to serve their people. In Afghanistan, for ex-ample, these firms have been engaged to provide expertise to help Afghan officials design and carry out the country's public sector reform efforts.

Although these are respected major players in the international develop-ment scene, there are also persistent questions about how these powerful organizations operate. An example is a recent critique of one of the IFIs titled "Five Points to keep ADB relevant":

> Standing as one of the largest multilateral development banks operating today, the Asian Development Bank has carved out a niche for itself in the arena of international development, serving the world's poorest nations and helping them achieve sustainable economic progress and genuine growth. Or at least, that's what the bank should be doing. Today, the ADB and other large finan-cial institutions such as the World Bank and the International Monetary Fund are in danger of losing their relevance, especially as the international community goes through a whole string of inexorable changes. The old method of giving aid to developing countries is no longer as effective as it may have been a decade ago.[68]

Other critiques are more scathing in that they assert that the structural adjustment and privatization processes called for by the IFIs reflect an ideology that is actually causing many of the social, cultural and economic disruptions that produce the unrest that requires international interven-tion to maintain peace and stability. This is a serious issue, as noted by the World Council of Churches:

> The rules and norms of the neo-liberal ideology perfectly serve the needs and interest of corporate business and finance and de-mand the transfer of power from the state to the private sector in general and transnational corporations and financial institutions in particular. Taken as the iron law of economics, they assume religious status, justifying massive exclusion and sacrifice of hu-man lives and nature in the name of economic growth through

privatization and the liberalised and de-regulated market... Buying into the growth syndrome, the specific cultural and economic context and the limits set by nature were simply neglected with the consequence of social fragmentation and environmental destruction. Focusing on export led growth, top-down approaches and an unsubstantiated belief in the so called "trickle down effect", the role of just and sustainable communities as the basis and necessary context for life in dignity of the majority of the people was misjudged.[69]

This assertion that the IFIs' policies are causing social unrest and contributing to the collapse of the state is a large topic that is well beyond the scope of this monograph. It is, however, a significant issue with major security implications. An example is the Colombian rebel group *Fuerzas Armadas Revolucionarias de Colombia* (FARC) which was reported as having its origins, at least in part, in a desperate attempt by dispossessed landless peasants to reverse the effects of an IFI-supported policy to encourage market reforms which promoted a shift from small subsistence-level family farms to large-scale cash cropping of sugar cane. A good source of further information in this area is IFIwatchnet, an online compendium of films and other resources that focus a critical eye on the IFIs.*

International non-government organizations (INGOS)

This section briefly describes a few of the many international non-government organizations that are active in humanitarian relief and development in Afghanistan and in most countries where the military is involved in peace and stability operations. Most of these organizations operate on funds raised from the public as well as from government sources.

CARE International

CARE International is one of the larger humanitarian and development INGOs, coordinating the activities of its 12 national affiliates operating a range of development projects in some 70 countries. CARE affiliates have worked in Afghanistan and the region since 1989, and continued operations throughout the Taliban era, providing a broad range of humanitarian and

---

* See: *IFIwatchnet Home Page.* <www.ifiwatchnet.org/?q=es/films>, (30 January 2008).

development services. The UK affiliate is helping educate over 60,000 Afghan children, about 66 per cent girls, and operates some 283 schools in remote regions of the country. Almost 99 per cent of CARE staff in Afghanistan are Afghans, providing good connections with the community and increasing skills levels of staff who will remain a permanent resource for the country's development.[70]

Oxfam

Oxfam international is a confederation of 13 independent non-government organizations working with about 3000 partners in some 100 countries to eliminate poverty and justice. They strive to increase worldwide public understanding that economic and social justice is crucial to sustainable development, and to shift public opinion to give equity the same priority as economic growth. They also work with people affected by humanitarian disasters, with preventive measures, and provide emergency relief. Their work includes helping the poor organize to gain better access to opportunities, supporting research and lobbying to change international policies and practices to ensure the poor have rights, opportunities and resources to improve and control their lives, and carrying out campaigns to raise public awareness of solutions to global poverty and foster a sense of global citizenship.[71]

The International Development Law Organization (IDLO)

IDLO carries out projects to strengthen legal and judicial systems in developing countries. These can include helping improve legislation, training judges and other court personnel, and other measures to increase the capacity of the government's justice department.

In the years following the ouster of the Taliban government, IDLO specialists provided training and organizational development services to strengthen the courts and other Ministry of Justice operations in Afghanistan. These services were provided by legal systems specialists from a variety of IDLO member countries.[72]

Médecins Sans Frontières

MSF is an international humanitarian aid organization that works to provide emergency medical assistance to populations in danger in more than 70 countries.

The organization's activities extend into areas beyond emergency relief and into longer-term development support. In countries where health structures are insufficient or even non-existent, MSF collaborates with authorities such as the Ministry of Health to provide assistance. It works in rehabilitation of hospitals and dispensaries, vaccination programs and water and sanitation projects. MSF also works in remote health care centres and slum areas, and provides training of local personnel. All this is done with the objective of rebuilding health structures to acceptable levels – activities that go well beyond emergency aid.

MSF also engages in advocacy work: it seeks to raise awareness of crisis situations and acts as a witness and will speak out, either in private or in public about the plight of populations in danger with whom they work. In doing so, the organization strives to alleviate human suffering, protect life and health, and restore and ensure respect for human beings and their fundamental human rights.

MSF has been one of the more vocal agencies complaining about the linkage between military objectives and humanitarian services to a population.[73]

Aga Khan Development Network (AKDN)

The Aga Khan is the spiritual leader of the Ismaili Muslim community, a sub-group of Shia Islam whose members live in some 25 countries, mainly in West and Central Asia, Africa and the Middle East as well as in North America and Western Europe. They see their faith as having a distinctly practical, applied dimension that manifests itself in a variety of ways, including involvement in international development.

The Aga Khan Development Network (AKDN) is a group of ten organizations focusing on social development, health, microfinance, economic development, planning and building services, humanitarian assistance, education, a trust for culture and the operation of two universities based in Pakistan and Kenya, and operating in at least 8 countries.

> The Aga Khan has emphasised the view of Islam as a thinking, spiritual faith, one that teaches compassion and tolerance and that upholds the dignity of man, Allah's noblest creation....In consonance with this vision of Islam and their tradition of service

CHAPTER 6

to humanity, wherever Ismailis live, they have elaborated a well-defined institutional framework to carry out social, economic and cultural activities. Under the Aga Khan's leadership, this framework has expanded and evolved into the Aga Khan Development Network, a group of institutions working to improve living conditions and opportunities in specific regions of the developing world. In every country, these institutions work for the common good of all citizens regardless of their origin or religion. Their individual mandates range from architecture, education and health to the promotion of private sector enterprise, the enhancement of non-government organisations and rural development.[74]

The organization has an enviable reputation in the development field, and receives considerable support from government agencies that have confidence in AKDN's ability to design and implement effective development projects that are consistent with national development priorities. An example is a partnership with CIDA (announced in October 2007) to strengthen girls' education in central and northern Afghanistan, a project with a total budget of some $9.3 million, with $8 million being provided by CIDA.[75]

This is a partial list of some of the larger international agencies – each of these and many other international humanitarian and development organizations has its own ideology, funding sources and mode of practice. While some may appear to be relatively similar, such as Oxfam and CARE, for example, there also are widely differing modes of operation in this group, all of whom may be active in the same region that is the focus of a UN-mandated peace and security operation.

National development agencies

Most industrialized countries have their own international development units as part of their foreign affairs operations. Relatively new players in this field include India, Malaysia and South Korea, as well as a number of former members of the Soviet Bloc. Many of the major contributors to international development assistance are members of the OECD.

An indication of their level of involvement with development is their annual expenditures in this area, which are available from OECD's Development

Co-operation Directorate. The Statistical Annex of the 2007 Development Co-operation Report provides an interesting overview of these countries' allocations to the various avenues through which development assistance is distributed. It also shows how well countries are performing in relation to the UN's target of having industrialized countries spend 0.7 per cent of Gross National Income (GNI) on development assistance. The Annex also shows which countries received assistance from OECD member states.

One of the many tables and two graphs in the report's Annex are included here as an indication of the information available on the size and scope of international development activity.

	2006		2005		Per cent change
	ODA	**ODA/ GNI**	**ODA**	**ODA/ GNI**	**2005 to 2006**
	USD million	**%**	**USD million**	**%**	**in real terms**
	current		**current**		
Australia	2 123	0.30	1 680	0.25	22.5
Austria	1 498	0.47	1 573	0.52	-6.9
Belgium	1 978	0.50	1 963	0.53	-2.2
Canada	3 684	0.29	3 756	0.34	-9.9
Denmark	2 236	0.80	2 109	0.81	3.0
Finland	834	0.40	902	0.46	-9.0
France	10 601	0.47	10 026	0.47	2.9
Germany	10 435	0.36	10 082	0.36	1.7
Greece	424	0.17	384	0.17	5.9
Ireland	1 022	0.54	719	0.42	36.9
Italy	3 641	0.20	5 091	0.29	-30.6
Japan	11 187	0.25	13 147	0.28	-9.1
Luxembourg	291	0.89	256	0.86	4.8
Netherlands	5 452	0.81	5 115	0.82	4.2
New Zealand	259	0.27	274	0.27	0.5
Norway	2 954	0.89	2 786	0.94	-1.9
Portugal	396	0.21	377	0.21	2.0
Spain	3 814	0.32	3 018	0.27	20.7
Sweden	3 955	1.02	3 362	0.94	14.7

cont...

Switzerland	1 646	0.39	1 772	0.44	-7.4
United Kingdom	12 459	0.51	10 772	0.47	11.7
United States	23 532	0.18	27 935	0.23	-18.2
TOTAL DAC	**104 421**	**0.31**	**107 099**	**0.33**	**-4.5**
Average Country Effort		0.46		0.47	
Memo Items:					
EC	10 245		9 390		6.2
DAC-EU countries	59 035	0.43	55 750	0.44	2.9
G7 countries	75 539	0.27	80 809	0.30	-8.0
Non-G7 countries	28 882	0.51	26 290	0.50	6.3

TABLE 4 – DEVELOPMENT ADVISORY COMMITTEE MEMBERS' NET ODA IN 2006[76]

The following figures illustrate the amount of ODA of OECD member countries in 2006, and the percentage of their GNI they spent on this aid.

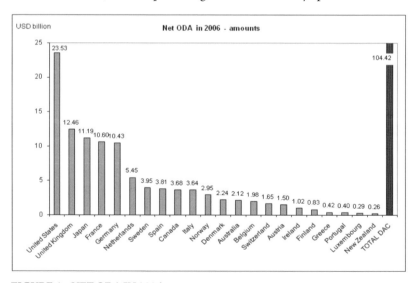

FIGURE 4 – NET ODA IN 2006.

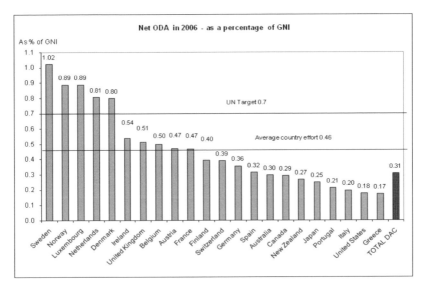

FIGURE 5 – NET ODA IN 2006 – % OF GNI.

These OECD figures illustrate the amount of resources dedicated to ODA and the relative commitment of member countries to international development assistance. This includes funds distributed through multilateral organizations (the UN, WB, EC, etc.) as well as by these countries' own development agencies. Only five countries have exceeded the UN's target of spending 0.7% of GNI on ODA. This does not indicate the degree of impact of countries' development efforts: the sheer size of the US contribution ($23.53B) is significant, even if is only 0.18% of GNI, the second-lowest among OECD countries. The cost of development-related efforts by the military through avenues such as CIMIC, some of the PRTs' activities and the SAT are not included in these figures.

A brief summary of four national development agencies' activities in Afghanistan follows.

USAID

USAID is the largest development agency in Afghanistan, with a budget of almost $2.6B for fiscal year 2007-2008[77] and a staff of some 600 people working in their offices in Kabul and elsewhere in the country. The size of this operation is intentional, as stated in their plan for 2005-2010:

CHAPTER 6

> Afghanistan will continue to be a fragile state with high though
> diminishing security risks and extreme poverty throughout the
> country during the next five years. The culture of corruption re-
> mains and without attention will continue to be an obstacle to
> positive change. Because of this precarious situation, USAID/Af-
> ghanistan will continue to require a funding mechanism that al-
> lows it maximum flexibility and the ability to move funds quickly.
> It will also need a high level of funding that reflects US national
> interest in retaining its current position as the lead donor, giving
> it critical influence on the way Afghanistan recovers from its past
> and moves forward. To ensure the success of recovery, this high
> level of funding... is required over the five year strategy period.[78]

During this period of recovery, "symbolic" projects, such as schools, clinics, roads, and other physical infrastructure, designed to show the Afghan
people quick and beneficial short term impacts, will continue. The visible
impact gains interest and support for longer-term capacity building efforts,
which are the key to recovery and the follow-on transformation development strategy.

While some may question the US approach to development in Afghanistan
and elsewhere, the first 15-page section of their concise (26-page) *Afghanistan Strategic Plan* spells out in clear terms what they see as being required
to build a stable democratic capitalist state. If the plan succeeds, there will
be significant improvements in the lives of the Afghan people.

Their three main strategic objectives are:

1. a thriving economy led by the private sector;

2. a democratic government with broad citizen participation;
   and

3. a better educated and healthier population.

The Plan also clearly defines how the US intends to make all this
happen – it is unabashedly directive in its language and approach, and this
philosophy is reflected in how many USAID-funded projects operate.

USAID staff working as DEVADs in PRTs had considerable freedom to design and fund community-level projects that supported American strategic
and tactical-level interests. In Jalalabad, for example, they collaborated with
representatives of other US agencies (Department of State, of Agriculture,
US Army Civil Affairs) to develop a strategy to allocate funds in a way that
maximized security in the region.

The agency also contracts large consulting firms such as Bearing Point,
Chemonics International, ARD Inc. and others to implement many of its
projects. While CF personnel in HQ and the PRTs may work directly with
USAID officials, in the communities and in government ministries their
primary contact is likely to be with employees of these consulting firms.

Three of their contractors, Bearing Point, ARD Inc. and Development Al-
ternatives Incorporated (DAI), for example, have been engaged to implement a Local Governance and Community Development (LGCD) project
in rural Afghanistan, and some have hired Afghan-Canadians and Afghan-
Americans as director-level managers in their field offices in Kandahar and
other provinces. These managers could move relatively freely within the
population and implement culturally-appropriate projects at the community level, even in areas where insurgents were active. DAI described the
project, which was "engaging local communities in their development and
stability," as follows:

> The objectives of this task order are to: 1) assist the Government
> of Afghanistan to extend its reach into unstable areas and engage
> at-risk populations by building the capacity of provincial and lo-
> cal government officials to deliver services and address citizen
> needs; 2) create an environment that encourages local com-
> munities to take an active role in their own development; and 3)
> promote stability by addressing the underlying causes of violence
> and support for insurgency.

> LGCD is working with the Provincial Reconstruction Teams
> and provincial authorities in the Eastern and Southern regions to
> build the capacity of individuals to generate income, familiarize
> *shura* councils with transparent oversight of development activ-
> ities, and enhance the skills and experience of local businesses. In
> addition, the DAI team is working with local labour to produce

C H A P T E R   6

tangible infrastructure improvements, such as irrigation systems, roads and bridges, health clinics, schools, market centres, and agricultural processing facilities, and is training people to operate and maintain them.

LGCD helps villagers and tribes resolve conflicts and enhances local capacity to continue to do so in the future. The LGCD team uses development projects as an incentive for conflict resolution between villages and sub-tribes, to reduce the resource limitations that motivate much conflict and to reach people at risk of participating in conflict. The goal is to leave behind an enhanced understanding of the underlying tensions that cause conflict; skills in conflict prevention, mitigation, and resolution in the provincial governments and nongovernmental organizations; and a stability plan framework for each of the provinces.

The DAI team is working to enhance the capacities of provincial governments to plan and implement community-based development activities and to provide essential services. This will in turn increase the governments' legitimacy and contribute to nation building and stability. Capacity-building efforts include hands-on experience with real issues of allocating resources, resolving issues, participating in project implementation, monitoring progress, and dealing with constituents. The DAI team is also helping provincial governments create their own development plans and adopt transparent budgeting processes.[79]

This is one example of many. Another contractor worked with the ACSI to design and deliver training in Financial Management, IT, Training-of-Trainers and Training Needs Analysis. As with the several other donor-provided training programs at ACSI the intention was that their resources and personnel will be absorbed into the permanent public service training program when external funding runs out. The ability of the Afghan government to do its part and establish the budgets and supervisory systems required to absorb these programs is an open question.

While there is no doubt that USAID and other donors with similar attitudes are accomplishing a great deal, there are persistent concerns about the effectiveness of USAID's aggressive approach and the ability of the host country to absorb what is being provided.

While progress is being made, the US is still investing huge amounts of money without adequate consultation with the local population. For example, schools have been built without teachers available to teach in them, or are built in a location that is so far away no students can actually reach them. These structures are then occupied by the Taliban insurgency, and consequently destroyed by the very coalition that built them in the first place.[80]

An example of this is noted in the email from the US soldier quoted at the end of the Preface of this monograph – the empty school house he described was probably built by a contractor who was being paid to construct facilities without adequate consideration having been given to the ability of the host government to provide the many other resources required to make full use of the well-intentioned contribution. This is a common problem in development project design – construction projects are far easier to carry out than the more complex capacity development needed to operate the programs these facilities are intended to house. There are limits on the host environment's absorptive capacity and the sustainability of these efforts is in question.

DFID

DFID is the UK's main international development agency and is a significant contributor to the reconstruction of Afghanistan. Since 2001, it has spent over £490M, making the UK Afghanistan's second largest bilateral donor (after the US). Over the last three years, the size of DFID's program has grown substantially and further increases are planned. In 2007/08, it expects to spend £107M and £115M in 2008/09.[81]

The UK is supporting Afghanistan's security, reconstruction, good governance and counter-narcotics work. Their efforts are coordinated by the Foreign & Commonwealth Office, the Department for International Development and the Ministry of Defense – a 3D operation.

The UK's program differs from the US approach in that a significant portion of its aid funds are routed through the Afghan government and support its priorities, as set out in the Interim National Development Strategy:

1   Building effective state institutions;

2. Improving economic management and the effectiveness of aid to Afghanistan; and

3. Improving the livelihoods of rural people.

[DFID believes] [t]he best way to achieve these goals is by supporting Afghans to help themselves – which is why 80% of [their] aid goes directly to the Government of Afghanistan.[82]

DFID funds also support the WB's public sector reform initiatives, and like USAID and other donors, it contracts with large international consulting firms to carry out development projects. For example, Adam Smith International has several capacity development projects with the public service and is providing strategic planning supports for counter-narcotics programming in the provinces. Military personnel in the field are more likely to encounter TAs hired by these firms than the relatively few DFID staff working in the country.

The UK's PRTs operate somewhat differently from those run by the US: they focus more on development and less on security, and have larger civilian staff in proportion to their military complement.

CIDA

CIDA is the main development partner of Canada's 3D or "Whole of Government" approach, and has significantly increased its assistance to Afghanistan since 2001 – by early 2008 it had become Canada's largest bilateral aid recipient. Canada is one of the world's top donors in Afghanistan, having pledged more than $1.2B in aid for 2001–2011. In 2006–2007, CIDA's bilateral assistance to Afghanistan totaled more than $179M. Of this, $49M was disbursed to the province of Kandahar.

CIDA provides considerable support for multinational development activities managed by international agencies such as UNDP. A significant portion of CIDA's funds ($48M in 2006/07) was allocated to the WB-administered Afghanistan Reconstruction Trust Fund (ARTF) and routed through the Afghan system to support a variety of government operations.

CIDA's projects are in the following major categories:

- sustainable rural livelihoods and community-based development;

- democratic development and effective governance; and

- role of women and girls in society, including education.

Their website describes it this way:

> CIDA funds support projects whose objectives are aligned with the three pillars of the Afghanistan Compact: security, governance and socio-economic development. As the basis of CIDA's approach to rebuilding Afghanistan is to help Afghans help themselves, the majority of funds support Afghan-designed national programs such as the National Solidarity Program, Microfinance Program in Afghanistan and Afghanistan Reconstruction Trust Fund.[83]

Following the introduction of the "Whole of Government" approach, CIDA established an Afghanistan Task Force, a special high-level operating unit that coordinates with counterparts in DFAIT, the PCO, the CF and other departments working in Afghanistan such as Correctional Services Canada (CSC) and the RCMP. As with other countries that are coordinating their civilian and military operations in Afghanistan and elsewhere, Canada is finding establishing well-integrated policies and administrative machinery to support the "Whole of Government" approach to be quite a challenge, particularly in the intense political climate surrounding the mission.

CIDA is under pressure to invest in Kandahar to balance the large expenditures for the military and to show the Canadian public that Canada is committed to development as well as security. This is a difficult due to conditions in the province, limited absorptive capacity and restrictions on movement of CIDA personnel "outside the wire", which prevents development staff from visiting villagers and Afghan officials with whom they are working. Locals come to the Kandahar PRT to discuss projects with CIDA staff – an arrangement which is less than ideal but is seen to be necessary given the security situation in the area.

C H A P T E R   6

Korea International Cooperation Agency (KOICA)

South Korea is a relatively new member of the international donor community, and through their development agency, KOICA, they have supported training and public sector reform projects in Afghanistan since 2002, when it launched a special assistance program for Afghanistan in keeping with the $45M commitment made by the Korean government at the 2002 International Conference on Reconstruction Assistance to Afghanistan.

KOICA offers a unique assistance model based on its own experience in postwar reconstruction, focusing primarily on improving public healthcare and strengthening vocational training:

> Assistance to Afghanistan has included the construction of vocational training institutes and hospitals, the provision of a variety of equipment as well as financial contributions to the trust fund administered by the [WB].

> KOICA has also helped build an efficient administrative government in Afghanistan. In addition to what is currently being done, KOICA plans to invite high-ranking Afghan officials to Korea to attend training courses that will share with them Korea's experience in post-conflict reconstruction and longer-term economic development.[84]

The Koreans are enthusiastically promoting a vision of development that is based on their own remarkable progress since the mid-1950s, and while they have made major contributions, they seem to have a limited understanding of how to adapt their inputs to the context and culture of quite different societies. For example, they supported the construction of two major educational facilities in Kabul – a vocational school and a civil service training institute – both of which had not been adequately absorbed into the mainstream operations of the public service a year or more after they opened their doors.

Afghans who have participated in training and orientation missions in Korea reported that while some of the content was useful, there were other elements that missed the mark entirely, such as the group-based calisthenics designed to foster team spirit and increase motivation to dedicate their

energies to the country's advancement. There are marked differences between a Confucian/Buddhist-based culture and the Islamic patterns at the
root of Afghan society, and the Koreans seem to need some more experience before they learn the culturally-appropriate strategies that are linked
to sustainable development.

These four examples – USAID, DFID, CIDA and KOICA – illustrate similarities and differences among major national development agencies that
are working in the same environment. There are others – the Germans
with GTZ, Denmark's DANIDA, Swedish SIDA, Norway's NORAD, and
more – each with their own way of operating.

Non-government organizations

In 2006, it was estimated that there were over 800 international and indigenous NGOs operating in Afghanistan, offering a broad range of services that the new Karzai government could not provide:

> …a wide range of international humanitarian and development
> NGOs are involved in providing humanitarian relief, rehabilita-
> tion, reconstruction, development and peace building assistance
> to Afghans, often working directly with communities at the grass-
> roots level. Some of these have been providing humanitarian
> relief to Afghans for decades, while others have begun programs
> only since 2001.

> The majority of NGOs are Afghan, but the largest programs are
> implemented by established international relief and development
> NGOs, staffed overwhelming by Afghan nationals, with a hand-
> ful of expatriate staff. Some of the largest NGOs employ over
> 1000 people, making NGOs a significant source of employment
> for Afghans.

> The main sectors of NGO programming span the continuum
> between relief and development, focusing on health, educa-
> tion, food security, school reconstruction and educational pro-
> gramming, livelihoods and economic development, agriculture
> and capacity building and the government's community

C H A P T E R 6

development effort, the [NSP]. Some NGOs are active in governance programs, mine action, peace building efforts, and elements of security sector reform as well. Given the acknowledged lack of implementing capacity in the Afghan government, NGOs are deemed to be indispensable to the implementing of aid efforts by both donors and the Afghan government alike.[85]

Military actors working in an area need to identify, understand and establish appropriate relationships with these influential organizations as they exercise their mandate to improve security and foster progress in the regions in which they are deployed.

Simply identifying all the NGOs can be a major challenge – in 2006 ISAF devoted considerable time and resources to prepare a database of all the NGOs and donor-supported contractors working in Afghanistan, and after months of work still had not identified them all. A similar effort launched in 2004 by UNDP and the Ministry of Finance to develop a Donor Assistance Database appeared to have been abandoned by early 2008.

In mid-2006 it was difficult for the military to get a comprehensive list of donors and NGOs in the field. One of the Kabul-based US officers working on Political-Military Integration (PMI) as part of Operation Enduring Freedom (OEF) described his attempts:

> I don't know what the ISAF folks had and from what I could find when I was there, nobody had even the slightest idea what was going on. But there may have been someone that I didn't stumble across.... I found that USAID, CIDA, and the corresponding agencies for Britain, Germany, South Korea, Japan ...UNAMA, and UNDP, didn't have a list.... I never met anybody that had one and I asked many people. Maybe I asked the wrong people or not enough.

> On the Afghan side, neither the Civil Service Commission nor the Ministry of Interior for Administrative Affairs had that information either. Of course, I was focused on training initiatives, rather than a long list of all NGOs.

Perhaps the Canadian officer in charge of PMI would know since he talked to all of the PMI officers and one of them might have found a master list or an attempt at one.[86]

Many of the major international NGOs (Oxfam, World Vision, CARE, etc.) as well as the more established Afghan NGOs are members of the Agency Coordinating Body For Afghan Relief (ACBAR), an "umbrella" organization that represent 97 organizations from the national and international humanitarian, reconstruction and development NGO community working in Afghanistan. In its efforts to be a responsible coordinating body ACBAR has developed a code of conduct in an attempt to sift out fly-by-night operations, and it collaborates with government efforts to exercise some quality control in this sector. It also advocates for improved development policies and strategies in Afghanistan, and lobbies for better conditions for NGO operations in the country. A directory of member organizations is available online.

Although NGOs are active throughout the country and some have considerable influence in the areas in which they operate, many are not members of ACBAR and it is difficult to identify and establish appropriate relationships with them all. Agencies that have a long-term presence in an area will likely have information about most of the others in their part of the country – it can take some time for military actors to develop a good sense of which NGOs these are and to learn something about how and where they work. Also, some NGOs operate for relatively short periods, only as long as their funding lasts, so there can be significant changes in a region's NGOs from one year to the next.

The NGO community represents a broad range of ideologies and mandates and one should not expect similarity and unity in this group of organizations. The NGO sector is as it should be: diverse, mission-driven and self-governing, and working with them can be frustrating. It is not a straightforward and well-ordered component of the international development system.

Relationships between NGOs and the military

Relationships among NGOs can vary from highly cooperative to nasty interagency conflict. Some NGOs are thinly-disguised fronts for entrepreneurs

CHAPTER 6

who want to take advantage of readily-available donor funds (including from the military) and do not take kindly to sharing this bounty with others.

In situations where several NGOs in the same geographical area are operating in complementary fields (such as agriculture, health and literacy) they tend to get along relatively well. Where they are competing for the same limited pool of funding and human resources and are working in areas where there are relatively few good places to invest their energies, their relationships can be difficult. They may use their linkages with powerful external agents, such as the military, to seek advantage over their competitors.

They can also have different types of relationships with the military. These relations are, to say the least, complex, and can sometimes be contentious. Difficulties are based in part on factors such as differing missions and purposes among NGOs:

> Humanitarian NGOs, those focused on providing short-term lifesaving relief, are used to operating in situations of open conflict and are more concerned that when the bullets start to fly, the humanitarian response be separate from the military and political response so that they can still provide assistance to civilians caught in the crossfire. Development NGOs have had less concern with this issue as their work has traditionally been focused on working with recognized governments on national development priorities. However it bears noting that these once strict distinctions between humanitarian and development NGOs are much blurred these days as many NGOs are involved in both spheres in what is seen as a continuum between relief and development with many overlapping stages and roles.[87]

Challenges in relationships are compounded when the military and the development community do not adequately understand each others' values and ways of operating. Two of the key issues are the notion of the "humanitarian space"– a core concept in assisting populations that are living in conflict zones – and what has been called the militarization of aid.

Humanitarian Space
And The Militarization Of Aid

There are two large and complex issues associated with military-development collaboration in peace and security missions – the notion of a neutral "humanitarian space" and the link between military activity and development. There is considerable controversy around these aspects of counter-insurgency campaigns, which have a major non-kinetic dimension that overlaps with the activities of development agencies.

The concept of "humanitarian space" which was introduced earlier in the section on ICRC is based in part on the belief that all needy civilians caught up in a conflict have a fundamental right to receive assistance, and this is supported by a variety of laws and policies in virtually all countries. Olson analyzed this in her paper:

> By humanitarian space they mean the independence and neutrality from military and political forces that has allowed NGOs and to some extent the United Nations itself, to provide lifesaving aid to needy civilians on all sides of a conflict. The fundamental principles of humanitarian action as spelled out in numerous conventions and codes of conduct are 'the right of citizens of all countries to assistance', the 'independence of aid from political and religious standpoints' and the 'impartiality of aid, to be given on the basis of need alone'. In countless wars and disasters, the acceptance by governments and belligerents that humanitarian groups follow these principles has been the biggest source of security for NGO personnel operating in conflict areas and has meant that humanitarians can gain access to needy people on all sides of a conflict.[88]

The mission of agencies providing humanitarian assistance is to be able to impartially serve all civilians in a conflict zone and they do not want to be seen as supporting either side in the conflict. Their independence is essential: although many humanitarian organizations receive funds from government they should not been seen as sub-contractors implementing donor countries' political agendas. This core principle is jeopardized if they become involved in political or military-related activity.

The military, on the other hand, wants to use aid to serve their objectives, such as force protection (reducing the hostility of a population), to win hearts and minds and increase support for government – in a carrot-and-stick approach with clear tactical and political objectives.

These two mutually-exclusive sets of objectives are the subject of considerable debate. NGO personnel often assert that the militarization and politicizing of aid is eroding the humanitarian space and putting their personnel at risk: this is often heard in a variety of criticisms of the military's role in the conflict.

When humanitarian workers are harmed as they go about their business, their agencies often withdraw from the conflict zone. MSF, for example, withdrew from Afghanistan after five of their workers were killed by insurgents. They linked this tragedy to the militarization of aid:

> Tragically, on June 2, 2004, five MSF staff members were shot and killed on the road between Khairkhana and Qala-i-Naw in northwestern Badghis province. After weighing the options, MSF sadly decided to close all of its medical projects in Afghanistan by the end of August 2004. Most activities were handed over to local groups, international NGOs or the ministry of health.

> Although Afghan officials presented MSF with credible evidence that local commanders conducted the attack against the three international volunteers and two national staff members, these officials had done little to bring the perpetrators to justice. In addition, after the killings, a Taliban spokesperson claimed responsibility for the murders and later stated that organizations like MSF work for US interests and are therefore targets for future attacks.

> MSF believes that humanitarian assistance is only possible when armed actors respect the safety of humanitarian workers, more than 30 of whom have been killed in Afghanistan since the beginning of 2003. The targeted killing of MSF staff, the government's failure to arrest the culprits and the false allegations made by the Taliban made it impossible for MSF to continue providing assistance, despite the great needs.

The violence directed at humanitarian aid workers in Afghanistan comes amid consistent efforts by the US-led coalition to use humanitarian aid to build support for its military and political aims. MSF has repeatedly denounced the coalition's attempts to do so. The organization has also spoken out against the military's attempt to usurp humanitarian aid.

In May 2004, MSF publicly condemned the coalition's decision to distribute leaflets in southern Afghanistan that conditioned the continued delivery of aid on local people's willingness to provide information about the Taliban and Al-Qaeda.[89]

The "neutrality from military and political forces" at the root of humanitarianism is difficult to maintain, especially in environments where provision of services that improve living conditions can be seen as a sign that things are progressing and, by inference, that the government is extending its influence into previously un-serviced areas. Rebuilding an irrigation system, for example, improves the local economy – some may see this as strengthening government, and it could be considered as political since it appears to support one side in a conflict.

The distinctions can be difficult for the military to appreciate. A former officer in the Australian forces who subsequently worked for ICRC put it this way:

I think that the CF members in Kandahar – and I visited them there as well as being a regular at the Mirwais (ICRC-run) hospital – have little comprehension of why the humanitarian community doesn't like to see arms carriers in what used to be "humanitarian space."

This issue is fundamental to the different approaches of humanitarians and the CF, or other forces for that matter. Military people use humanitarian and development activities to support/achieve a military mission. Humanitarian organisations are fundamentally differently motivated! This is the issue where the major difference exists. I have been on both sides of this fence.[90]

It is easy to see why the military and others concerned about peace and stability can have difficulty with this issue, since the humanitarian stance can prevent the use of available resources to increase the ability of government to serve the people. An example is in efforts to strengthen governance and administrative capacity at the sub-national level, which is a major challenge in Afghanistan. The PRTs have skilled personnel who could help with this, and as such they present a potential capacity development resource that could be tapped to strengthen the operations of Governors' offices across the country. When discussing the possibility of facilitating these linkages as part of a UNDP public sector reform project, one of their officials said they did not work with soldiers in uniform[91] – a structural barrier to tapping available resources to solve a major development challenge.

On the other hand, humanitarian organizations want to be seen as neutral and as such avoid affiliating themselves with the military and do not use armed guards and other protective measures so they can move freely and serve civilians throughout the conflict zone. Their security comes from their neutrality. MSF expressed this concern as follows:

> As an independent humanitarian organisation MSF stands by the core principle of humanitarian action: unconditional assistance to those in need without regard to their political or military allegiances.

> It is the responsibility of all parties in the conflict to allow humanitarian action to happen – and to ensure the safety of humanitarian workers and access to needy people that are outside of the conflict. By targeting aid workers, obstructing aid workers' access or trying to manipulate aid to serve one set of military or political objectives – parties to the conflict undermine humanitarian action and show disrespect for human dignity in times of war and a willingness to disregard the Geneva conventions.

> MSF calls on all parties in the conflict to respect the basic dignity and needs of ordinary people caught up in this violent crisis – and thereby to respect and enable the necessary neutrality and impartiality of humanitarian work and the safety and access of those trying to deliver it to people in need in Afghanistan.[92]

As long as all parties respect this neutrality humanitarians can continue to operate. When it breaks down, things become quite challenging. In some cases humanitarian agencies are in a position where their own actions contribute to difficulties, such as when they request military assistance in delivering aid to areas where security is a problem. This puts them in a position of reliance on one side of the conflict and compromises their neutrality.

The respect for humanitarian space requires all belligerents to abide by the values embedded in the Geneva Conventions. If this is not the case and, as a senior CF officer serving in Afghanistan said, "Everybody is a target," demanding that actors observe humanitarian values can be somewhat ir-relevant – in Afghanistan it seemed there was no humanitarian space to respect.

Whether this situation was preventable or not is the subject of much de-bate. The nature of conflicts may be changing and humanitarian agencies might no longer have the neutrality-based protection they once had. Per-haps better strategies can be learned so this collapse of the humanitarian space is not repeated in the next countries in which civilian and military organizations find themselves interacting on peace and security missions. A key ingredient is effective communication among the various parties so they can better define and understand their respective risks, roles and approaches. Since the non-kinetic dimension of these campaigns is signifi-cantly larger than the war fighting function, the military would do well to reach out to these other actors and find ways to engage in authentic and respectful consultation on how each party can operate to best reflect their values as they strive to meet the needs of the people they serve. An inter-mediary that is respected by all parties may be able to help, but usually it is best to do this direct. If, as is sometimes the case, humanitarian agencies do not want to interact with arms-bearers, leaving the armour, weapons and uniforms back at camp might be a helpful way to proceed.

To say this is a contentious and challenging matter is an understatement: it is a large subject about which much has been said and written. This brief overview hopefully provides sufficient information to help military actors begin to navigate through this complex issue in the areas in which they operate.

CHAPTER 6

Impact Of Humanitarian And Development Assistance On Aid Workers

As is the case with many in the military, this work has a significant impact on those who do it, whether they are involved with long-term development or short-term emergency relief in a crisis situation (the third block of the Three Block War). As noted earlier, the boundary between these two types of inputs is not precisely-defined – one form of aid merges with the other, depending largely on how the funding and work are organized for the particular organizations and environments in question. However, it is evident that many of the people providing this assistance are strongly impacted by their experience.

Humanitarian assistance in crisis situations can be a turbulent business indeed, providing quite an adrenaline rush – one form of aid is portrayed in the 2003 movie, *Beyond Borders*, starring Angelina Jolie and Clive Owen, which was nominated for the Political Film Society's Peace Award in 2004. The film depicts several humanitarian aid situations (Ethiopia, Cambodia and Chechnya) and its powerful impact on people providing this assistance.

Some humanitarian and development professionals become so engaged in their work that they have difficulty adjusting to "normal" life when they return to their home societies. This also occurs with DEVADs in areas like Afghanistan. For example, one of the ISAF DEVADs in Kabul in 2006 who had years of field and administrative experience including a previous tour in Iraq put it this way:

> Working in places such as Afghanistan and Iraq, I have such a strong sense of purpose, and feel part of something much bigger than myself. After each deployment, it is difficult to return to "normal" life back in the UK and it takes awhile to readjust.[93]

After she had completed her first mission in Iraq she sought other similar postings – and was happy to be working alongside the military in Afghanistan, and subsequently went on to another assignment in Iraq. For many who have worked in this field the problems at home seem trivial compared to what they were doing in the field and they want to continue doing what they consider to be more substantive work. This business can be addictive.

This addiction can also be dangerous, as noted by a seasoned NGO administrator working in Ethiopia who commented on the preceding paragraphs:

> I've lived in a conflict zone (Burundi) and have dipped in and out of other conflict zones for brief periods (DRC [Democratic Republic of the Congo], Angola, Mozambique) over the years. I can thus relate to the premise of your piece that is very true and real. I've known of a number of aid workers in conflict zones whose perspective on reality became skewed. Being constantly under the adrenaline rush of operating in a high-stress conflict zone they find it hard to adapt to a more "normal" way of life when they come out of it. While there, the addictive nature of the experience causes them to gradually assume risks that can be dangerous to themselves and others. Frequent short R&Rs away from the work zone are a necessity to keep such people grounded in a more normal reality. Given the addictive nature of the experience, some may even refuse to benefit from these escapes, but superiors should not accept refusals. These situations can become so surreal that attitudes and actions get moulded in a jaded way, to the extent that psychological stability can become an issue if not checked and monitored.[94]

While the military has a fairly well-developed system to support personnel who have experienced negative impacts of extensive periods of service in high-stress environments, most development agencies, and the consulting firms that carry out many of their projects, have not learned how to systematically address these issues. The result can be that returning staff are left to fend for themselves as they go through re-entry, a process that can be exceedingly difficult.

Summary

This section has described part of the cast of characters that are likely to be exerting influence in an AO: it is a diverse and varied scene indeed. Achieving some sort of alignment of this energy is a challenge.

In just one group, the many international and national aid agencies that are active in the field, this variety can be difficult to comprehend let alone manage. Each agency has its own ideology and methods of operation, and is guided through its own administrative structure to exert its influence in the manner it sees fit.

Unlike the military where even in multinational missions there is often a central organizational hub, in development there is no overarching command system obliging these actors to adhere to a clearly defined set of objectives. Within each agency there likely is little that is comparable to the military's chain of command – particularly in the larger aid agencies where the different parts of their operations can function in varied and sometimes contradictory ways. Agencies that operate through large international development consulting firms bring an added measure of complexity to the field: each contractor has its own way of interpreting and carrying out the projects they have been assigned, and has its own internal management structure that determines how it operates. Attempting to achieve coherence in this scene is somewhat like trying to herd a bunch of cats: it is very difficult to do.

Although the national PRSP is designed to foster alignment of inputs on a common set of priorities, and most aid agencies do make reference to this document, the operational reality both within the host government and among aid agencies can be inconsistent with this plan. As noted earlier, in one Afghan minister's office the ANDS was not even a blip on the radar, and the only people in the office who referred to the plan in their work were three foreign technical advisors. The efforts of the Joint Coordination and Monitoring Board (JCMB) do not appear to be reaching all the line ministries. This is an indication of how much work there is to be done to foster alignment of all major actors toward a common set of objectives.

The situation in Afghanistan makes alignment particularly difficult. Although improved coordination has long been sought, a UN effort in early 2008 to place a forceful individual (the UK's Lord Paddy Ashdown) in that role was not successful. The SRSG's office does not appear to be able to provide the leadership required to effect this collaboration – it is difficult to know the reasons behind these challenges.

What is clear is that in fostering the advancement of a society along its trajectory of growth the influence exerted by outsiders needs to be consistent with indigenous initiatives and processes:

In the long-term, for successful development to take place in Afghanistan, it must be an endogenous process – development cannot be imported on the back of a truck. International actors operating in Afghanistan, such as USAID also need to adopt a culture of strategic consultation and situational awareness with each other and with the local population.[95]

The strategy needs to be similar to a client-centred approach in social work, where multiple external inputs need to work together to reinforce the host system's latent capacities to manage its own affairs. This calls for awareness of how the host environment operates – the focus of the next chapter.

CHAPTER 7

How Does this Place Work?

Introduction

The military's concept of "situational awareness" has a somewhat similar equivalent in development. Simply put, development agents need to find out enough about what is going on in a community or region to get a sense of how the place works so they can figure out how to help the situation improve. They must find ways to see into a rather opaque foreign system and identify community norms and patterns of relationships, power and influence, assess the potential of that system to move in a beneficial direction, establish entry points, and then make whatever inputs they can to help this movement happen.

This chapter summarizes a few of the major challenges in development. Some of these are due to the lack of skilled human resources, and others are part of trying to understand the culture and patterns of behaviour and belief in the environments where external actors are called upon to carry out peace and security missions.

Having some awareness of these internal factors is essential in understanding a population's capabilities and complex motivations and behaviours, carrying out effective interventions, and in setting realistic expectations of the results of efforts to help the situation improve.

Distribution Of Skills In A Developing Society

One of the key factors in understanding how a system works is knowing something about the range and depth of skills in the society and how much local talent is available to do the work that needs to be done. In his groundbreaking 1973 book, *Small is Beautiful: Economics as if People Mattered*, E. F. Schumacher describes some of the key differences between industrialized countries and less developed societies like Nigeria.

CHAPTER 7

Schumacher said the rapid recovery of Japan and Germany following their defeat and devastation at the end of World War II could not be replicated in countries in Africa largely because of the differences in the distribution of skills in these two types of societies. He said that industrialized societies have a skill distribution that resembles a pyramid, while in under-developed societies the distribution is more like a fat inverted "T"[96] (see Figure 6).

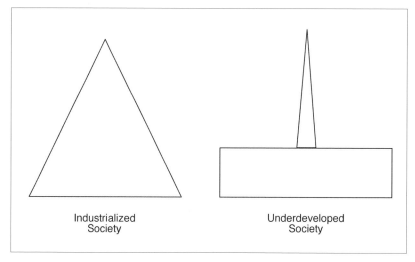

Industrialized
Society

Underdeveloped
Society

FIGURE 6 – SKILL DISTRIBUTION IN INDUSTRIALIZED AND UNDER-DEVELOPED SOCIETIES.

While there may well be highly educated visionaries and leaders in both types of societies, in the underdeveloped states there is much less planning and implementation capacity, with relatively few technicians and middle-level managers who can translate high-level vision into reality by preparing work plans and lines of action that coordinate the efforts of large sectors of the population into streams of coherent productive activity.

At the end of WWII, the various levels of education and skills that were present in the Japanese and German populations were quickly mobilized and engaged in productive activity, soon resulting in two of the strongest economies in the world. These skilled human resources simply do not exist in a developing country.

This is evident in Afghanistan, where in 2006 it was estimated that only about 30 percent of the aid available to the Afghan government had been absorbed and applied to the development needs of the country. The problem is not so much that there is a lack of funds: it is more a question that there are not enough skilled people in the system who know how to turn resources into concrete activities that benefit the poor and improve conditions in the country. Increasing the host society's absorptive capacity is a key factor in effective development.

While outsiders can do some of this work (it is what most foreign TAs and contractors do, at great cost!) this is capacity replacement rather than capacity development, and therefore not a permanent solution to the country's challenges. Sustainable development leading toward autonomous healthy growth requires the full range of skills and institutions that are present in any functioning society, and it takes generations to create these human resources and structures.

Trying to force the process by pushing resources into a system that cannot properly absorb and distribute them causes distortions that often slow down the pace of productive growth. People who can manipulate the system for personal gain may become more interested in cashing in on the available wealth than in doing the work necessary to put the resources to good use to build a healthy society.

Sometimes less is more – providing a little bit of what is available may be better in the long-run than overwhelming an area's systems with a well-intentioned flood of resources that will increase appetites to unsustainable levels and result in disillusionment when resource flows cease. And sometimes providing mentoring or coaching in things as basic as setting up an administrative office's filing system or conducting productive decision-making meetings is better than high-level theory related to development economics or lofty-sounding and complex national policy or strategy development processes.

Sustainable capacity development needs to build on what is already present, and if what exists is at a rather basic level, then that is where the work needs to begin. As the saying goes: "the big things depend on the little things" – if the little things, like literacy and simple project management skills, for example, are not in place, the big things just can't happen. This is why it is so important to get accurate information about how things work (or don't work) – it increases the likelihood that inputs will be appropriately designed to match existing conditions in the system.

CHAPTER 7

Working With Communities In A Counter-Insurgency

Understanding community dynamics and how to shift a population's attitudes is a major part of a counter-insurgency campaign. As noted earlier in this monograph, the general population's central role in an insurgency was expressed in Field Marshal Templer's statement on the Malayan campaign. He stated, "...the shooting side of the business is only 25 per cent of the trouble and the other 75 per cent lies in getting the people of this country behind us."[97]

Both sides of the conflict need the community's support. The primary purpose of military and development activity in places like Afghanistan is to strengthen the government and increase its ability to serve the people. The insurgency has the opposite objective. Both sides involve the population in their campaigns, and success is linked to community support for their intentions.

The objective of development in a counter-insurgency campaign is to reinforce individual, small group or community norms required to eliminate support for the insurgency, increase the people's trust in government and ultimately foster a peaceful and open society. It is helpful to consider a continuum along which these norms and behaviours can be positioned:

1. At one end of the continuum the entire population cannot conceive of a society other than that portrayed by the insurgents and will not harbour any thoughts or discussions that may lead to another state of being. Active participation in the insurgency by locals is encouraged and rewarded by community members. Intelligence about government forces is fed to the insurgents.

2. At another stage the community appears to be neutral: most of the insurgents are not locals and they use the threat of violence to get the support needed to carry on their anti-government activities. While there may be some information about insurgent activity fed to government forces, most of the significant intelligence flows to the insurgents.

3. Somewhere in the middle there is increasing unhappiness about the insurgency and community members passively tolerate the insurgents,

who are outsiders and use violence to get required supports. Information about insurgent and government activity flows both ways in roughly equal measure.

4. At another point on the continuum the community is becoming increasingly resistant to the presence of the insurgents, and while they may harbour some insurgents it is through fear rather than ideological commitment. Most significant intelligence flows to the government forces.

5. At the other end of the continuum virtually all community members are openly opposed to the insurgency, and no members are involved in anti-government activity. Insurgents seeking community support are unwelcome and are driven away. No significant intelligence flows to the insurgents, and community members provide high quality information to support counter-insurgency activities.

Development inputs are essentially an intervention in a system to foster a desirable shift in individual, group or community norms and behaviours. In traditional development work, the resources that flow into a community are designed to do things such as helping people recognize they have the capacity to change, improve living conditions, reduce inequality among sub-groups, strengthen cohesiveness and local decision-making institutions and foster self-determination. Material and educational inputs reinforce certain beliefs, attitudes and behaviours and discourage others so the community's trajectory changes for the better, and this change becomes self-sustaining.

Although some in the aid community would argue otherwise, development intervention can also be used as a weapon in a counter-insurgency campaign, with the added key element of encouraging a shift of norms in a positive direction similar to that described in the five-point continuum above. These inputs can be inducements to change attitudes and behaviours as part of a carrot and stick strategy to achieve a desired effect. This overtly utilitarian and manipulative use of resources is seen by some in the development camp as outright heresy since in some quarters (as noted earlier) there is a notion that assistance should be impartial. The development work required in a counter-insurgency campaign is necessarily partial: it seeks specific results – strengthening the government, reducing support and hospitality for insurgents, protecting the population and increasing the flow of reliable intelligence about insurgent activity to government forces.

Environments that are at varying levels on the continuum above will require different types of influences – those which have norms at the low end of the range might require a combination of material and psychological inputs to shift in a desired direction. Increased security and concrete evidence of effective government and the benefits of resisting the insurgents coupled with more subtle communications strategies can demonstrate the possibility and viability of alternative ways of life.

Once these mindsets and behaviours have begun to change, other inputs demonstrating the value of changing norms even further can reinforce this shift. Individuals and small groups may start to move in a positive direction and begin countering insurgents' messages and provide useful information to the government, often at considerable personal risk. This shift can be accelerated as the sustainable benefits of co-operation become more clearly evident and government-related messages are conveyed by formal and informal leaders and others who are held in high esteem by residents.

Ultimately the community, with the help of government, needs to take ownership of this transition and become the prime agent in a material, social and psychological shift that has legitimate formal and informal local leadership in charge of the change process. External inputs can continue but these should be designed and managed in a way that fosters unity among the inhabitants of the community through consultative processes in which the various sub-groups, especially women, have a voice and each has their fair share of the community's resources.

Equitable access to the benefits of development by all sub-groups in a community is of strategic importance: alienated sub-groups can provide support or be a haven for insurgents even in communities where the majority of the population supports the government. The opposite can also be true: alienated members of insurgent-friendly communities can support the government.

Although most communities are likely to accept all the assistance and services they can get, considerable care is needed to avoid pouring so much into the community that its internal balance and self-sufficiency are negatively impacted by the support. Inputs should be targeted to those symbolic or practical areas that will have maximum return on investment in terms of achieving a desired change in attitudes, beliefs and behaviours. However, absorptive capacity has its limits, and inputs that create a dependency or unsustainable lifestyles can have a counter-productive effect when the resources are no longer available: a disillusioned population may increase its support for the insurgents.

Development and internal community dynamics

Communities (and organizations) usually have differing levels of internal coherence, with their sub-systems or groups being in varying degrees of alignment as they move through time: these all work together to determine how a population conducts its affairs. Some sub-groups may strongly support a particular set of norms, while others might have quite different views about important matters such as trust in government or support for an insurgency. These preferences and motivations are a form of social energy that should be understood and which can be selectively reinforced, tapped or released to achieve particular purposes.

An understanding of a system's patterns of social energy is particularly important in situations where the interveners have relatively low levels of influence or power, as is the case in most community development projects. These interveners strive to reinforce and align existing community energies that tend in the direction of a desirable trajectory. Low-power instigated norm shifts that are consistent with and build upon a community's traditional way of operating are likely to be sustained after external inputs are no longer available.

High-power inputs such as injecting large amounts of money and material resources into a community may achieve a short-term desirable result but in the long term can be counter-productive if the change is not sustained and if the intervention damages long-standing beneficial indigenous patterns of community functioning.

Patterns of domination and subordination are often present among sub-groups even in the smallest communities. There usually are differing levels of adherence to predominant community norms, and the more oppressive the dominant sector is the higher the likelihood there will be sub-groups

CHAPTER 7

with norms that differ markedly from the system's formal or informal leaders. These variations are rarely evident to outsiders who are accustomed to dealing only with visible community leaders, or with individuals who seek the outsiders' attention and who might not have beneficial influence within the community. Insurgents and locals, including members of host government agencies, are often well aware of these internal dynamics and can use them to their own advantage.

Development inputs usually target sub-systems that are (or have the potential to be) aligned in a direction consistent with the objectives of the intervener, with a view to accelerating the system's movement along a desired trajectory. The variety of views held by community members on issues such as support for the government or the insurgency may be associated with different sub-groups or individuals who are likely to be moving at different rates – and possibly in different directions – along the five-step community norms continuum described above. Depending on a variety of factors (such as the level of corruption of local police) these attitudes and beliefs may reach a tipping point which will result in large-scale or collective shifts in perceptions and behaviours, for better or for worse.

Counter-insurgency related development inputs can be made in a variety of physical, social and psychological points to achieve a desired effect on a system's trajectory. Examples could include repair of irrigation systems, improving government operations and schools, and communication strategies directed at particular sub-groups to increase their perception of the credibility of government.

The selection of appropriate points for intervention depends on the nature of available development inputs and at least three factors: where the intervener has direct or indirect access to the system, where the desired effect is to be manifested, and the internal networks and connections between the point(s) of intervention and the desired point(s) of effect. These choices are influenced by the intended scope, depth and duration of effect – whether it be on individuals, small groups or larger collectivities and whether the impact is to be superficial and temporary or profound and permanent.

These intervention strategies are also influenced by the characteristics of available agents of change, the people and systems that are key actors in the intervention process, especially the people who can help external agents see more clearly into the communities and organizations with which they want to work. Some of these helpers are called interpreters or "cultural brokers" – they play an essential role in a development intervention that merits considerable discussion.

Cultural Brokers

As noted earlier, both military and development workers face much the same challenges when beginning to operate in an area: they need to know enough about the internal dynamics of the local system to understand how things work so they can have some confidence that they know how to design and carry out their intervention. Identifying and navigating about in the complex set of individual, group, organizational or community norms and capacities, and configuring appropriate inputs to help these shift in a desired direction, requires accurate and relevant knowledge of the community.

To obtain this information, collaborative relationships need to be established with people who know and understand the system, and their input is required at all stages from initial conceptualization through design and implementation to monitoring, evaluation and extracting lessons learned for future cycles. In the development field the term "cultural broker" is used to identify these helpers.

Cultural brokers are usually members of the recipient community who can communicate with external interveners to help configure and deliver inputs. There can be other non-indigenous cultural brokers or helpers who can provide useful information on the internal workings of a system – these could be other development workers who have good information about the system, or other observers who have relevant knowledge of the AO. Each of these has its own strengths and weaknesses, and each person's analysis is necessarily a partial view of what is really going on in the system.

Communities are rarely homogenous entities – there may be quite different conditions in the various sub-systems of an area in which an intervention is to take place. Although it is essential to work with local leaders, it is not safe to assume that the formal leadership of a community speaks for all its members, and that the picture conveyed by the leaders is shared by the entire population. While the formal leadership needs to be engaged in

CHAPTER 7

an intervention, it is often the informal leadership that exercises meaning-ful influence in a community. Informal leaders can be difficult for external agents to identify, and they may be reluctant to collaborate with the inter-vention. Without their support, however, most interventions are likely to have minimal effect. Local co-workers or others with knowledge of the area are key to identifying and establishing productive relationships with the community's informal leadership.

Because of the likelihood of a community having sub-groups which have their own ways of thinking and acting, a single cultural broker will rarely be able to provide an adequate picture of how a community works. Multiple points of access are advisable, using several cultural brokers who have dif-ferent types of access to formal and informal leaders in key sub-groups, so the external actors have more than one view or entry point into the system.

The external agency also has its own cultural brokers, development or mil-itary personnel who know how to establish relationships with local helpers – these cultural brokers build bridges between the two sets of actors in the intervention process. There may be several layers or links in a chain of rela-tionships between an external agency and the point of impact of the inter-vention. Information flows both ways along this chain of relationships, and can provide the external agent with insights on how best to configure the flow of resources to achieve the desired effect. It also helps the recipient of aid to better understand how the external agency works.

Each cultural broker is likely to be seen as linked to a particular part of a community or organization. Becoming too closely identified with a broker who is part of one sector of a community's power structure might alienate other sub-groups and prompt them to provide additional support for the insurgency even while some members of the community are shifting away from this pattern of belief and behaviour. Having multiple points of entry with several cultural brokers who are linked with the various sub-groups can mitigate the negative effects of this selective distortion process and will present interveners with a broad array of information on which to base their initiatives.

Many locals who choose to work with the military do so at considerable personal risk. The insurgents can easily discover their identities and often target them in their campaigns. Care is needed to protect these valuable resources from potential harm while they act as information conduits between the military and the people and systems that need to change.

Each potential cultural broker will have his or her own priorities that may or may not have the best interests of the population or government in mind. While some may be motivated by a high-minded commitment to their people, others may see their relationship with powerful external agents as enhancing their own position and increasing their ability to manipulate the situation to their own advantage. Interpreters are in particularly powerful positions that they can (and often do) exploit to their personal benefit. Each will provide points of entry to the community in a manner than suits their interests, and careful selection of cultural brokers and entry points is essential in an effective campaign. It cannot be assumed that the various people who become cultural brokers in an area have good relationships with each other – they may have long-standing internal conflicts that are invisible to the development agent and could distort the information they provide.

Establishing authentic relationships with potential cultural brokers is a key to an effective intervention. Most bilingual locals who are in cultural broker roles have considerable experience working with foreign nationals – some have done so for years, remaining employed with agencies such as the Canadian military while foreigners rotate through on their relatively short tours of duty. Most cultural brokers have identified a range of stereotypes into which they classify foreigners, and will tend to relate with them on the basis of these categories. While each external agent hopes to be seen as a unique individual, it takes considerable time and effort to break through the stereotypes and establish authentic relationships with locals who have seen so many foreigners come and go over a period of years. Some are reluctant to invest the emotional capital required to establish close personal relationships when they know these will end in a few short months.

There is no quick way to cut through these normal barriers to effective intercultural relations and to quickly determine whether a cultural broker is providing the straight goods. One of the best strategies is for the foreigner to behave in as authentic a manner as possible, and to create conditions where the local person is in the teacher or leader role and sharing information on his or her view of life and the situation at hand. Many locals are pleased to respond to foreigners' interest in learning about their culture. This open two-way communication coupled with a high tolerance for ambiguity while accessing multiple sources of information will provide an array of inputs that the intervener can use to chart a course.

Cultural brokers are key agents of both short-term and long-term change in any cross-cultural development initiative, and establishing effective relations with them is central to achieving a mission's objectives.

Interpreters: Language Assistants Or Cultural Brokers?

Most military training includes a component on working with interpreters based on the concept of language assistant (LA). An LA is usually presumed to be a bilingual person who acts as a communication bridge between a foreigner and locals, and is not assumed to be doing much more than translating conversation back and forth from one language to another. What actually happens in the field is considerably more: interpreters not only translate messages back and forth, they control the communication and, where they deem necessary, the foreigner's behaviours as well, to achieve a desirable outcome. They also provide information related to security and community attitudes related to the mission.

Credit: DND Image AR2006-A020-0010a.jpg. Combat Camera website.

PHOTO 3:   INTERPRETER AT WORK – AFGHANISTAN.

CHAPTER 7

In essence, they are the foreigner's guides as well as their eyes, voice and ears. External agents are completely dependent on their interpreters for far more than language – interpreters effectively become their handlers and are in positions of enormous power. They often are active agents in carrying out the mission and central to its success.

When the military uses interpreters in a cultural broker function, they can be providing their services at considerable personal risk. Roy Thomas has written extensively on this topic. An example:

> **Sarajevo, 1993: A Dangerous Investigation Demands an Interpreter**
> Interpreters can mean the difference between life and death. In one instance, the Serb Liaison Officer refused to go further! Quite rightly he felt that mines and trip wires would be difficult to detect in the falling darkness. A violation was alleged. However, the team's 'United Nations' status was less clear in the fading light. "Last light" is when belligerent or prohibited activity can be expected. The Bosnian Serb lady who acted as the UN military observer interpreter was asked, "Do you wish to stay with him?" meaning with the Liaison Officer. "Who will talk to the Bosniaks if soldiers are there?" the interpreter responded, as she moved forward to share the dangers facing the unarmed UN military observer team.[98]

When working in a conflict zone it is important to do whatever possible to see that cultural brokers and interpreters are not put in harm's way. Support for interpreters is an under-appreciated factor given the risks they take. In another article, Roy Thomas comments: "Since the United Nations Interim Force in Lebanon was formed in 1978, as many as 35 interpreters may have died working with the Irish contingent alone." Most peace and security missions have extensive provisions for dealing with the needs of their international personnel – health care, medical evacuations, disability supports in case of accidents, etc. Locally hired interpreters face much the same dangers but do not have anywhere near the same level of support and protection if they come to harm. They also are vulnerable once the mission has left if the contending parties seek them out for retribution for the work they did during the mission. These locally-hired gems are the mission's windows on the world in which they operate, and they deserve all the support they can get from the organizations they serve.

Beyond interpretation – capacity development

Interpreters usually do more than simply translate communication – they can augment the message, for better or worse. If they have an appropriate background they can also become skilled enough in the subject matter to do some of the work themselves, in their own language and in a culturally-appropriate manner.

An example is the young lady in the photo below, who helped with a series of basic interpersonal communications courses for public servants in Kabul. After interpreting for several sessions she became a co-trainer as well as an interpreter, and made significant input that increased the effectiveness of the training. When she became familiar with the instructional design at the root of the training she made suggestions for improvement and also conducted some of the participatory exercises herself.

PHOTO 4:   INTERPRETER HELPING WITH INTERPERSONAL COMMUNI-
CATION TRAINING FOR PUBLIC SERVANTS – KABUL, MAY 2006.

Working With Interpreters And Cultural Brokers

Most communication between external agents and locals in peace and security missions involves working through interpreters. The translation strategy used in development work is usually sequential rather than simultaneous, as would be the case where the interpreter is in a sound-proof booth and microphones and earphones are used. In virtually all development-related field activity the communication takes place in relatively short sequential bursts of information, given by one or the other speaker and translated by an interpreter as it goes from one to the other. This interrupted back-and-forth pattern of exchange of information has a major effect on the accuracy and richness of the communication.

Interpersonal communication between two native speakers of the same language is tremendously complex, especially considering that at least 80 per cent of the meaning that is transmitted in ordinary communication is not in the dictionary definition of the words, but in other parts of the exchange, including the context, power relationships and non-verbal communication.

It is difficult enough to establish effective communication between speakers of the same language – exchanging information using an interpreter to link people of different cultures and who speak different languages is considerably more complex, and the likelihood of error is much higher. The large parts of the message conveyed by the context and non-verbal components of communication vary with culture and language, and much of this major portion of interpersonal communication is lost or distorted when the exchange is going through an interpreter.

The more completely all parties understand the dynamics of working through interpreters, the more likely it will be that the communication will be effective. Many community leaders and others who interact frequently with foreigners have considerable experience with this difficult form of communication – it is the military member or the development agent who may be relatively new to this process and who may have much to learn to make sure their end of the exchange is handled properly. This is a large topic that merits more attention than is possible to give in this monograph – the following basic components of working with interpreters will help improve the effectiveness of exchanges with locals and others working on peace and security missions.

Quality of relationships

The effectiveness of the communication exchange is directly linked to the quality of the relationship on a speaker-interpreter team. Before engaging in mission-critical exchanges it is highly desirable for the pair to spend some time together informally to get some sense of each other's mode of communication and to establish some basic protocols defining how the discourse will unfold. The interpreter should be asked how he or she likes to receive and transmit information, clarifying issues such as the length of each unit of discourse, seating arrangements, debriefing processes and other similar factors linked to effective interpersonal communication.

As noted earlier, many locals who are employed as interpreters and cultural brokers have worked in the AO for some time, often with the same organization, usually for considerably longer than the development worker or military member who is ostensibly in the supervisory role. They know more about the environment than the external agent and usually have to spend considerable time and effort to orient the newcomer to the situation; especially in the beginning, when the "subordinate" is actually the more knowledgeable party in the relationship.

This can make for awkward interpersonal dynamics in a command-and-control structure, particularly if the newcomer may be somewhat insecure and needs to show that he or she is in charge of what is going on. This might limit the quality and content of communication between the two. In a counter-insurgency campaign this can have dangerous consequences: if the leader does not know how to listen and adjust operations accordingly the results could be disastrous. The supervisor needs to consciously create the conditions that will make it possible for others to speak freely and openly so the needed information will be provided, and to demonstrate the ability to incorporate this information in appropriately-designed operations.

Caution is required, however, in adopting this learner position in the exchange: there can be a delicate balance between demonstrating openness to receive needed information without giving the impression that the supervisor does not know enough to exercise appropriate leadership. There is a fine line between openness to input and being perceived as incompetent and losing credibility, and this varies from one culture to another. Care is required when moving into a new environment, since these assessments and images are established during the first few encounters with local staff.

Most of the foregoing presumes a relatively honest and altruistic interpreter. This is not always the case. The outsiders' dependence on interpreters and cultural brokers puts these local staff in positions of extraordinary power and they can, and often do, take advantage of their position for personal gain and to enhance their standing in their own community. They are in a position to direct resources to their friends who may be giving them kickbacks or other benefits because of the contracts they send their way.

There may also be questions as to the interpreter's true loyalties – they are in a position to convey sensitive information to the other side in the conflict. Roy Thomas commented on this from his experience in the Balkans:

> Thus in the case of locals hired as interpreters, these individuals could indeed be conduits of information for their communities and no doubt, at minimum, low level intelligence operatives. However, for every betrayal of information (and only one interpreter had to be dismissed under these conditions in Sarajevo from October 1993 until July 1994) there are countless examples, which to this day should not be openly discussed, in which locals working as interpreters provided warnings or other information which assisted in the security and protection of UN military observer team members.[99]

In some cases the difficulties in relationships with interpreters and cultural brokers arise from a simple limitation of competence on the part of the locally hired person. They may not be malevolent at all, but just don't know how to do what is being asked of them, and it may take some time for the foreigner to figure this out.

It is difficult for external parties to navigate these potentially perilous waters and to accurately assess the competence and motivation of the locals who are hired to help the mission. This is compounded by the relatively short rotation of military personnel, since it often takes about six months in an environment before a newcomer starts to get a sense of how the place works. In some cases that understanding begins to happen when they are ready to pack up and leave for home, just as they begin to be able to properly assess the quality and performance of their locally hired personnel. They pass on their impressions – whatever they may be – of their interpreters and other local contacts to their replacements.

Most development operations (including the PRTs in Afghanistan) are seen by many locals as producing ripe fruit that is easy picking – there often is a circle of local business people hovering about ready to capitalize on the contracts for development work and the other benefits available from the wealthy outsiders. When development workers manage to bypass this cluster of eager local agents to do their projects they often find they can get work done for substantially less than they have been accustomed to paying, indicating they have been subjected to inflated prices – something that has likely been done with the knowledge of their interpreters and cultural brokers.

This is all part of what some cynically call "Aid Incorporated" – a jaded view of development where all parties seem to be more interested in milking the system for their own benefit than in providing needed services to a population. While much of what goes on in the development field is noble and well done, in some cases it is difficult to avoid this trap. Local staff hired as interpreters are as likely to fall into this negative self-serving pattern as anyone else.

Content and pacing of discourse

Interpretation is a difficult art and requires collaboration between the speaker and the interpreter to increase the likelihood that the communication is effective. Most interpreters are working from English (or another western language) back and forth to their native tongue – the western language usually is not their mother tongue and they are likely to have a relatively limited vocabulary. Basic and straightforward terminology should be used that avoids jargon or colloquial figures of speech. Jokes and humorous comments should be kept to a minimum, as they usually do not translate well.

The amount of information transmitted at any one time varies with the skill and preferences of the interpreter. In most cases, the speaker should organize his or her thoughts into "chunks", clearly defined clusters of concepts that can be expressed in a few sentences at a time, preferably not longer than a minute or so for each chunk. Pauses should be frequent and long enough to permit the interpreter to grasp the essence of the main ideas and convey the concepts to the other, and to receive and return the response. There may be times when the interpreter does not adequately grasp the ideas being transmitted and the message needs to be re-stated in a more comprehensible and clearer form that the interpreter can handle. This forces the sender to be clear on what he or she wants to say.

Eye contact should be primarily with the other main party in the communication rather than with the interpreter, although it is wise to keep the interpreter in view to see how the exchange is going.

Interpretation is mentally tiring and stressful and it is common for translators to experience high fatigue levels after even a short period of work. If interpreters get overly tired they are likely to be less accurate, so it is wise to offer to take breaks every once in a while. This can be set up beforehand, during the initial relationship-building process between the interpreter and the speaker.

Debriefing after meetings

Time should be made to have regular debriefings after meetings to reflect with the interpreter on how the exchange went and to determine how to improve the quality of communication. This can be a central part of building the relationships required for effective work with an interpreter and an orientation for team members who have relatively little prior experience to working with interpreters in that context.

Learning from the interpreter

Interpreters who have considerable experience working with development agents or members of the military have accumulated a lot of potentially relevant knowledge, and means should be instituted to encourage them to share their thoughts and insights. External actors might unwittingly be doing things that interfere with the main purpose of their work and interpreters may be reluctant to share their concerns for fear of punishment from making their leaders or supervisors lose face. If the supervisor can model an appropriate level of openness to constructive criticism in a hierarchical relationship this may have a positive spin-off effect on the interpreter's overall approach to management in general and beneficially effect the organizational climate wherever the interpreter may be working after their current job is done.

Interpreter as a long-term indigenous capacity development agent

It should constantly be borne in mind that ultimately it is the local people who must do the development work in the communities or organizations that are the focus of a mission's interventions, and the cultural broker has a long-term role in helping this process. Often the unintended by-product of an intervention has the most significant and sustainable impact on a society – the cultural broker will learn much from working with external agents on several lines of action: those skills will remain in the community after the development project has ended, and, if appropriate values are present, they can be of long-term benefit to the people.

External agents should see their relationships with interpreters and cultural brokers as part of the overall development process – as time passes these individuals are likely to rise to positions of leadership in their home communities or organizations, and will take whatever they have learned from working with foreigners (both the good and the bad) into these organizations with them as they progress through life. Interpreters and cultural brokers should be seen as part of the development agency's delivery system as well as indirect but key recipients of the agency's development inputs.

Summary

External agents need to know enough about how a community or region operates to configure their inputs to reinforce constructive elements in the situations with which they are working. Most areas where there are peace and security missions are likely to have relatively few human resources capable of translating good ideas and resources into well-managed lines of action, which is one of the reasons for the low absorptive rate of donor funds in places like Afghanistan (estimated at about 30 per cent in 2006). This is one of the reasons communities are not seeing much fruit from the development funds expended in their own country, and that in turn contributes to insurgents' ability to operate in an area. Anything that increases an area's capacity to manage its own growth is likely to have positive impacts on security.

There are capable people in every group, and some are eager to work with external agents to improve conditions in their societies. Many who have appropriate language and technical skills seek jobs with aid organizations and the military for both personal financial reasons and, in most cases, because of a genuine interest in helping improve the lot of the people in their communities. Some of these become cultural brokers, people who act as a bridge between external agents and the local communities and organizations, and they play an essential role in the intervention. They are the external agents' eyes, ears and voice, and have enormous influence on how the intervention is carried out.

Working with cultural brokers and interpreters (who often are much more than LAs) takes some skill and good interpersonal communication on all sides. The quality of interaction along the chain of relationships of which they form an essential link is one of the major elements influencing mission success and the sustainability of the changes sought by the intervention.

CHAPTER 8

What is the Mission?
A Change of Mindset

Introduction:
What Mindsets Need To Change?

This chapter addresses the complex issue of clearly defining the purpose of the mission in Afghanistan, and by inference, the objectives of other similar peace and security operations in fragile states. It also discusses the challenges associated with the change in mindset that is required to achieve victory in this type of conflict. Two groups of mindsets need to be changed: both the military and the development agencies (and likely also the other participants) need to adjust their thinking and operations to combine their energies toward a common objective.

This purpose should define priorities and guide the activities of all major actors in the AO. There is a lack of clarity on this fundamental issue, and this is a problem: in their 2006 paper on PRTs, Major-General (MGen) Roger Lane and Emma Sky defined the challenge this way:

> ...there is not yet a common understanding or shared vision of the causes of instability in Afghanistan, the outcomes (effects) required to deliver stability, (how) to deliver stability processes and outputs at provincial level, and the selection of security, governance and development inputs for stability.[100]

While the purpose of the military's mission may seem obvious to most, on closer examination it seems things need to be clarified and better focused. As noted earlier in this monograph, after almost a year as a senior officer in ISAF HQ in Kabul, BGen Pepin reflected on his experience (repeated here for ease of reference):

> I am of the view that the military is able to adapt itself, whether it is to respond to a threat or an enemy and to find ways to win

173

> when confronted with this threat, and they are also able to adjust themselves to a development environment (as they did successfully in Bosnia, for example).
>
> The challenge that is relatively new is to be able to do both at the same time. From my experience in Afghanistan I've seen that the military (both Canadian and American) has a tendency to be more comfortable with kinetic than non-kinetic activities such as development. That is why when a situation arises where both types of interventions are necessary, kinetic operations receive more attention.
>
> This being said, my comments on changing the "mindset" referred to the capacity to develop an ability to act in both roles at the same time.[101]

While it is a natural tendency for any organization's leaders to focus on things they know how to do well and to give less attention to things that are outside their normal sphere of activity, the changing nature of military operations – shifting from third-generation to fourth-generation warfare – is requiring a major shift in perception of what a mission is really all about. This has implications for the purpose of the military itself, now that the era of two opposing standing armies seems to have come to an end. The Commander of the Canadian Defence Academy, MGen Daniel Gosselin, put it this way, "Fragile states – that's our future."[102]

Working in fragile but relatively peaceful states has long been part of the development community's mindset and operations: these struggling societies are its past, present, and also its future. Most members of that community, however, are accustomed to thinking that the military has no business acting in their field of operation – that they exist in two separate spheres. The notion that there are bad guys who need to be neutralized or killed is alien to most. However, development workers also know they cannot operate where the level of violence is above a certain point, and the military's support is required to achieve beneficial results in these environments. The development field must become accustomed to seeing the military as essential partners in their work in fragile states where there are insurgencies – their mindset and ways of operating also need to change to accept and work with this reality.

This is likely to be a challenge because most development workers are not accustomed to seeing their activities as part of a counter-insurgency campaign. In fact, some are quite allergic to this notion – a CIDA analyst with years of experience in a variety of countries recently asked with some incredulity, "What does counter-insurgency have to do with development?" Many would ask the same question. This indicates a profound lack of understanding of what is required to establish and maintain stability in some of the more troubled parts of the world.

Just as the military tends to focus on its area of expertise, the kinetic dimension, the development agencies also focus on their area, the non-kinetic – governance, social and economic development and other similar aspects of an intervention. Each party has relatively little understanding of the realities in which the other operates, and yet these two quite different entities need to combine their talents to achieve desired effects in successful peace and security operations. One of the key things they need to accomplish this is a clear and common understanding of the purpose of the mission.

What Is Counter-Insurgency?

The US Army's *Counterinsurgency* manual describes a broad range of elements involved in this type of mission:

> A counterinsurgency campaign is… a mix of offensive, defensive, and stability operations conducted along multiple lines of operations. It requires a mix of familiar combat tasks and skills more often associated with nonmilitary agencies. … (Soldiers) are expected to be nation builders as well as warriors. They must be prepared to help reestablish institutions and local security forces and assist in rebuilding infrastructure and basic services. They must be able to facilitate establishing local governance and the rule of law. The list of such tasks is long; performing them involves extensive coordination and cooperation with many intergovernmental, host-nation, and international agencies.[103]

The manual continues with a description of required changes in mindset:

> Western militaries too often neglect the study of insurgency. They falsely believe that armies trained to win large conventional

175

wars are automatically prepared to win small, unconventional ones. In fact, some capabilities required for conventional success – for example, the ability to execute operational maneuver and employ massive firepower – may be of limited utility or even counterproductive in COIN operations. Nonetheless, conventional forces beginning COIN operations often try to use these capabilities to defeat insurgents; they almost always fail....

The military forces that successfully defeat insurgencies are usually those able to overcome their institutional inclination to wage conventional war against insurgents. They learn how to practice COIN and apply that knowledge...

In COIN, the side that learns faster and adapts more rapidly – the better learning organization – usually wins. Counterinsurgencies have been called learning competitions.[104]

And they go further to describe what is required to achieve victory:

Before most COIN operations begin, insurgents have seized and exploited the initiative, to some degree at the least. Therefore, counterinsurgents undertake offensive and defensive operations to regain the initiative and create a secure environment. However, killing insurgents – while necessary, especially with respect to extremists – by itself cannot defeat an insurgency. Gaining and retaining the initiative requires counterinsurgents to address the insurgency's causes through stability operations as well. This initially involves securing and controlling the local populace and providing for essential services. As security improves, military resources contribute to supporting government reforms and reconstruction projects. As counterinsurgents gain the initiative, offensive operations focus on eliminating the insurgent cadre, while defensive operations focus on protecting the populace and infrastructure from direct attacks. As counterinsurgents establish military ascendancy, stability operations expand across the [AO] and eventually predominate. Victory is achieved when the populace consents to the government's legitimacy and stops actively and passively supporting the insurgency.[105]

To summarize two central points: according to the US *Counterinsurgency* manual, the desired effect of the military's mission – victory – is achieved "when the populace consents to the government's legitimacy and stops actively and passively supporting the insurgency." Also, the way to accomplish this is for the military to become a nimble, responsive, learning organization while carrying out its mission.

This calls for concerted attention on two dimensions of external and internal activity:

1. External: working with agencies and individuals in the AO to increase the capacity of the host society's government to provide the services that establish its legitimacy in the eyes of the population.

2. Internal: undertaking the structural and cultural changes within the military that are needed to become a nimble learning organization, and to either become more of a development agency or to be an effective partner with others who can do the capacity development work that is outside the military's scope of expertise.

Equivalent changes of mindset are required on the development side of this relationship – they also need to become nimble, responsive learning organizations, and to stop being allergic to the military. Most development agencies are not accustomed to seeing themselves as having a role creating conditions where the "populace consents to the government's legitimacy and stops actively and passively supporting the insurgency" – they usually operate in environments where this is already established and taken as a given. They do development, and that usually does not include being engaged as full collaborating partners in a counter-insurgency. Terms such as "victory," "defeat" and "enemy" are not central concepts in their vocabulary, and attending joint planning meetings in a room full of soldiers who arrive wearing armour and carrying a variety of weapons is not part of their habitual pattern of work. As some of those soldiers might say, the development agents need to get over it, take their place at the table and get on with the task at hand. If the development workers won't do it, the soldiers will go ahead on their own, likely with sub-optimal results.

CHAPTER 8

Insurgents Or Institutions? A Contest For The Ungoverned Space

BGen Pepin's comments noted earlier about needing to focus simultan-eously on both the kinetic and non-kinetic aspects of security are reinforced in the paper by MGen Lane and Emma Sky, who go even further and assert that it is actually the non-kinetic objectives that should be paramount:

> Understanding the problem is everything; ... It seems to us that it is not so much that the sources of instability are strong, but that the nascent government institutions are weak. Most people are behind the government and yearn for leadership and a genu-ine sense that it will protect and serve them. We are therefore engaged in a contest for the ungoverned space – not only in the physical domain, but in the cognitive domain of the minds of the population, and in time. Many of the anti-government actors are not offering the population anything tangible; but given the scale of the challenges, the government struggles to offer them anything in this contest. Collectively, we need interventions that allow the population to reject the cause of instability – especially the insurgents – and give them the confidence to withstand some of the pressures upon them.[106]

While dealing with insurgents is essential, these anti-government forces are able to operate largely because there is an administrative vacuum that should be filled by well-run institutions that foster a healthy economy. Much the same could be said about counter-narcotics work, which is most effective when there are supports for alternate and sustainable lifestyles – productive legal agriculture with access to markets, credit, transportation, and so forth – in addition to functioning policing and justice systems.

Lane and Sky continue, describing the implications of this focus for both military and development actors in a manner compatible with the US Army's *Counterinsurgency* manual:

> Set against this complex web of causes of instability, each of which needs to be correctly identified if the appropriate interven-tions are to be used, it is possible to identify four broad strands required for stability in Afghanistan:

- legitimate and effective governance;

- capable Afghan security forces;

- mitigation and marginalization of threats to stability; and

- conditions for sustainable and legitimate economic growth.

Recognizing these complex causes and responses is an acknowledgement of the limitations of the military security agencies in delivering long-term stability (although crucial at the outset), the absolute requirement for an effective law enforcement system, and the requirement for an interagency, multinational, coherent and coordinated approach from the outset. This has profound implications for the manner in which governments formulate their strategies, train and educate their officials, as well as how they interact between ministries. It suggests that the elegant linear progression of phases so beloved of some militaries is no longer relevant, and it also raises the question of how international organizations and NGOs fit into this new paradigm.[107]

In describing the possible role of the PRT in building up institutional capacity, their personnel's knowledge of local dynamics could make it clear that what might at first seem to require a kinetic approach may well be better addressed with a non-kinetic response to resolving the causes of instability:

> By thoroughly analyzing the causes of conflict, the PRT may also help its resolution. For instance, where the seeds of dissent are caused by local officials who ensure that (only) family and fellow tribesmen are given jobs, patient talking about the value of representation in local government is likely to be more effective than a close air-support strike against a group of what we think are insurgents, but in reality are under-represented peoples.[108]

The military needs to establish and maintain effective collaborative relations with people who have the required expertise, and to know when to stand aside and let others handle issues. Lane and Sky say this can be a challenge due to the military not understanding their own limitations, compounded by difficulties brought on by aspects of their culture:

Too often military officers are providing advice in areas that they are not expert. The military approach tends to be to 'solve' the problems themselves – and in the process create a raft of unintended new problems – rather than in supporting Afghans to help solve their own problems. The consultative process is laborious but is crucial to achieving the required effect.[109]

As noted earlier, if development inputs are not available, the military will do what it deems necessary to solve a problem, and will take action even if, from a developmental perspective, it might be better to do something different than the military proposes. Sometimes deciding to *not* take action is the best way to support the constructive trajectory of the society. If skilled development advice is available, the military needs to heed it and not take initiatives that may well be counter-productive.

How Much Is Enough – Who Decides?

How much development is enough to achieve victory? It depends on who is asked – the answers cover quite a range. At one end of the continuum there are discussions of the ten core functions of a sovereign state, as described in a paper by Ashraf Ghani and others.[110] These include the following macro-level elements of governance:

- a legitimate monopoly on the means of violence;

- administrative control;

- management of public finances;

- investment in human capital;

- delineation of citizenship rights and duties;

- provision of infrastructure services;

- regulation of the market;

- management of the state's assets (including the environment, natural resources and cultural assets);

- international relations (including entering into international contracts and public borrowing); and

- rule of law.

At the other end of the continuum is the citizen who just wants a society that works, which includes having a way to make a decent living, access to basic health care, education, shelter, security, and above all, a measure of social order and hope for a better life for the next generation. In development this is known as a sustainable livelihood, some elements of which are included in the MDGs described earlier.

The standards chosen to determine the extent to which any of these are at an acceptable level vary widely. An example is the "rule of law" in Ashraf Ghani's list – one might well ask, "which law?" An answer that is likely to bring some stability to a region may be the establishment of order through application of Sharia Law, which is rooted in the faith of the population.

Sharia Law was used as an example in a discussion of a problem with international interventions, and a pragmatic solution, in a presentation on Afghanistan by Col Steve Noonan before an audience of university students in late 2007. He argued that one problem with the mission in Afghanistan is the American's desire to institute government in the same form as in the US. He suggested that it might be wiser to reinforce locally-acceptable forms of government that did not result in the violation of basic international principles. He said this could even be Sharia Law that, unlike American democracy, is deeply rooted in local culture.

This pragmatic position says basically that the development agent should not care how locals achieve stability as long as the effect of doing so results in acceptance of the government and does not violate internationally accepted norms. The external agent's job is to help the situation progress to that point. However, this stance assumes that there actually is something called an international community and that this "international community" has agreed on what these norms are and abides by them. Unfortunately it is not that simple, as becomes clear once these assumptions are closely examined. Nonetheless, the pragmatic stance is likely the most desirable, even if there are problems with the foundation of the argument. If it helps achieve a generally acceptable form of order and reinforces effective government in a region, it's good enough: that is about as clear as it gets in this business.

Who Has Agency And Takes Initiative: Shifting Locus Of Control Inward

Another area where a change in mindset is required is linked to the notion of "agency" – the question of who is doing the acting and who is being acted on. Most military discourse reinforces the notion that 'we' act on 'them'. The military draws on intelligence, it decides what needs to be done, and then others in the field receive their ordinance(s). This structure is not surprising considering the historical uses of military planning, but it is not well suited for Fourth Generation Warfare, especially the 75 per cent that is non-kinetic.

In development work, particularly at the non-directive and low-power end of the continuum of intervention strategies, agency is seen to rest with the host environment, and development workers do whatever they can to strengthen the local system's ability to take initiative and act. This can often be difficult, particularly in situations where the people have not been accustomed to freedom of choice and action beyond a limited sphere of influence. The more oppressive the power relations in an environment, the smaller the sphere of influence of the powerless. This is one explanation for high levels of family violence and alcohol abuse in colonized societies – these are often the only ways the powerless can exercise agency; in their households and on themselves.

The realization of being able to effect change in one's condition, coupled with a desire to do so, is a prerequisite for healthy development, and development agents should do whatever possible to shift the perception of the location of control from external to internal. That is, the way eternal agents operate should reinforce the power and initiative of the host system rather than decrease the host's ability to initiate action, even if it means achieving some tangible result more slowly than by doing it themselves. This can be difficult in a recovering fragile state given the fact that most of the resources and power are in the hands of outsiders.

Sustainable development requires ownership of the initiative by the host system rather than by the external party. While it may be difficult for military actors to refocus their approach, the more the local agencies believe in their own capacity and demonstrate their ability to take initiative and implement beneficial changes in their circumstances, the sooner victory will be achieved.

Development And The Concept Of "Adversary"

The concept of "adversary" which is a taken-for-granted foundation of most military discourse on Fourth Generation Warfare, is not a part of most development workers' thinking. This difference is another part of the change of mindset that military colleagues need to make as they strive to better understand the development dimension of counter-insurgency.

Most military analysis seems focused on dealing with an adversary to reduce its ability to do what it wants. In development thinking, the concept of adversary is not as evident as it is among the military, and this forms a foundation-level difference in approaches to the "mission". Development workers tend to see an entire region or community as an environment with which they are being invited to work, and there are positive, neutral and negative forces or energies in that environment that need to be taken into consideration and worked with as they try to help it move in a desirable direction. To base an intervention strategy on the idea that the main thing needed is to overwhelm or neutralize an adversary is foreign to how they think about their activities.

That does not mean that development workers ignore barriers to the changes they are trying to promote. Part of development thinking uses a force-field analysis strategy to identify negative and positive elements that tend to inhibit or promote a change from one level to another in an environment's condition. They try to help the people in the communities or organizations in which they work to weaken the resisting forces and strengthen the positive ones to achieve a desirable change in the situation. This is perhaps as close to "adversary" as they come.

In other intervention design models based on General System Theory (described earlier) they use the concept of open and closed boundaries between systems and sub-systems to identify where influence (both constructive and destructive) can flow to effect some change in the system's

CHAPTER 8

trajectory. They try to help the system's inhabitants do what they can to modify boundary conditions and the dynamics within relevant sub-systems to achieve alignment in a desirable direction. Factors linked to maintaining appropriate boundary conditions, where the appropriate amounts and kinds of influences can flow back and forth among sub-systems, are analyzed and incorporated in intervention strategies. The "adversary," if there is one, in systems models are factors linked to destructive, divergent and inappropriate flows of energy across boundaries – either too much or too little, or of the wrong kind and going to the wrong place (the narco-economy fuelling part of the insurgency in Afghanistan is an example). Development workers try to help the system use its own forces to bring those disruptive factors into a more constructive way of influencing how the system moves through time. The example of the narco-economy is a particularly complex and difficult situation that indicates the weakness of seeing things through a black-and-white "adversary" lens.

The concept of "adversary" is of limited use in the business world as well, as noted by a management consultant working in a very competitive environment (the high-tech sector) after reading a few articles on Fourth Generation Warfare.

> I was struck by the same concept of "adversary" and how it is so different from most non-military thinking. Even in the corporate world, the concept of adversary is usually toned down to "competitor", and competitors are always potential partners or merger/acquisition candidates.[111]

This indicates that part of the change of mindset that the military needs to make involves a shift away from looking at the world in terms of over-coming an adversary to a more complex and less-polarized way of thinking about working with the various actors and forces in an environment.

The unpredictable pattern of shifting allegiances that marks the history of conflicts in places like Afghanistan reinforces the limitations of the simple classification of groups into two camps – us and them, good guys and bad guys. There are many who may be in between these two poles, and today's adversary might become tomorrow's ally, depending on their perception of where their interests will be best met. Intervention strategies need to take this factor into account and the military should not operate in ways that make it difficult for any positive peace-oriented shifts to happen.

Development workers have their own changes to make in this regard: they have been characterized as "Pollyannas" who see all the local actors as members of the society who will listen to reason and who can be enlisted in programs to improve the system. Unfortunately there are people who do not want to be part of any programs they are offering and who will do everything in their power to resist their efforts, including committing atrocities such as beheading 13-year-old girls for going to school. When these brutal characters are on the scene it is clear there *is* an adversary, an us-and-them, good guys and bad guys, and the military's traditional concepts and tools are entirely appropriate.

While it may be difficult for the military to see an AO in any way other than through the "adversary" lens, it may be just as challenging for a development worker to recognize that the "Pollyanna" lens sometimes is not appropriate and that the use of deadly force may be required to help a community move forward along the development trajectory, especially when the level of violence in the society is at the lower end of the ten-point scale mentioned earlier. Both groups need to know when and how to change their mindsets in this regard.

Monitoring And Evaluation Of Effects

Appropriate monitoring and evaluation are essential in any effective development project or military campaign. "Appropriate" means measuring the right things and then doing the right things with the results of the analysis. This is not always taking place. A study of PRTs in Afghanistan and Iraq by a Princeton University team noted that evaluation of their activities measures inputs rather than outputs and their effects on their environments.[112] They usually report on the number of hours of training provided or amounts of funds spent rather than on the community's perception of these activities and the extent to which they move the situation toward victory by reinforcing the population's acceptance of the government and rejection of insurgents.

The capacity development analysis framework described in Chapter 4 provides a basis for description of the multiple levels and dimensions of functionality required in a well-performing society – these are potential areas for activity and assessment. Also, the notion of an institution as a lattice-like structure of roles and relationships that needs to be appropriately populated and activated to become a working organization can establish targets toward which an intervention can attempt to move a system. Properly-done impact evaluation can identify the extent to which priority areas are beginning to function appropriately and link inputs to effects (or lack thereof).

To minimize distortion caused by the observer effect, assessing community-level results of development interventions calls for indigenous assessment processes that are not obviously linked to the inputs being assessed. A goal-free strategy using evaluators who do not directly associate their inquiry with specific development activities can gather data on how communities have changed over the period in question, and attributions to specific in-puts can be made later, after responses have been collected and partially analyzed. In Kandahar, for example, household-level or neighbourhood-based assessments could be conducted by appropriately-trained local university students as part of their social and economic development-related field research work.

Indicators of achievement should include direct and indirect impacts of ac-tivities, since the indirect and unanticipated impacts may well be the more significant and sustainable results. Interpreters, for example, often learn things that increase their capacity to be of service to their communities and they take these skills with them when they move to other jobs. These by-products of an intervention are often more beneficial than the stated intention of the project.

There is another side to the monitoring and evaluation issue that needs to be taken into consideration: although cultural brokers are essential partici-pants in a stability initiative, in some cases their reports of effects should be taken with more than a grain of salt. The same holds true for government officials and community leaders. It can be difficult to determine the extent to which they are being forthright and their information can be taken at face value, or if they are telling the external agents what they think they want to hear. Since most foreigners are rather blind, deaf and dumb without their assistance, it is essential to reach beyond these windows and screens to find out more about what is really happening. An effective independent community-based monitoring and evaluation system is essential to mis-sion success.

Becoming A Learning Organization – Applying Results Of Evaluation

The US Army *Counterinsurgency* manual clearly defines becoming a learning organization as a strategic requirement in Fourth Generation Warfare. As noted earlier, they state, "In COIN, the side that learns faster and adapts more rapidly – the better learning organization – usually wins. Counterinsurgencies [sic] have been called learning competitions."[113]

Development workers with backgrounds in capacity development and organizational change would say there is a major challenge in this area. According to the Princeton University study of PRTs, one of the problems with the Afghan mission is a lack of systematic evaluation of neighbourhood-level impacts of PRT activities related to helping the population accept the legitimacy of government, which is an element required for "victory." There is not enough reliable information for systematic feedback loops to guide the system so it can learn from analysis of its performance and chart its course accordingly. It seems that while part of the system is saying it needs to become a learning organization, its operations (as reported in the Princeton study) are not demonstrating that capacity.

The literature on organizational change offers a rich array of methods for helping large systems become nimble learning organizations and a detailed review of this area is beyond the scope of this monograph. A few sources and comments will suffice.

An early classic is *When Giants Learn to Dance*, which documented changes made by IBM, Kodak and others to stay alive in rapidly changing environments.[114] The works of Chris Argyris are particularly useful – especially the concept of double-loop learning, which has also been promoted by Peter Senge and others. Also, authors who apply Chaos Theory to management have much to offer. Margaret Wheatley, for example, has worked with the US military to help open up the feedback loops across the ranks that make essential field-level information available to senior-level planners so they can properly direct their troops. She has also used Chaos Theory to analyze self-organized networks in the war on terror.[115] These all have something to offer counter-insurgency leaders who recognize that their systems need to constantly adapt to mirror the structures and strategies of anti-government forces.

However, it is well known that talking about change is easier than having it actually happen. Many organizations know they need to change when their feedback loops present them with information for which they are ill prepared, and even though they make valiant efforts to adjust themselves to new realities these shifts are often exceedingly difficult to implement. BGen Pepin's earlier statement about a change in mindset has deeper implications than might appear at the outset. The issue applies to communities as well as organizations.

One of the main factors contributing to resistance to fundamental change in organizations is their employees' natural desire to maintain the integrity of their personal structure of meaning, the cultural and psychological framework that defines their place in the social universe. This is especially prevalent among senior managers and leaders who derive much of their identities from the organizational contexts they have sacrificed the best years of their lives to build – in their own images. As these senior staff move toward retirement, many use targeted selection and grooming of culturally similar junior staff who are likely to replace them to maintain the integrity of the systems they have built – this is one reason for the persistence of an organization's structure and cultural traits from one leadership cadre to the next.

This factor is particularly evident in organizations that have a strong corporate culture, and whose members have relatively few pillars on which they base their identities. The military is a classic example of such an organization, with subliminal and powerful cultural factors that will try to undermine or subvert the changes required to adapt to the realities brought into the system by the feedback loops which are a core feature of a nimble learning organization.

This is because organizational change often means identity change, and most people will resist going through this process because it hurts – a lot. The psychological impact is akin to the bereavement cycle. Most normal people will avoid this process if they possibly can: this is one of the major factors underlying resistance to change and inhibiting the shift to becoming nimble learning organizations.

It is easy to say that a counter-insurgency is essentially a competition between two learning organizations and to assume that the military can learn and adapt faster than the insurgents – in reality this can be an exceedingly difficult dimension of the operation. As noted in the Princeton PRT study and other reports, counter-insurgencies have the added complexity of not being carried out by a single organization – they have to bring together a number of quite different agencies in an integrated, coherent effort, and to share and extract lessons from their varied experience that can influence how each of them work. Each participating agency has its own challenges in this area and needs to adjust its operations to be part of a nimble collective effort to help the host society move forward. The nature of this collaboration, and the extent to which each party needs to change how it usually operates to make it work, is a key to an effective campaign.

Collaboration – Is It Cohabitation, Assimilation Or Integration?

Collaboration with other agencies working in an AO can take different forms, which can be placed on a continuum marked by three types of relationships: cohabitation, assimilation and integration. The points on the continuum denote the extent to which the parties are expected to change how they operate so the relationship can be maintained. Each form of collaboration has its particular cultural and organizational dynamics and power relationships, and its own set of advantages and disadvantages.

Cohabitation

Cohabitation is a situation in which two parties coexist and may be aware of each other's activities, but this awareness does not contribute to any meaningful change in the internal workings of either party. Each continues operating in the manner to which it has become accustomed. There may be superficial and polite (or not so polite) interaction at their points of contact but they do not exert significant influence on each other's internal processes.

Examples of cohabitation in Canadian society could be ethnic enclaves in a large city where language and family patterns continue to reflect the cultures of origin, or the traditional Mennonite, Hutterite and Doukhobor communities in various parts of the country. In peace and security missions it could be the relationship between the military and humanitarian aid agencies that want to remain neutral in a conflict. There may be occasional contact between the two groups but there is little significant exchange of information or influence that will prompt either party to change how it operates. It is essentially a two-solitudes type of relationship.

Advantages

The advantage of cohabitation is the apparent lack of inconvenience experienced by either party: each goes on working with little impact from the other, and nobody is overly influenced or inconvenienced by how the other operates. It appears to be a comfortable, no-change situation.

Disadvantages

The disadvantage of a cohabitation relationship is that there is no significant exchange of information or skills that would increase the performance of either party. They cannot benefit from each other's expertise and adapt the lessons learned by one group to improve the practices of the other. Also, there is a security dimension: if this relationship exists in a society in which there are extremes of wealth and poverty, and the poor can see the conditions in which the other party lives but they do not have access to an adequate share of the wealth in the society, the situation can become dangerously unstable – the poor may take extreme measures to disrupt the existing social order. Examples are the urban riots by unemployed immigrant youth in France in 2007 and in the black ghettos in the US during the 1960s.

Assimilation

The classic assimilation model is the American melting pot, where the larger party is in control and the smaller party is absorbed into the majority. The weaker party adapts itself so it can coexist with the larger group, whose culture and traditional practices are not much changed by the presence of the smaller group. In some sense it is a win-lose model, where the weaker party loses something to be part of the larger whole.

The underlying idea seems to be something like, "This is my field (or game) now, and if you want to play on my field you'd better learn my rules. If you don't want to play by my rules, go find another field." There is an assumption that the characteristics of the larger group are to remain unchanged and smaller groups are to acquire these traits to have the relationship.

Advantages

Assimilation seems convenient, particularly to members of the larger or stronger group, because they do not have to change. Members of smaller groups sometimes also find the arrangement desirable because they can become like the majority and partake of its benefits. It is a common model of intergroup dynamics among entities that have unequal levels of power.

Disadvantages

Although assimilation seems desirable, there are major difficulties with what is essentially a win-lose model of intergroup relations. It can contribute to problems especially when the minorities begin to think they are being asked to give up too much to remain part of the society (as in French Canada). In some cases they rebel – many of the civil wars in the world are related to difficulties associated with assimilation. Also, the weaker party needs to learn and use the language and thought patterns of the majority to remain in the relationship, and as such they cannot fully express themselves and the richness of their full and free voice cannot be heard. This limits the potential for growth in the system and deprives the majority of the potentially essential contributions of the minority.

Integration

Integration is a situation in which both parties change – in mathematics the definition is "to make whole by a combination of parts." This is a win-win (or lose-lose) model in relationships in which everybody gives up something so they can be united.

Advantages

Integration is an equitable but rare model of intergroup relations. Once both parties agree to make the sacrifices they need to make to achieve harmony and equity, the relationship is usually more effective than the other two models. It promotes what is known as "hybrid vigour" in which the total is actually greater than the sum of its parts, as in genetics, where the mixed-breed offspring often is superior to either of the purebred parents. Hitler was dead wrong: the master race is the mongrel, not the pure breed. Multi-disciplinary teams that achieve integration are more productive than others that operate on an assimilation model.

CHAPTER 8

Disadvantages

Integration is difficult to achieve, particularly in situations where there is a history of inequitable power relationships. It requires identity change by all parties and can take more time and effort than most people are willing to give. The introduction of the *Official Languages Act* in Canada is an example – the majority was unexpectedly inconvenienced by the fact there were French-speaking people in the country and public servants had to learn French if they wanted to progress in their careers. Some unilingual Anglophone senior public servants resigned or took early retirement in response.

Groups that try to achieve open, authentic and meaningful levels of interaction as they come together usually find they must go through the difficult but ultimately rewarding process of integration. It can be particularly challenging for people who have been accustomed to being in a position of control, such as in the military's chain of command.

Implications For Development-Military Collaboration

Ideally the concept of integration should be applied at all levels of an intervention, from the policy formulation and conceptual phase through all steps to the application of a country's resources and expertise in the field. This would call for joint policy and planning groups in the host country, as is the case with the UK's PRT, and shared control of funding and operations at all levels down to the personnel working in the communities. Most collaboration missions do not have this high a level of integration. Some of the PRTs, for example, have multiple lines of management with each function reporting separately to their respective head offices. This makes collaboration and coordination of the intervention's strategy, operations and tactical level activity difficult. Others ensure effective integration by requiring signatures from the three main agencies – defence, diplomacy and development – before money can be spent. In some the bulk of the budget is controlled by the development sector, putting the military in an essential but subordinate position in the power hierarchy.

The ideal version of 3D or the "Whole of Government" approach implies that CIDA's development workers, DND personnel and DFAIT staff and members of other participating agencies should form collaborative units at each level that enable their diverse contributions to merge in a single integrated output. There is considerable work needed to implement the "Whole for Government" approach – the administrative machinery of all participating agencies needs to be changed to operate in an integrated fashion rather than in the parallel stovepipes to which they have been accustomed. They are shifting from cohabitation toward integration, and hopefully they will not become stuck in assimilation along the way.

Military As Partner Rather Than Leader Of Mission

The concept of 3D or the "Whole of Government" approach entails a change in roles which may be a challenge for the military and for other normally autonomous government agencies – they all need to shift from being independent to being a partner in how a mission is to unfold. This is a quite different stance than is implicit in most military vocabulary and its underlying culture, which is clear that the military assumes it acts on the environment rather than working with the various other actors in an AO including the recipient of its efforts. Development agents, on the other hand, are supposed to work with rather than on the host environment – a quite different non-directive orientation that might easily be misread by the more directive military partners as weakness and indecision and they may tend to run roughshod over their development colleagues as a result. This is not collaboration but domination, and needs to be countered in an integrated mission.

ISAF operations and CIDA's unit in Kandahar had a way of ensuring that an appropriate level and type of collaboration was a feature of their activities. To operationalize the equal status of the major collaborating agencies in the eyes of the military, equivalent rank status was accorded to the head of the development unit. The ISAF DEVAD, for example, had equivalent brigadier-general rank. The same principle was instituted in Kandahar, where the senior CIDA representative had full colonel rank. This rank equivalent gave the DEVADs complete access to meetings and senior personnel, and ensured lower rank military officers responded to them in an appropriate manner when asked to provide information or assist with their operations.

This indicates that the way to ensure the military sees the other parties in the collaboration as full partners is to give their unit heads the same equivalent rank as the senior military officer. While this may be required by the military on a joint mission, it was the cause of some bemusement to the development staff (both were young women) since the notion of rank and much of what is implied in a chain of command was foreign to how they were accustomed to operating. They soon became accustomed to it, however, and found that fitting in to the military structure helped get the job done.

This strategy is more in the assimilation category above than integration, in that the powerful party (the military) accorded the weaker parties high status on the military's terms, so there would be minimal disruption of the military mindset as they went forward. It could be seen as an identity-maintenance strategy on the part of the military that the development workers accepted, and given the circumstances it seems to make sense. The military way of seeing the world did not have to change much to make this work.

However, if in another situation other actors take the lead, such as the representative of DFAIT, for example, and their hierarchy structures are imposed on other parties such as the military, police and development workers, the adjustment may be more difficult. The military may have difficulty knowing how to relate to these other actors if they are not given equivalent rank and placed in a known pigeon-hole in the military's view of the social universe. Some of the other PRTs in Afghanistan have joint leadership structures which place the military in a parallel or even subordinate support role. These relationships are difficult to manage.

To make any of these partnerships work it has been found that interpersonal relationships and key individuals' personalities must be taken into consideration. A number of PRTs described in the Princeton report were not functioning well because of personality issues that could probably not have been resolved even if appropriate structures and rank equivalents were in place.

The change in mindset described by BGen Pepin and highlighted in the Princeton report (and by others) as a requirement for effective multi-agency counter-insurgency operations is a challenging issue – it requires concerted effort to establish appropriate structural and interpersonal relationships to ensure the mission is to be an effective partnership of the military and other key agencies.

Summary

Being able to think about both kinetic and non-kinetic activities at the same time is a challenge requiring considerable effort, good interagency and interpersonal communication, and a clear and shared understanding of the purpose of the mission. While the temptation to move quickly and use kinetic measures in response to a situation may be paramount in a commander's thinking, a development worker's approach may be quite different. As noted earlier in the example given by Lane and Sky, a group of angry villagers confronting a local official may be simply demanding an equitable distribution of resources that the official had been giving only to his own sub-group in the area. A number of visits by a development worker who drinks multiple cups of tea while patiently urging the official to grasp basic concepts of good governance is likely to achieve a more sustainable beneficial effect than a kinetic response to that official's panic call for an air strike on the angry mob of villagers that is besieging his office.

Military and development actors need accurate information about the communities they serve so they can know which strategy to use at a given time. Reliable community-level analysis is required to properly assess local conditions and the impacts of counter-insurgency inputs, and to know the extent to which these inputs help move the situation toward victory – the population's acceptance of the government and cessation of support for the insurgents. When fostering change in the community, external actors need to be in the background, leading from behind, and the local agencies should be the prime visible actors.

Accurate feedback loops need to influence how the international agencies operate and, if necessary, promote changes in their ideologies, perceptions and behaviours. This can be difficult in part because it might provoke deep level change and evoke the natural tendency to maintain the integrity of one's structure of meaning, the foundation of one's identity. Identity is particularly strong in the military, with the whole command structure creating physical, cultural and psychological spaces in which people live. Resistance to significant organizational change is a normal part of identity maintenance, which can be overcome in part by entering into authentic shared-power relationships with other participants in the counter-insurgency campaign.

Subtle use of power is not a universal military skill and can elicit identity change processes in people who are accustomed to being in control. Moving into unfamiliar power relationships with development workers who don't know the meaning of "sir" and all that goes with it can be a challenge but it is possible if conditions are right and the mix of personalities is appropriate.

The obedience factor in the military can help in this regard: members will usually do new things if they are ordered to do it and they may learn new patterns of thought and behaviour by osmosis, through frequent collaboration with others on whom they depend to achieve a desirable result – the behavioural-level interaction can produce the attitudinal-level change of mindset that is required.

Leadership in these integrated missions requires collaborative personalities, members who are better at listening and fostering creative problem solving in others than in telling them what to do.

The multiple actors in a counter-insurgency should have a clear vision of the path to victory in the local context, and need to believe that each is really dependent on the others to get the job done. Working together on a common urgent task builds bridges across many gaps and can weld the disparate members together into a cohesive integrated unit whose members reflect both the military and developmental perspectives and know when one should lead and the other follow. If they work well together the result will be an acceleration of movement of the local area along a desirable trajectory of growth.

There are several tools that can be used to identify appropriate personnel and to increase the cohesiveness, alignment and effectiveness of a multi-agency group of professionals in a counter-insurgency campaign: these are described in the next chapter.

CHAPTER 9

Tools of the Trade

Introduction

This chapter describes a few of the many tools available to increase the effectiveness of an intervention in an AO. It begins with summaries of two approaches used in development: an asset-based strategy and a sustainable livelihoods approach. It then discusses intercultural relations and personality issues, and closes with an example of a culturally and contextually appropriate approach to strategic planning that was used to good effect in a unit of the Afghan government.

Deficit-Based Versus Asset-Based Strategies

Most development activity begins with a needs analysis of some sort that usually produces a long list of what is wrong and needs to be fixed. Inputs are then based on this analysis of the deficits in a community or organization. While there is no doubt that there are many problems to be addressed, a deficit-based analysis does not focus on what is right about the way a community or organization operates nor does it set out to build on existing capacities to reinforce its strengths.

Capacity development needs to build on what *already exists*, and to use the energies and skills of the local people to help the system progress. There are a variety of ways of identifying an area's strengths and capacities, several of which are outlined below.

Appreciative inquiry

Appreciative inquiry (AI) is a process of working with a population to identify and reinforce its strengths that acts as a motivator that spurs them on to further achievements:

> [AI] is a strategy for purposeful change that identifies the best of "what is" to pursue dreams and possibilities of "what could be." It

is a co-operative search for the strengths, passions and life-giving forces that are found within every system – those factors that hold the potential for inspired, positive change.

The appreciative approach involves collaborative inquiry, based on interviews and affirmative questioning, to collect and celebrate the good news stories of a community – those stories that enhance cultural identity, spirit and vision. [AI] is a way of seeing that is selectively attentive to – and affirming of – the best and highest qualities in a system, a situation or another human being. It involves an appreciation for the mystery of being and a reverence for life.[116]

There are other descriptions that are somewhat less poetic – the general idea is to identify, appreciate and reinforce a system's strengths.

Asset-Based Community Development Institute

The Asset-Based Community Development Institute is based at the Institute for Policy Research of Northwestern University in the US. This Institute has a network of practitioners and provides a variety of resources to support its vision of development, which is:

[To challenge] the traditional approach to solving urban problems, which focuses service providers and funding agencies on the needs and deficiencies of neighbourhoods, … (the Institute has) demonstrated that community assets are key building blocks in sustainable urban and rural community revitalization efforts. These community assets include:

- the skills of local residents
- the power of local associations
- the resources of public, private and non-profit institutions
- the physical and economic resources of local places.[117]

Asset-based strategies are more empowering than the usual deficit-based approach and the assessment and intervention tools they provide are useful. Nevertheless, some practitioners can be rather messianic about their work and need to be approached with a bit of caution.

Sustainable livelihoods approach

Many development agencies are applying a sustainable livelihoods approach that uses a whole-system framework to identify and strengthen the many factors affecting the quality and standard of living in an area.

> [It] places people, rural poor people in particular, at the centre of a web of inter-related influences that affect how they create a livelihood. Closest to the people at the centre of the framework are the resources and *livelihood assets* that they have access to and use, which can include natural resources, technologies, their skills, knowledge and capacity, their health, access to education, sources of credit, or their networks of social support. Access to these assets is strongly influenced by their *vulnerability context*, taking into account trends (for example, economic, political, technological), shocks (for example, epidemics, natural disasters, civil strife) and seasonality (for example, prices, production, employment opportunities). Access is also influenced by the prevailing social, institutional and political environment, which affects how people combine and use their assets to achieve their goals. These are their *livelihood strategies*.[118]

A variety of tools are available from the Institute of Development Studies in the UK, which operates "Livelihoods Connect", a web-based resource and distance learning program based on the sustainable livelihoods approach to eliminating poverty. Materials are available in multiple languages including Dari and Pashto.

The approach is driven by a set of principles which include being people-centred, holistic, dynamic, building on strengths, promoting micro-macro links, encouraging partnerships and aiming for sustainability. It is a broad-based approach to identifying and reinforcing the array of factors linked sustainable ways of improving livelihoods in a region. It is one of the foundations of most constructive counter-narcotics programs, which seek to replace opium cultivation with other marketable crops and to address the range of other supports required to make the replacement viable.

Participatory rural appraisal

Participatory rural appraisal (PRA) is one of several similar techniques to engage locals in assessment and implementation of development initiatives.

Based on the work of Robert Chambers and others, it is a well-known method with a large body of supporting literature, and it can be applied to urban as well as rural communities. This method has been described as follows:

> [PRA] is a label given to a growing family of participatory approaches and methods that emphasize local knowledge and enable local people to make their own appraisal, analysis, and plans. PRA uses group animation and exercises to facilitate information sharing, analysis, and action among stakeholders. Although originally developed for use in rural areas, PRA has been employed successfully in a variety of settings. The purpose of PRA is to enable development practitioners, government officials, and local people to work together to plan context appropriate programs.

> Participatory rural appraisal evolved from rapid rural appraisal – a set of informal techniques used by development practitioners in rural areas to collect and analyze data. Rapid rural appraisal developed in the 1970s and 1980s in response to the perceived problems of outsiders missing or miscommunicating with local people in the context of development work. In PRA, data collection and analysis are undertaken by local people, with outsiders facilitating rather than controlling. PRA is an approach for shared learning between local people and outsiders, but the term is somewhat misleading. PRA techniques are equally applicable in urban settings and are not limited to assessment only. The same approach can be employed at every stage of the project cycle and in country economic and sector work.[119]

Intercultural Relations Skills

Effective intercultural relations are key to mission success – these issues effect relations between external agents and the local population as well as among varied members of a multinational military coalition, and with other types of agencies such as development-related NGOs and other organizations working in the AO. According to the literature on multinational military missions:

> …cultural differences in cognition and in world view can seriously impede smooth coordination among allies….multinational forces

are often used during... (operations that) include goals as varied as deterring hostile actions, combating terrorism, and providing relief from natural disasters. These missions are undertaken by coalition forces from divergent national cultures but also including non-governmental organizations and private voluntary organizations... Each member of the coalition may have its own agenda and its own leadership expectations and style. Multi-national missions vary in goals, while the participants vary in their agendas and command structure....Cultural differences... affect planning, problem detection, situation awareness, uncertainty management, and decision making. If commanders assume that others interpret and react as they do, manage uncertainty as they do, and think about real and hypothetical issues as they do, there can be problems...[120]

This quote refers to cultural issues among the various interveners in an AO – it does not refer to relationships with the people who are the permanent inhabitants and administrators of that area, a factor that would make the issue even more complex.

There are two main approaches to intercultural training that can be termed trait-based and relational. The trait-based approach is the more common description of a variety of characteristics that are presumed to be broadly representative of the way of life of the people in the area in which a mission will operate. While this strategy has some utility and seems to be popular, it has major limitations. It does not account for the variability of patterns of thought and belief that exist in any group of people, and it does not usually include any significant reference to the culture of the external agent that is intervening in the society.

No large group of people is homogenous and there are major differences within any country or region: poor labourers or farmers have a quite different way of thinking and behaving than do the upper classes, for example. Also, there are major similarities across groups. Military personnel of one country often have more in common with another county's military personnel than they do with artists or social workers in their own society. The same holds true for development workers – they likely have more in common with their counterparts from other countries than they might with stockbrokers or soldiers from their own country (see Figure 7 on p. 202).

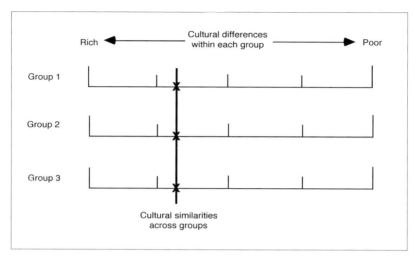

FIGURE 7 – CULTURAL DIFFERENCES WITHIN GROUPS & SIMILARITIES ACROSS GROUPS.

The relational model is useful in addressing these aspects of intercultural issues. The model acknowledges that there are differences within any identifiable group of people, and that while it is necessary to have some sense of the major features of the society, these are usually taught in the form of stereotypes which are based on national-level units of analysis (Greeks are like this, the French are like that, etc.) and may not be accurate for the individuals and small groups with whom one is working.

A clear example of the limitations of the trait-based approach is the generally accepted notion that women are dominated by men in Afghan society and they have no voice in the affairs of state. While that may be so in the majority of cases, there are families in which the husband is the primary care-giver for the children and the wife is the energetic, out-going professional who may be a senior government official and is active in meetings with members of the military and development organization personnel. It would be a major error to relate to such women leaders as if they were oppressed and had no voice in their domestic and national environments.

In these cases the information received in the typical pre-departure cross-cultural briefing does not apply. There is a need for an approach that increases the likelihood of an external agent establishing a productive relationship with people whose cultures are quite different than their own, regardless of where the local person may be on their society's range of cultural characteristics.

This relational strategy focuses more on what is happening within the external agent than on trying to pigeon-hole the traits of the host-country national to match a set of behaviours that were taught in a workshop back home. It is designed to permit the external agent to establish and maintain an effective relationship while gathering information during the interaction so it is possible to figure out what is going on and how to behave to keep the relationship productive. The strategy applies in any interaction with people from any cultural group: it is not ethno-specific.

This more fluid strategy is based on self-management in out-group relations so a person can figure out what is going on while it is happening and manage their own end of the interaction as effectively as possible to keep the relationship going. It entails monitoring one's own emotional state while communicating with the other, and observing and catching troublesome emotions before they surface and negatively influence behaviour. It is a mindful suspension of judgment that allows more information to accumulate and perceptions to be verified before potentially problematic reactions occur. It is based on the fact that one's emotions are a window into the deeper and largely subliminal sets of rules that form the foundation of our personal culture – when interaction is taking place with a person who is of a culture similar to one's own, there are relatively few significant violations of the subliminal rule sets used to manage the interaction – both are on much the same wave length so the rules are largely transparent and usually elicit no emotions. However, when interacting with a person from another cultural group (such as a foreigner or a member of another professional group in one's own society) there may well be infractions of these subliminal rules – they will provoke emotions such as insecurity, frustration, anxiety or anger, any of which can have an impact on the quality of interpersonal communication at the time. Observing these emotions and preventing them from negatively influencing one's own behaviour is a key self-management skill in relating with people of other cultures (outgroups). It has also been called a temporary "suspension of judgment" to allow more information to accumulate so appropriate behaviours can be selected to optimize the quality of the relationship. It is relatively easy to learn this approach in a short intercultural relations training workshop.

The ability to self-manage in this way, and other characteristics linked to effective intercultural relations, are not evenly distributed in a society: some people are better suited to this than others. Some of these capacities are measurable and it possible to identify people who would be more or less effective in an intercultural encounter.

Multicultural Personality Questionnaire

The Princeton PRT study repeatedly noted that personalities play a huge role in effective PRTs and other civilian-military operations: cross-cultural relations competency is a key element in these relationships. The Multicultural Personality Questionnaire (MPQ) is a personality assessment instrument that was constructed specifically to describe behaviour when one is interacting with people from different cultures and can be used to predict how easily people are likely to adjust to other cultures and come to feel comfortable with them. It is a proven psychometric test that assesses five dimensions of personality related to effective intercultural relations. This applies as much to cultural differences among professions and organizations within the same society as to international or inter-tribal dimensions of inter-group relations.

The MPQ has been reviewed by the CF and has been found to be a soundly designed instrument with good potential for improving how the CF operates in situations where intercultural relations competencies are important factors in ensuring operational effectiveness.[121]

A short description of each of the five personality factors assessed by the MPQ follows.

Cultural empathy

This scale assesses the capacity to identify with the feelings, thoughts and behaviour of individuals from different cultural backgrounds. To function effectively with people of other cultures, it is important to acquire some understanding of those cultures, and cultural empathy seems important to "reading" other cultures.

People who score high on cultural empathy are able to identify with the feelings, thoughts, and behaviours of people and groups who are part of different cultures. People with a low score have difficulties in identifying with the feelings, thoughts and behaviours of people and groups with different cultural backgrounds.

Open-mindedness

This scale assesses people's capacity to be open and unprejudiced when encountering people outside of their own cultural group and who may have different values and norms. This ability, just like cultural empathy, seems vital to understanding the rules and values of other cultures and to coping with them in an effective manner.

People who score high on open-mindedness have an open and unprejudiced attitude towards other groups, cultural values and norms and are open to new ideas. People who score low are characterized by a predisposed attitude and a tendency to judge and stereotype other groups.

Social initiative

Social initiative denotes people's tendency to approach social situations actively and to take initiative. This determines the degree to which they interact easily with people from different cultures and make friends within other cultures.

People who score high on this scale have a tendency to be active in social situations and to take initiative. They will tend to be outgoing when in another culture. People who score low on this scale are less inclined to take initiative. They will be rather reserved and stay in the background.

Emotional stability

This scale assesses the degree to which people tend to remain calm in stressful situations. When working in another culture it is important to be able to cope well with psychological and emotional discomfort. A variety of factors (political system, procedures, lack of means and resources, impediments) may cause things in different cultures not to work in the same way as they do in one's own culture. When things do not go the way they do in one's own culture, this may lead to frustration, tension, fear, social detachment, financial problems and interpersonal conflicts.

People who score high on this scale tend to remain calm in stressful situations. People who score low on this scale exhibit strong emotional reactions to stress.

Flexibility

This scale is associated with people's ability to adjust their behaviour to new and unknown situations. When working in another culture it is important to be able to change strategies because customary and trusted ways of doing things do not always work in a new cultural environment.

People who score high on flexibility perceive new and unknown situations as a challenge. They are able to change behavioural patterns in response to unexpected or constrained circumstances within another culture. People who score low are quicker to see new and unknown situations as a threat. In addition they tend to stick to trusted behavioural patterns. Consequently they are less able to adjust their behavioural pattern in reaction to unexpected or constrained circumstances in another culture.[122]

Summary

The MPQ is consistent with the relational approach to intercultural relations training described above. It is not ethno-specific and focuses more on the characteristics of the intervener than on the traits of the people with whom she or he may work.

Personality is a key success-related factor in multidisciplinary and interagency operations. Situations of high ambiguity require leaders who are open, flexible, and collaborative, and who know they need all the information they can get from others before making decisions. The personality characteristics of these effective leaders are often not those that are associated with high visibility in an organization, a factor which is often linked to promotion and career advancement.

This can contribute to difficulty in organizational effectiveness. In the legal profession, for example, the mid-career lawyers who come to the attention of superiors usually are the aggressive A-types whose competitive nature has been recognized by receiving one promotion after another. At some point these people who have been rewarded for their barracuda-like personalities are put in charge of a team of strong-willed professionals and asked to create a collegial working environment. They are expected to shift overnight from being aggressive and competitive to being supportive and collaborative, which is often difficult to achieve. The soldier who rises quickly through the ranks and has been rewarded for aggressive, competitive traits is likely not the most suitable candidate to lead a collaborative multidisciplinary team which has members who don't know the meaning of the word "sir" and all that goes with it.

The MPQ has the ability to identify a range of personality traits that can be used in the selection of personnel who are suitable for leadership and membership in the highly ambiguous environments in which development and military personnel find themselves collaborating to strengthen the host society's ability to manage its own affairs.

Appropriate Approach To Strategic Planning

This section is a summary of a planning method used with good effect in late 2007 to help the ACSI develop a strategic plan a year after the building was completed and they had moved in and set up operations. Normally such planning is done well before an architect is commissioned, but as often happens in international development, a donor wanted to build a public service training facility and received necessary approvals on the assumption that the more complex planning work was being done in parallel. This did not happen and it was necessary to create a plan for an organization that was already in some sort of operational mode without a comprehensive framework in place. This called for a contextually appropriate approach to strategic planning.

Although the military has well-established planning methods, they do not always suit the context in a developing country. The need for alternate approaches was cited by a member of the third SAT group after reading an earlier draft version of this monograph:

> Another thing that resonated with me is the differences in approach that you describe between the military and civilian actors. The drive by military actors, in particular ISAF, to see concrete results of progress over their relatively short tours often just results in a waste of effort and eventual frustration. In particular,

> ISAF has been pushing for an overall plan for the transition of
> civil aviation to Afghan authorities, since all of the airports
> and airspace in the country are effectively run by various foreign
> military entities at the moment. This plan, according to ISAF,
> must include definitions of all required activities with timelines,
> responsibilities, etc. The problems with this are numerous – not
> least of which is that it fails to realize that public sector reform
> must make substantial progress before the Afghans are even ca-
> pable of helping with, nevermind overseeing or leading, imple-
> mentation of such a thing. To me, this is where the concept of
> "management by groping along" comes into play. Everyone
> knows, roughly speaking, what the end state must be – however
> coming up with an all-encompassing plan to actually get there is,
> to my mind, impossible in the current environment. By constant-
> ly spending time trying to draft this plan and forcing the issue on
> the [Government of Afghanistan], ISAF is actually making things
> worse and creating friction and conflict. They would have more
> success, in my opinion, by putting a focused effort into analyzing
> the situation in more depth with a view to discovering opportun-
> ities where their help could make substantial contribution.[123]

There are many approaches to strategic planning, the best of which are
highly participatory and suited to the realities of the organization's environment. A well-known method is to create a vision of a fully-functioning
organization at some time in the future (usually five years hence), carry
out an analysis of current internal and external conditions (e.g. Strengths,
Weaknesses, Opportunities & Threats [SWOT]), and then to prepare
short-term and medium-term work plans to fill in the gaps between current
conditions and the vision of the future organization.

As noted in the above quote, in the planning of military training the process
usually begins with a detailed analysis of desired outputs or competencies
and the numbers of students completing training in a given period, and
works backwards from there to design the entire training program. While
there is nothing fundamentally wrong with it, this traditional linear approach to strategic planning presumes that the future is predictable and
people can provide the required information. It is not appropriate where
the future is uncertain, resource levels are unpredictable, desired outputs
are not clearly defined at the outset, and the steps required to produce
these results are likely to be full of unforeseen circumstances.

The standard approach also presumes that the host country can answer the basic questions that normally underpin linear strategic planning. As noted in the above quote, many don't have that information, such as knowing how many graduates they want, with what skills and over what period of time, so the plan cannot be anchored on that level of analysis – a more fluid and open-ended model is needed to help them get to that point.

In the current turbulent environment of Afghanistan, a more flexible planning approach is appropriate, based on the works of Ralph Stacey (*Managing the Unknowable*) and others. This approach defines a general mission or purpose for the organization, and uses a participatory method by which a series of short-term plans are created to guide the organization along its path in the direction of that mission.[124] This approach is more compatible with Afghan cultural processes related to planning than is the typical longer-term linear approach previously described.

This strategic plan defines the Institute's mission, a number of desired outputs or services, and describes the participatory procedure and work plans the organization needs to move in a coherent fashion toward its objectives.

Organizational Context Of A Strategic Plan

An organization's strategic plan is part of a broader set of elements as illustrated in the following figure:

FIGURE 8 – ORGANIZATIONAL CONTEXT OF A STRATEGIC PLAN.

These elements are described as follows:

- Most organizations have a "vision" – a lofty ideal to which they aspire, which is supported by their mission statement, usually a short sentence describing their purpose or reason for existing.

- Each unit has a work plan with a mission or purpose that supports the organization's mission, with desired results expressed in measurable terms, and the supports needed to accomplish those results.

- Employees have job descriptions that define their reporting relationships and 4 to 6 main areas of responsibility. They also have work plans for specific time frames that describe activities in each area of responsibility and their intended results, again in measurable terms, and the supports they need to do their work.

- Performance management guides employee activity during the work plan period; the performance evaluation periodically assesses employees' results and describes why they were greater or less than in the work plan.

- Information from performance reviews and from new elements in the broader environment (changes in technology, etc.) contributes to staff development programming.

- Organizational development is influenced by external factors as well as findings from staff development, and in turn can contribute to changes in the organization's vision and mission statement.

Each component is linked to the others.

A strategic plan defines three of these elements: the organization's vision and mission statement, unit-level missions and work plans, and employee job descriptions and work plans, with its primary focus on the first two. The plan also describes how the organization will evolve as it moves forward in time, by indicating changes in these three components.

Method

The following is a description of the method used to prepare this strategic plan.

An ongoing cycle of planning

Strategic planning is a cyclical activity that continues as long as an organization exists. Put simply, it is a periodic consultative process that produces a plan document that answers four questions:

1. Where do you want to go?

2. Where are you now?

3. How are you going to get from where you are now to where you want to go?

Once these questions have been answered, the last question completes the planning cycle:

4. Where do you want to go next?

The answer to this fourth question starts the next cycle of the planning process, which begins again with the first three steps, and the entire process repeats itself at regular intervals – whenever required, usually every six months, and at least annually – as the organization moves forward in time and appropriate plans are prepared for each time period.

All relevant stakeholders, especially senior staff and others who have reliable information about the organization's purpose, resources, operations, clients and environment are involved in this process.

Components of the plan and its implementation

A number of steps are involved in preparing and implementing a strategic plan:

1. define the organization's vision and mission;

2. conduct a baseline analysis – a description of current conditions;

3. define desired services and outputs or deliverables – the organization's activities and results – to the extent possible under the circumstances;

4. conduct a "gap analysis" between the baseline and desired outputs;

5. carry out an institutional design and development process to bridge the gaps; and

6. plan program activity: prepare unit work plans and senior-level job descriptions.

These first six steps produce a plan document. The next two steps implement the plan and prepare for the next cycle of the planning process:

7. implement and guide program activity based on work plans; and

8. do regular monitoring, evaluation and feedback to guide the organization's progress and contribute to the next cycle of the planning process.

Activities for each unit in the organization are recorded in the following format, and these are updated whenever required.

SAMPLE UNIT WORKPLAN FORMAT

Work unit name: _____

Mission/Purpose: _____ _____

Reporting relationship: _____

Workplan period: _____

Work Unit Respon- sibilities	Main Activities	Anticipated Results	Method of Measure- ment	Authority & Account- ability	Supports Required
Duty 1	Activity 1.1				
	Activity 1.2				
	Etc.				
Duty 2					
etc.					

FIGURE 9 – SAMPLE UNIT WORKPLAN FORMAT.

Preparing these unit workplans to manage operations and address the gaps identified earlier completes the strategic planning process. The next steps will be the implementation of the plan as indicated in each of the unit workplans. Unit performance monitoring is recorded in the following format.

SAMPLE WORK UNIT PERFORMANCE MONITORING FORMAT

Work unit name: _____

Mission/Purpose: _____

Reporting relationship: _____

Workplan period: _____

Work Unit Responsibilities	Main Activities	Anticipated Results	Level of Achievement	Reasons for Variance	Authority & Accountability
Duty 1	Activity 1.1				
	Activity 1.2				
	Etc.				
Duty 2					
etc.					

FIGURE 10 – SAMPLE WORK UNIT PERFORMANCE MONITORING FORMAT.

Engaging local staff and the organization's leaders in filling out these workplans so they present a realistic picture of the system produces relevant plans and helps local staff better understand and take charge of the planning process. It is a capacity-building exercise as well as a planning process.

Afghan managers and staff said they understood this planning framework, and it would be effective in helping the Institute's personnel set out a number of stepping stones to identify the work needed to guide the organization's operations.

Summary

This chapter has briefly described a few of the tools used by development specialists in their services to the communities and organizations they help to strengthen. They encourage workers to identify and build on existing capacities rather than focusing only on the weaknesses in the host country's systems. It has also described an approach and a resource that can be used to increase the effectiveness of the many intercultural dimensions of peace and security missions.

One of the major factors to consider in achieving mission success is that cultural differences within one's own cultural group, such as between two members of the same society who have conflicting values and personality styles, often have greater negative impact that cultural differences between members of two quite different societies. One expects the latter and readily considers that interpersonal difficulties may be linked to culture. However when one has difficulties with people from one's own society or a country with a similar way of life (such as Canada and the US, for example) the possibility of there being a cultural dimension is rarely considered – it is more likely that the difficulties will be attributed to personal or professional shortcomings rather than thinking there may be subtle differences in cultural patterning at the root of the problem. Effective cross-cultural training based on the relational model coupled with staff selection guided by the results of the MPQ (or any similar instrument) will reduce the likelihood that problems with intercultural relations will negatively impact organizational effectiveness.

While the military uses a number of proven organizational tools to guide its operations, these are based on a rich context with a vast web of pre-existing conditions, many of which are simply taken for granted by most in the service. When working in an emerging post-conflict state it is essential to recognize that this assumed foundation is probably not yet present, and that planning and organization development strategies need to begin at a point that may differ markedly from the systems with which the foreign worker is familiar.

The approach to strategic planning described above was well understood by the Afghans with whom it was used, and produced guidance frameworks that were well suited to the emerging nature of their organizations. They could not specify how many graduates they wanted and the particular competencies required, but they had a general idea of the types of services they wanted the Institute to provide. The plan helped them develop a roadmap to follow so they could approach the level of operations that could define the specifics one would normally expect in a plan for a public service training institution.

Beginning where the situation currently is, and building on its strengths to help the society move itself in a constructive direction are two of the foundational principles of development. This is particularly challenging in fragile states with an active counter-insurgency, since the world has not yet acquired the full range of institutions and resources needed to address these issues. This institutional framework, and the training and administration for "Whole of Government" missions are discussed in the next and final chapter.

CHAPTER 10

The Way Forward

Introduction

As humanity progresses from one stage to the next along the difficult path toward global peace and security, it is becoming clear that a number of normally distinct and separate fields of practice must better understand each other so they can collaborate in helping fragile and post-conflict states improve the quality of life of their citizens. Canada's 3D or "Whole of Government" approach is one country's response to this requirement. The political, policy and administrative instruments to implement this integrated way of operating are gradually being designed and put in place.

Whereas over the past several decades each part of the government has worked relatively independently in the international arena, these stove-pipe arrangements are not well suited to resolving problems in places like Afghanistan, Somalia, Darfur, and others. An integrated approach is required where the skills and resources of multiple domains can come together in a coherent, collaborative multidisciplinary approach to helping a society improve its performance. The focus of this book has been on two of the major actors in this approach, international development and the military, fields that have relatively little experience in working together to achieve a common objective.

Although it is clear that military resources are required to reduce the level of violence in a troubled society, sustainable peace will not be established with weapons alone – a functioning government and a healthy economy are prerequisites for stability. Development resources need to be applied to help the society progress, and this work sometimes must take place in a non-permissive environment. If development does not occur, the violence is likely to continue. However, there are limits on the extent to which civilians can function in dangerous situations – their training and organizational supports are not well suited to those contexts.

The military needs to become better informed of the principles and practices of development so that it can support – and where required provide – services that are normally in the domain of development. It needs to know how to go beyond the third block of the Three Block War and do more than ensure the delivery of survival-oriented humanitarian aid. As stated in the US *Counterinsurgency* manual, soldiers need to be nation builders as well as warriors. However, a major problem with this line of reasoning is that nation building is a complex business and the military is not in the best position to do a good job of it on its own – it is not a long-term solution to helping strengthen a fragile post-conflict state.

There are limitations on how far it is desirable to stretch the mandate of an organization designed primarily for functions that are quite different than nation building, which includes activities such as drafting legislation, cross-cultural organizational development, running an education system and providing literacy training to women in remote villages. Mission creep can be a problem. This work is at the edge of the military's habitual realm of operation. They can operate in an insecure environment, but the development, diplomacy and other work that is needed is normally somebody else's business.

Development workers feel much of that work is their business, but they can't operate in a violent environment. The same holds true for the diplomats and the others. They have the tools but can't apply them because of the security problem.

The skills and resources are there, ready to be provided to a society that needs them but which is in no condition to receive the people who can help them acquire these capacities. It is as if there is a big donut with the military, development agencies, diplomats, and others all around edges and wanting to help, and with the violence-plagued society somewhere in the middle pleading for assistance. The military can move about in that environment, but its tool kit does not normally contain the governance and socio-economic development resources the society needs to put an end to the turmoil. The development agents and others can go into the region but their work is constrained by the violence so they usually have to operate "inside the wire" which is far from an ideal state of affairs.

This is a large-scale capacity development issue: new tools need to be developed that can do the job properly. In the capacity development field, when it becomes clear that there is a need that is not being properly attended to, the response is to look at the administrative framework and resources around the situation, and to see if there are institutional gaps that need to be addressed. The inability to fully tap the civilian resources required to help a society move away from violence and toward peace and prosperity is an indication of such a gap – the skills are present but they can't be applied. The agencies that are able to operate in the environment don't have all the appropriate skills or mandates.

This calls for a new set of institutional arrangements which make it possible to apply the required resources in an environment even if there is violence – a hybrid of some sort, possibly an integrated team of soldiers, development workers, diplomats and others who can protect themselves, and a globally-sanctioned, permanent and well-funded system that can move sufficient appropriate resources into position rapidly, regardless of the security concerns. The world needs to build something that can do this work. The PRTs in Afghanistan and Iraq come close, but there is still lots of room for improvement, and a need for a global system to govern these instruments and to help them apply best practices to the contextually-appropriate operation of each of these units.

New International Institutions For Fragile States

This new institutional arrangement has been the subject of considerable thought. Former Minister of External Affairs Lloyd Axworthy, for example, said Canada should help draft a new map to deal with situations facing the world:

> And what might be some guideposts to place on that map? Let's begin by rejoining international efforts to rehabilitate UN peace-keeping efforts using the Responsibility to Protect principle endorsed by the world summit in 2005. This involves rewriting the rules of engagement for the protection of people, primarily by setting up international means of prevention to support fragile states before they fall into turmoil, equipping regional and UN peacekeepers with appropriate equipment to suffocate conflicts before they grow, and providing major aid quickly to post-

conflict regions as recommended by British Prime Minister Gordon Brown just a few weeks ago.[125]

The North-South Institute had a similar suggestion, as noted earlier:

> Multilateral organizations (the UN, international financial institutions) and regional groups (the African Union [AU], OAS [Organization of American States]) are better placed (than Canada) to deal with failed states or poor performers. However, there is currently no accepted approach to such countries – no acknowledged or proven way of helping "poor performers" turn into "good performers." Canada should take a leadership role in the multilateral organizations and in working with regional groups such as the AU to spearhead initiatives to deal with such countries satisfactorily.[126]

Thomas Barnett, in a video presentation linked to his book, *The Pentagon's New War*, described the lack of an institutional framework to deal with post-conflict societies, and said that we need a "rule set for the world as a whole for dealing with politically bankrupt states. We have them to deal with economically bankrupt states, (the IMF, etc) … but we don't have them for processing politically bankrupt states."[127]

It is well beyond the scope of this monograph to do more than identify the need for a global mechanism to address the situation in countries like Afghanistan and the many other areas where development, diplomatic, military and other resources should collaborate in a well-planned and properly-funded intervention to establish peace and stability in a country. The current rather uncoordinated ad hoc arrangement seems inefficient to say the least. Having the military take the dominant role is somewhat like using the courts to deal with family matters, the instrument is not always well suited to the need. Likewise, development workers lack the full range of tools to do the job. Something new is called for, and in time no doubt it will be implemented. It is all part of the evolution of global governance.

In the meantime an interim solution is required, and this monograph contributes to this process. One of the obvious needs is new forms of administration and training for "Whole of Government" operations.

Administration Of "Whole Of Government" Operations

Developing an integrated delivery system calls for collaboration at all levels of the multiple organizations that are part of the process to ensure that the parallel lines of authority and accountability are appropriately merged into a single well-managed operation. Some parts of the Canadian government have recently developed a "Task Force" approach which is special operating units within CIDA and DFAIT, with the senior policy level guided by a new unit in the Privy Council Office. As with many organizational development processes in government, this seems to be taking a long time – the first SAT mission was in September 2005, some two years after 3D started to enter government terminology, and when this was written in early 2008 the integrated systems were not yet fully functional. The Princeton PRT study reported a variety of similar coordination efforts in the central ministries of the countries operating in Afghanistan and Iraq.

Implementing a global mechanism is likely to take even longer, as each country has its own approach that will need to be accommodated in some fashion, a process that usually involves a lot of negotiation before action can be taken. As implied above in Lloyd Axworthy's comments, the ideal solution would be for the UN to have its own well-resourced permanent integrated cadre of development workers, diplomats and military units, and the mandate to rapidly deploy these assets as required to prevent fragile states from falling into chaos, and to help rebuild those which need assistance to achieve stability.

It would be a large-scale capacity development SWAT team with teeth – at some point the world will realize this is needed and it will be done. As Tom Barrett states, there already is a global mechanism to deal with states that are in financial difficulty, so a comparable mechanism to intervene in states facing serious social and political difficulties is in the realm of possibility.

Training For "Whole Of Government" Missions

Training for "Whole of Government" missions calls for development of a broad-based realistic curriculum and preparation of a carefully-selected cadre of skilled human resources that can be rapidly deployed to serve in Canadian peace and security operations worldwide.

The military currently provides extensive preparations for its forces before they are deployed, and has long offered to include staff from CIDA, DFAIT and other departments in its training sessions. There are difficulties in securing participation of civilian personnel, since their employers' normal operations require all available staff to be online and fully engaged in the work. The military has whole units than can go "off-line" for months to prepare for the next mission: other departments do not have that type of staffing configuration. Having a senior CIDA or DFAIT officer take more than a week away from his or her regular job to attend a training session is a major challenge. These ministries need to develop the depth of human resources required so deployable staff can participate fully in the pre-departure orientation and training sessions provided to the military. They need to learn to work as integrated teams from the inception of the mission and throughout its duration.

Most civilians have never been in an active military environment, and the immersion learning experience from spending time in a camp cannot be replicated in a comfortable seminar room in Canada or even on bases like Petawawa or Gagetown – there is no substitute for being in a place like Kabul or Kandahar. Training needs to be realistic and experience-based rather than simply theoretical. The curriculum needs to reach all levels, cognitive, affective and behavioural, and to specifically include team-building based on the integration model described earlier.

Part of the program can be similar to cross-training the members of a multidisciplinary team in a workplace, where a process is implemented to ensure that all the members of the team know enough about each others' skills that they can be fully supportive and if needed step in and do some of the others' work when that member is not able to do his or her normal job. Members do not have to become fully knowledgeable of the skills of others on the team – a compressed version of each member's skills can be provided. This is consistent with the well-known 80/20 principle used in a number specialized areas which is based on the notion that it is possible to do 80 per cent of the work with 20 per cent of the skills – the other 20 per cent of the work needs the additional 80 per cent of the skills provided by a fully trained professional.

If a large cadre of development workers is not available, it may be appropriate to train some members of the military (such as those in CIMIC) in more advanced development-related skills. Because of the living conditions, work environment and the culture of the military, it is likely that it will be easier to provide military personnel with an appropriate amount of development training than to have seasoned development workers learn to function and survive in a military environment. The training should help military personnel learn enough to know when to call on the fully-trained resource that can do the more demanding aspects of the work.

Providing development-related training to the military, especially senior-level staff, will help greatly in their understanding of the 75 per cent of the peace-building mission that does not require weapons – and this knowledge may prompt a decision-maker to think twice before launching a kinetic action when there is a possibility that a non-kinetic approach may be more effective.

As Canada develops its administrative and training resources to meet the challenges posed by fragile and post-conflict states it will be better positioned to make substantive input to the global search for solutions to a global concern. These unstable regions affect us all, and development is one of the tools required to remedy these situations. The military is at the front end of many of these interventions, and supporting an increase in the military's development-related knowledge and its ability to make the required shift of mindset is what this monograph is all about.

Hope it helps.

List of Acronyms

3D	Diplomacy, Development and Defence
3D+T	Diplomacy, Defence, Development and Trade (Canada)
ACBAR	Agency Coordinating Body for Afghan Relief
ACS	Australian Customs Service
ACSI	Afghanistan Civil Service Institute (Public service training facility)
ADB	Asia Development Bank
AFP	Australian Federal Police
AI	Appreciative Inquiry
AKDN	Aga Khan Development Network
ANDS	Afghan National Development Strategy
AO	Area of Operation
ARTF	Afghanistan Reconstruction Trust Fund
AU	African Union
AusAID	Australian Agency for International Development
CF	Canadian Forces
CFC-A	Combined Forces Command – Afghanistan (US Military)
CIDA	Canadian International Development Agency
CIMIC	Civil-Military Cooperation
CJTF-76	Coalition Joint Task Force 76
COIN	Counter-insurgency
CPB	Contracts and Procurement Branch
CSC	Correctional Services Canada
CSO	Civil Society Organization(s)
CUSO	Canadian University Services Overseas
DAI	Development Alternatives Incorporated
DANIDA	Danish International Development Agency
DEVAD	Development Advisor: usually a country's development agency employee
DFAIT	Department of Foreign Affairs and International Trade (Canada)
DFID	Department for International Development (UK)
DND	Department of National Defence (Canada)

LIST OF ACRONYMS

DOFA	Department of Finance and Administration (Australia)
EBAO	Effects Based Approach to Operations (NATO)
EC	European Commission: the executive arm of the European Union
EU	European Union
FAO	Food and Agriculture Organization of the UN
FARC	*Fuerzas Armadas Revolucionarias de Colombia* (Revolutionary Armed Forces of Colombia)
GNI	Gross National Income (UN has a target of 0.7% for ODA)
GTZ	*Deutsche Gesellschaft für Technische Zusammenarbeit,* Germany's main government development agency
I-ANDS	Interim Afghanistan National Development Strategy
IARCSC	Independent Administrative Reform and Civil Service Commission (Afghanistan)
ICRC	International Committee of the Red Cross
IDLO	International Development Law Organization
IDP	Internally displaced person/people
IFI	International Financial Institution (WB, IMF, ADB, etc.)
IMF	International Monetary Fund
INGO	International Non-Government Organization
ISAF	International Security Assistance Force (NATO's Afghanistan operation)
JCMB	Joint Coordination and Monitoring Board
JTF-A	Joint Task Force – Afghanistan (US Military)
KOICA	Korea International Cooperation Agency
LA	Language Assistant
LDC	Least Developed Country(ies)
LGCD	Local Governance and Community Development
M&E	Monitoring and Evaluation
MDGs	Millennium Development Goals
MOD	Ministry of Defense (UK)

LIST OF ACRONYMS

MoTCA	Ministry of Transport and Civil Aviation (Afghanistan)
MPQ	Multicultural Personality Questionnaire
MRRD	Ministry of Rural Rehabilitation and Development (Afghanistan)
MSF	Médecins Sans Frontières
NATO	North Atlantic Treaty Organization
NGO	Non-Government Organization
NORAD	Norwegian Agency for Development Cooperation
NSP	National Solidarity Program (Afghanistan)
OAS	Organization of American States
ODA	Official Development Assistance
OECD	Organization for Economic Co-operation and Development
OEF	Operation Enduring Freedom
PAR	Public Administration Reform (Afghanistan government)
PCO	Privy Council Office (Canada)
PMI	Political-Military Integration
PRA	Participatory Rural Appraisal
PRSP	Poverty Reduction Strategy Paper
PRT	Provincial Reconstruction Team
QIPs	Quick Impact Projects
RAMSI	Regional Assistance Mission to Solomon Islands (Australia)
RBM	Results-Based Management Performance Framework (CIDA)
RCMP	Royal Canadian Mounted Police
RFP	Request for Proposals
SAT/SAT-A	Strategic Advisory Team – Afghanistan
SC	Security Council of the United Nations
SIDA	Swedish International Development Agency
SRSG	Special Representative of the Secretary-General (United Nations)

LIST OF ACRONYMS

TA	Technical Advisor (a consultant provided by a development agency)
TDD	Training and Development Department of IARCSC
TORs	Terms of Reference
UK	United Kingdom
UN	United Nations
UNAMA	United Nations Assistance Mission in Afghanistan
UNDAF	United Nations Development Assistance Framework
UNDP	United Nations Development Program
UN-Habitat	United Nations Human Settlements Program
UNHCR	United Nations High Commissioner for Refugees
US	United States
USAID	United States Agency for International Development
WB	World Bank
WFP	World Food Program
WHO	World Health Organization
WID/GE	Women in Development/Gender Equity

Endnotes

1   Steifel, M. *Rebuilding After War. Learning from the War-torn Societies Project.* (Geneva: WSP/PSIS) cited in Barakat, S. and M. Chard. "Theories, rhetoric and practice: recovering the capacities of war-torn societies." *Third World Quarterly* 23, 5 (2002), pp. 817–35.

2   Major David Knellinger, SO2 Afghan Development Officer ISAF IX, to A. Tamas, 12 August 2006, via e-mail.

3   US Army, *Counterinsurgency*, FM 3-24/MCWP 3-33.5, (Washington, 2006), pp. 1–27.

4   See: Hammes, Thomas. "Insurgency: Modern Warfare Evolves into a Fourth Generation." *Strategic Forum*, No. 214 (January 2005). <www.ndu.edu/inss/Strforum/SF214/SF214.pdf>, (5 November 2007).

5   Brigadier-General Daniel Pepin, former ISAF Deputy Commanding General for Effects in Combined and Joint Task Force 76, to A. Tamas, 4 September 2007, via email.

6   Maslow, Abraham. "A Theory of Human Motivation." *Psychological Review* 50 (1943), pp. 370–96. See: "Maslow's Hierarchy of Needs." *Wikipedia.* <en.wikipedia.org/wiki/Maslow's_hierarchy_of_needs>, (5 November 2007).

7   Culpeper, Roy, David Emelifeonwu and Luigi Scarpa de Masellis. Appendix. *Architecture without Blueprints: Opportunities and Challenges for the Next Prime Minister in International Development Policy.* (Ottawa: The North-South Institute, 2004), pp. 29–30.

8   See: *UN Millennium Development Goals Home Page.* <www.un.org/millenniumgoals/>.

9   Clemens, M.A., C.J. Kenny and T.J. Moss. "The Trouble with the MDGs: confronting expectations of aid and development success – Do unrealistic expectations threaten to undermine support for aid?" *Center for Global Development Home Page.* 1 May 2004. <www.cgdev.org/content/publications/detail/2749>, (4 July 2008).

10   Ibid.

11   Culpeper *et al.*

12   Scott, Alison. "POVERTY REDUCTION STRATEGIES IN CONFLICT COUNTRIES: HOW ARE THEY DIFFERENT?" *The World Bank Home Page – PRSPs in Conflict-Affected Countries.* 8 November 2001. <web.worldbank.org/WBSITE/EXTERNAL/TOPICS/EXTPOVERTY/EXTPRS/0,,contentMDK:20200794~menuPK:384247~pagePK:64020865~piPK:149114~theSitePK:384201,00.html>, (4 July 2008).

13   Culpeper *et al.* p. 28.

14   Mintzberg, Henry. *The Rise and Fall of Strategic Planning.* (New York: The Free Press, 1994), p. 215.

15   Major R. Kamphius, Advisor to Afghan Minister of Transport and Civil Aviation SAT Roto 2, to A. Tamas, 8 December 2007, via email.

16   See: *Peacewomen Home Page.* <www.peacewomen.org/un/sc/1325.html>, (13 December 2007).

17   See: *The Official Documents System of the United Nations.* <daccessdds. un.org/doc/UNDOC/GEN/N00/720/18/PDF/N0072018.pdf?OpenElement>, (13 December 2007).

18   Cheshmak Farhoumand-Sims, Assistant Professor of Conflict Studies, St. Paul University, to A. Tamas, 5 September 2007, via email.

19   See: Beckett, Ian. *Encyclopedia of Guerrilla Warfare.* (New York: Checkmark Books, 2001), p. 98.

20   Brigadier-General (ret'd) Chris Day, former military attaché to the British High Commission, to A. Tamas, 2 December 2006, via email.

21   Keizer, Willemijn. *3D Security: From Policy to Strategy.* Draft Paper. June 2007.

22   Culpeper *et al.* pp. 24–6.

23   Behn, Robert D. "Management by Groping Along." *Journal of Policy Analysis and Management.* Fall 1988. pp. 643-63. A similar concept, "Muddling Through" is also well documented.

24   Keizer, *3D Security: From Policy to Strategy.*

25   Capstick, Mike. "A Year in Kabul: Strategic Advisory Team – Afghanistan." *On Track* 11, 3 (Autumn 2006), pp. 13–8.

26   Boutros-Ghali, Boutros. *An Agenda for Peace Preventive diplomacy, peacemaking and peace-keeping.* Report of the Secretary-General pursuant to the to the statement adopted by the Summit Meeting of the Security Council on 31 January 1992. <www.un.org/Docs/SG/agpeace.html >, (15 March 2007).

27   St-Louis, Michel-Henri. "The Strategic Advisory Team: A new capability in nation building for the Government of Canada – A new role for the Canadian Armed Forces." Master's thesis. Canadian Forces College, 2007, p. 22.

28   Ibid., pp. 31–2.

29   Dr. Wali Hamidzada, Director, Training and Development Department, IARCSC, personal communication to A. Tamas, October 2005.

30   St-Louis, pp. 33–4.

31   Capstick, pp. 13–8.

32   Michelle Parker, ISAF Development Advisor (USAID), to A. Tamas, 20 October 2006, via email.

33   Mintzberg, Henry. "The Fall and Rise of Strategic Planning." *Harvard Business Review*, (January-February 1994), p. 112.

34   Christina Green, former CIDA DEVAD, Kandahar, personal communication to A. Tamas, 1 November 2007.

35   Colonel Don Dixon, Commander SAT-A Roto 1, personal communication to A. Tamas, 31 December 2006.

36   Dr. A. Mushahed, Chairman of the IARCSC, as quoted in St-Louis, p. 41.

37   International & War CKA Canadian Forums. "Canada helps to shape Afghanistan bureaucracy." <www.canadaka.net/modules.php?name=Forums&file=viewtopic&t=13191>, (12 March 2007). Quoted in St-Louis, p. 41. The reference is to General Fraser's military campaign in southern Afghanistan in 2005.

38   St-Louis, p. 41.

39   See: Abbaszadeh, Nima *et al.* "Provincial Reconstruction Teams: Lessons and Recommendations." *Small Wars Journal.* (February 2008). <smallwarsjournal.com/blog/2008/02/provincial-reconstruction-team/ >, (29 July 2008).

40   AusAID. *Capacity Devlopment Principles and Practices.* 2004. Quoted in AusAID. Australian Government. *A Staged Approach to Assess, Plan and Monitor Capacity Building.* (2006), p. 2. Available from <http://www.developmentgateway.com.au/jahia/Jahia/pid/4116>, (30 July 08).

41   Barakat, Sultan, and Margaret Chard. "Theories, rhetoric and practice: recovering the capacities of war-torn societies," *Third World Quarterly* 23, 5 (October 2002), pp. 817–35.

42   Gordijn, Femke. "The 'What is' and 'How to' of Capacity Development." November 2006. <pso.nl/asp/documentsite.asp?document=801>, (6 November 2007).

43   Tamas, Andy. "Capacity Development Analysis Framework." *Tamas Consultants Home Page.* <www.tamas.com/samples/samples.html>, (6 November 2007).

44   Independent Administrative Reform and Civil Service Commission. Islamic Republic of Afghanistan. *Request for Proposal (RFP), Civil Service Reform Project,* Ref. No. IARCSC/601. (August 2007).

45   Office of the Coordinator for Reconstruction and Stabilization. United States Department of State. *Post-Conflict Reconstruction: Essential Tasks.* (Washington, DC: United States Department of State, 2005). Available from <www.state.gov/s/crs/rls/52959.htm>, (30 July 08).

46   AusAID. Australian Government. *A Staged Approach to Assess, Plan and Monitor Capacity Building.* (2006), p. 4. Available from <http://www.development-gateway.com.au/jahia/Jahia/pid/4116>, (30 July 08).

47   Barakat *et al.*, pp. 817-35.

48   Ibid., p. 818.

49   Comments made by Dr. Kérim Ousman on a panel at the "Suez Plus 50" conference, Queen's Centre for International Relations, Kingston, 15–17 May, 2006.

50   Fukuyama, Francis. *Trust: The Social Virtues and the Creation of Prosperity.* (New York: The Free Press, 1995).

51   Dr. Khalifa Mahmoud, an oncology specialist at Sunnybrook Hospital in Toronto, personal communication to A. Tamas, February 2007.

52   Bertalanffy, Ludwig von. *General System Theory.* (New York: George Brazilier, 1968). See also: Tamas, Andy. "Systems Theory in Community Development." *Tamas Consultants Home Page.* <www.tamas.com/samples/samples.html>, (6 November 2007).

53   Bardhan, Pranab. "Does Globalization Help or Hurt the World's Poor?" *Scientific American* 294, 3 (March 2006).

54   Barber, Benjamin. "Jihad vs. McWorld," *Atlantic Monthly* 269, 3 (March 1992), pp. 53-65.

55   FAAE. Government of Canada. "Government Response to the Eighth Report of the Standing Committee on Foreign Affairs and International Development." *House of Commons Committees Home Page.* 5 November 2007. <http://cmte.parl.gc.ca/cmte/CommitteePublication.aspx?SourceId=216092>, (8 November 2007).

56   United Nations Integrated Mission Staff Officers Course IV. Pearson Peacekeeping Centre, Cornwallis, Nova Scotia. (November 2006). © Copyright Pearson Peacekeeping Centre, 2006. Used with permission.

57   Major (ret'd) Tim Lannon, NATO Civilian-Military Relations Specialist, to A. Tamas, 1 November 2007, via email.

58   Brigadier-General D. Pepin, former DCG (E) Combined Joint Task Force 76 (CJTF-76) Afghanistan, to A. Tamas, 11 November 2007, via email.

59   Lieutenant-Colonel Pierre St-Cyr to A. Tamas, 10 November 2007, via email.

60   Ibid.

61   Ibid.

62   Paris, Roland, and Timothy D. Sisk. "Managing Contradictions: The Inherent Dilemmas of Postwar Statebuilding." *International Peace Institute Policy Papers Page*. November 2007. <www.ipacademy.org/publications/policy-papers>, (31 July 2008), p. 6.

63   Barakat *et al*., pp. 817-35.

64   Hofstede, Geert. *Culture Organizations: Software of the Mind*. (New York: McGraw Hill, 1997). For a summary, see: "Hofstede's Dimensions & Hall's Time" *Tamas Consultants Home Page*. <www.tamas.com/samples/samples.html>, (21 November 2007).

65   Dr. Tooryalai Wesa to A. Tamas, 25 December 2007, via email.

66   Michael O'Brien, former Afghanistan ICRC official, to A. Tamas, 30 January 2008, via email.

67   UNDP. "Overview of UNDP in Afghanistan." *UNDP Afghanistan Home Page*. <www.undp.org.af/WhoWeAre/UNDPinAfghanistan/index.htm>, (4 February 2008).

68   Development Executive Group. *The Development Newswire*. Email to A. Tamas 29 January 2008. See: Speltz, Paul, and Linda Tsao Yang. "Five ways to reform Asia's development bank." *Financial Times*, 28 January 2008. <www.ft.com/cms/s/0/2bf3d2b0-cdc0-11dc-9e4e-000077b07658.html?nclick_check=1>, (29 January 2008).

69   World Council of Churches. "Lead us not into temptation: Churches' response to the policies of international financial institutions." *Third World Social Forum*. Porto Alegre, Brazil, January 23–28, 2008. <www.oikoumene.org/en/resources/documents/wcc-programmes/public-witness-addressing-power-affirming-peace/poverty-wealth-and-ecology/neoliberal-paradigm/01-03-lead-us-not-into-temptation.html>, (30 January 2008).

70   CARE International. "About CARE." *Care International Home Page*. <www.care-international.org/>, (28 January 2008). See also: *Care International UK Home Page*. <www.careinternational.org.uk/?id=3497>, (28 January 2008).

71   Oxfam International. "About us." *Oxfam International Home Page*. <www.oxfam.org/en/about/>, (29 January 2008).

72   International Development Law Organization. "About IDLO." *International Development Law Organization Home Page*. <www.idlo.int/english/External/Idlo-Home.asp>, (16 January 2008).

73   Médecins Sans Frontières. "About MSF." *Médecins Sans Frontières Home Page*. <www.msf.org>, (29 January 2008).

74   Aga Khan Development Network. "About us." *Aga Khan Development Network Home Page.* <www.akdn.org/>, (30 January 2008).

75   See: Aga Khan Foundation of Canada. "New Partnership to Strengthen Girls' Education in Afghanistan." <akfc.ca/en/media_center/gesp.shtml>, (30 January 2008).

76   Development Co-operation Directorate. OECD. "Statistical Annex of the 2007 Development Co-operation Report." *OECD Home Page.* <www.oecd.org/document/9/0,3343,en_2649_34485_1893129_1_1_1_1,00.html>, (31 July 2008).

77   USAID. "Budget and Obligations." *USAID Afghanistan Project Home Page.* <afghanistan.usaid.gov//en/Page.Budget.aspx>, (7 February 2008).

78   USAID. "Afghanistan Strategic Plan 2005-2010." May 2005, p. 2. *USAID Home Page.* <www.usaid.gov/locations/asia_near_east/documents/countries/afghanistan/Afghanistan_2005-2010_Strategy.pdf>, (7 February 2008).

79   DAI. "Afghanistan Local Governance and Community Development (LGCD)." *DAI Home Page.* <www.dai.com/work/project_detail.php?pid=133>, (7 February 2008).

80   Clouston, Kate. "USAID in Afghanistan." *RUSI Newsbrief*, 27, 9 (24 September 2007). <www.rusi.org/publication/newsbrief/newsbrief/keywords:USAID%20in%20Afghanistan/ref:A46F7BCF649CEE/>, (31 July 2008).

81   DFID. "DFID in Afghanistan." *DFID Home Page.* 7 July 2008. <www.dfid.gov.uk/countries/asia/afghanistan.asp>, (31 July 2008).

82   DFID. "Afghanistan Programme." *DFID Home Page.* 7 July 2008. <www.dfid.gov.uk/countries/asia/afghanistan-programme.asp>, (31 July 2008).

83   Canadian International Development Agency. "Funding." *CIDA Afghanistan Page.* 10 June 2008. <www.acdi-cida.gc.ca/CIDAWEB/acdicida.nsf/En/JUD-12514411-QD6>, (31 July 2008).

84   Korea International Cooperation Agency. *KOICA Home Page.* <www.labfrontier.com/koica/koica/koica.htm#>, (9 February 2008). This desription was accurate as of the date accessed. KOICA subsequently agreed to withdraw from Afghanistan following a large hostage-taking incident.

85   Olson, Lara. "Fighting for humanitarian space: NGOs in Afghanistan." *Journal of Military and Strategic Studies* 9, 1 (Fall 2006), p. 6. <www.jmss.org/2006/2006fall/articles/olson_ngo-afghanistan.pdf>, (4 February 2008).

86   Lieutenant-Colonel Bruce Gunn, USAF, former Deputy Chief, Pol-Mil Integrated Governance Team, Kabul, to A. Tamas, 5 February 2008, via email.

87   Olson, p. 9.

88   Olson, p. 10.

89   Médecins Sans Frontières. "Afghanistan: MSF leave country following staff killings and threats." 16 December 2004. *MSF Home Page.* <www.msf.org/msfinternational/invoke.cfm?component=article&objectid=F446039F-4965-4FB0-9D21CF4C695F80C9&method=full_html>, (6 February 2008).

90   Michael O'Brien, former Afghanistan ICRC official, to A .Tamas, 30 January 2008, via email.

91   Abdul Bari, UNDP Assistant Country Director, Kabul, personal communication to A. Tamas, 6 February 2007.

92   Médecins Sans Frontières. "Afghanistan: MSF leave country following staff killings and threats." 16 December 2004. *MSF Home Page.* <www.msf.org/msfinternational/invoke.cfm?component=article&objectid=F446039F-4965-4FB0-9D21CF4C695F80C9&method=full_html>, (6 February 2008).

93   Emma Sky, ISAF DEVAD, to A. Tamas, 5 March 2008, via email.

94   David Rhody, Country Director, Ethiopia, CHF, to A. Tamas, 29 January 2008, via email.

95   Clouston. Ibid.

96   Schumacher, E.F. *Small is Beautiful: Economics as if People Mattered.* (New York: Harper & Row, 1973).

97   Quoted in Beckett, Ian. *Encyclopedia of Guerrilla Warfare.* (New York: Checkmate Books, 2001), p. 98.

98   Thomas, Roy. "There's No I in Team? Why and How Interpreters Must Be Made Members of the Team." *The Liaison* 3, 1. The Center for Excellence in Disaster Management and Humanitarian Assistance. <www.coe-dmha.org/Liaison/Vol_3No_1/Feat06.htm>, (31 July 2008).

99   Ibid.

100   Lane, Major-General Roger, and Emma Sky. "The Role of Provincial Reconstruction Teams in Stabilization." *RUSI Journal* 151, 3 (June 2006), pp. 46–51.

101   Brigadier-General Daniel Pepin, former ISAF Deputy Commanding General for Effects in Command and Joint Task Force 76, to A. Tamas, 4 September 2007, via email.

102   Major-General Daniel Gosselin, Commander, Canadian Defence Academy, personal communication to A. Tamas, 4 September 2007.

103   US Army. *Counterinsurgency* FM 3-24, MCWP 3-33-5 (December 2006).

104   Ibid., p. ix.

105   Ibid., pp. 1–3.

106   Lane and Sky, p. 47.

107   Ibid.

108   Ibid., p. 49.

109   Ibid., p. 50f.

110   Ghani, Ashraf, Clare Lockhart and Michael Carnahan. *Closing the Sovereignty Gap: an Approach to State-Building.* Working Paper 253. London: Overseas Development Institute, 2005.

111   Mishkin Berteig, Agile Work Management Consultant, to A. Tamas, 26 August 2007, via email.

112   Abbaszadeh, Nima, *et al. Provincial Reconstruction Teams: Lessons and Recommendations.* (Princeton University, 2008).

113   US Army. *Counterinsurgency* FM 3-24, MCWP 3-33-5 (December 2006), p. ix.

114   Kanter, Rosabeth Moss. *When Giants Learned to Dance: Mastering the Challenges of Strategy, Management , and Careers in the 1990s.* (New York: Simon and Schuster, 1989).

115   Wheatley, Margaret. "Leadership of Self-Organized Networks: Lessons from the War on Terror." *Performance Improvement Quarterly* 20, 2 (2007), pp. 59–66. See: <www.margaretwheatley.com/articles/Self-OrganizedNetworks.pdf>, (25 February 2008).

116   International Institute for Sustainable Development. "From Problems to Strengths." *IISD Appreciative Inquiry and Community Development Page.* <http://www.iisd.org/ai/>, (1 March 2008).

117   The Asset-Based Community Development Institute. "About ABCD." *The ABCD Home Page.* <www.sesp.northwestern.edu/abcd/about/>, (5 March 2008).

118   IFAD. "Sustainable livelihoods approach." *IFAD Home Page.* 20 April 2007. <www.ifad.org/sla/>, (1 March 2008).

119   The World Bank Group. "Appendix I: Methods and Tools – Participatory Rural Appraisal." *The World Bank Participation Sourcebook.* <www.worldbank.org/wbi/sourcebook/sba104.htm>, (5 March 2008).

120   Klein, Helen Altman, Anna Pongonis and Gary Klein. *Cultural Barriers to Multinational C2 Decision Making.* Proceedings of the 2000 Command and Control Research and Technology Symposium, Monterrey, California, June 24–28, 2000. <www.au.af.mil/au/awc/awcgate/ccrp/2000ccrts_klein_culture.pdf>, (29 February 2008).

121   Colonel Cheryl D. Lamerson, Director Human Resource Requirements, NDHQ, to A. Tamas, 4 January 2006, via email.

122   van der Zee, Karen I. and Jan Pieter van Oudenhoven. "The Multicultural Personality Questionnaire: A Multidimensional Instrument of Multicultural Effectiveness." *European Journal of Personality* 14, 4 (August 2000), pp. 291–309.

123   Major Robert Kamphuis, Advisor to Afghan Ministry of Transport and Civil Aviation, SAT Roto 2, to A. Tamas, 8 December 2007, via email.

124   Stacey, Ralph D. *Managing the Unknowable: Strategic Boundaries Between Order and Chaos in Organizations.* (San Francisco: Jossey Bass, 1992); Kiel, Douglas L. *Managing Chaos and Complexity in Government.* (San Francisco: Jossey Bass, 1994); Wheatley, Margaret. *Leadership and the New Science.* (San Fransisco: Berrett-Koehler, 1992); Mintzberg, Henry. *The Rise and Fall of Strategic Planning.* (New York: Prentice Hall, 1994).

125   Axworthy, Lloyd. "Finding Canada's place in the world." *Globe and Mail,* February 16, 2008. <www.theglobeandmail.com/servlet/story/RTGAM.20080215. wcomment0216/BNStory/specialComment/home>, (17 February 2008).

126   Culpeper *et al.* p. 28.

127   Barnett, Thomas P.M. *The Pentagon's new map for war and peace.* 2005. [Film.] *TED Ideas Worth Spreading Home Page.* <www.ted.com/index.php/talks/thomas_barnett_draws_a_new_map_for_peace.html>, (6 March 2008).

Index

INDEX